MYTHS OF LIFE & DEATH

MYTHS OF LIFE & DEATH

C.A. Burland

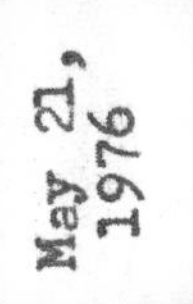

Crown Publishers, Inc.

Library of Congress Catalog Card Number 74-79865

Picture Research by Ann Davies

Published in the United States of America 1974
by Crown Publishers, Inc., New York
and in Great Britain 1974
by Macmillan London Limited
London and Basingstoke
Associated companies in New York, Toronto,
Dublin, Melbourne, Johannesburg and Delhi

Printed in Great Britain
by Jolly and Barber Ltd., Rugby
and by BAS Printers Ltd., Over Wallop, Hampshire

Contents

Preface

First we need a definition since the word myth has accumulated many meanings. For most people it has become a pejorative word and implies simply falsehood. But life and death are not falsehoods. The kind of myths presented here are stories about the gods and demons who influence the life of man. They reflect hopes and fears and dreams experienced by our fellow humans from many places and in many ages. They are stories which are told, and often acted, with some sense that they are reflections of reality.

The myths of mankind all come from one source, the flow of consciousness which is in all of us, and which in some mysterious way links us all at the level of what Professor Jung called the Common Unconscious.

In detail myths vary widely; though they may reflect archetypal themes they are conditioned by our experience of life and by the cultural level of the society within which we live. Long ago the philosophical poet said that no man is an island to himself. Here we find in the stories we have told ourselves some reflections on the mysteries of life and death. Here and there you will find mention of Eleusis, but Eleusis was always the home of the great mystery of death and life. We enact some of it in each life. We will never know the secrets told to the initiates in that sacred shrine, yet we can in some way see the vision of life which was presented to them in the form of an enactment of the story of Demeter the Corn Mother and her lovely daughter Persephone, the Spring Maiden. We experience the glory of the passage through the seasons whenever we can escape from our mechanistic civilisation. Alas, that is a hard escape, but necessary from time to time for us to see the stars. They are still there, moving in the night sky, with the planets and moon dancing among them.

There are many movements nowadays in which people seek to regain contact with another, more romantic reality. Religion gives some sense to life for millions, esoteric societies abound and spread philosophies, while on the basis of a simple love of nature we have naturists enjoying games in company without clothes, or sportsmen making glorious struggle worthwhile in a truly competitive Greek spirit. For all these ideas and movements there is a need for a rationale. It is usually no longer codified into a myth, but the old myths still can have meaning for those who will seek.

A myth is a truth in an irrational form. It tells a story, using pictures and thoughts in its own context; encapsulated truths, all the more palatable because of their disguises. So it is useless to seek a scientific aspect of their unreality. They are apparently factual, but when approached closely they turn into butterfly-fairies. Yet they remain obstinately alive in a most unsympathetic environment.

Of course there is a scientific aspect. We may compare similar myths from different peoples and find some rules about their occurrence. We may correlate the tales with the social structure of the tribes who told them. We may find echoes of long-past customs preserved intact, flies in amber, so to speak. By classification and inspection the specialist will learn much to be taught to future students.

In this book we had to make a plan for the presentation of a few from literally millions of myths. The chapter headings give a clue to the path we chose through the labyrinth. The tales are linked to the triple passage: the path through human life; the path of the seasons of the year; and the path of the seven directions: North, East, South, West, Upwards, Downwards, and to the heart of things in the Centre. There are naturally deviations from every aspect, but there *is* a plan, a thread running through this selection from an endless, labyrinthine library. And at the centre will we find the Minotaur? . . . One is hopeful of that, for in some way each one of us is the Minotaur, animal and sentient human all in one.

And apropos of that last thought, there is a good deal about sex in this book, because it is so frequently the subject of myths. But in the world from which myths come there is nothing about this aspect of life which is false, unnatural or filthy. Natural humans accept creative activity as something delightful, divine and laughable because it is joyous.

Neither do the mythmakers hide thoughts about death. It is inevitable and natural; indeed it may be noble. But death is also normally seen as a prelude to further adventures of the soul.

The labyrinth we explore has features in each chapter from each of the five continents. One hopes they will form some kind of link and do a little to show that in diversity there is yet unity; and understanding is a step to unity.

C. A. Burland
West Molesey,
February, 1974

1. The Powers Above

There seems to have been no primitive tribe which lacked the idea of the supernatural powers aiding the life of earthly peoples. It is hard to see the growth of grass in the spring, providing food for the animals we hunt, without thinking of some mysterious power which provides this annual miracle. The rains come and go, the herds follow the migration tracks: no one has ventured to explore beyond for fear of meeting hostile tribes. Moon and sun become symbolic beings in the sky who give light and heat according to their nature. The winds bring blessings or disasters which are seen not as accidents, but as an expression of the will of some great power, not a blind fate, but a sentient being who regards the need of the hunter or the farmer.

In the most primitive stages of which we have knowledge, the powers above were manifold, and they existed on a flat earth. There was neither beginning nor end to the Alcheringa time for the Australian aboriginal. The ancestors came in animal form from water-holes or clefts in the rock. They moved around and some assumed human forms, but for ever the link between the human being and the sacred animal form of the first ancestors was preserved. Thus men divided into totemic groups which intermarried according to the rules of the tribe. The only rule about the marvellous ancestral beings was that one did not eat the totem animals who were descended from one's own totemic ancestor. The whole was a projection from the unconscious at a level where the unity of all life was dimly experienced without making rationalizations about it.

A somewhat similar expression of an essential unity is apparent in many American Indian beliefs in a named but ill-defined entity. Wañkonda is a Dakota example. The white man translated the idea as the 'Great Spirit', but it really meant an overshadowing power of life and creation which had a personality and would be accessible to petitions of mankind asking for help from the great unknown. Such a sense of overarching power beyond the natural world seems to have been widespread among mankind.

Below: Wandjina of the Aborigines, who brought life to the people of the Kimberley Mountains

Left: An Aboriginal ritual dance impersonates ancestral spirits

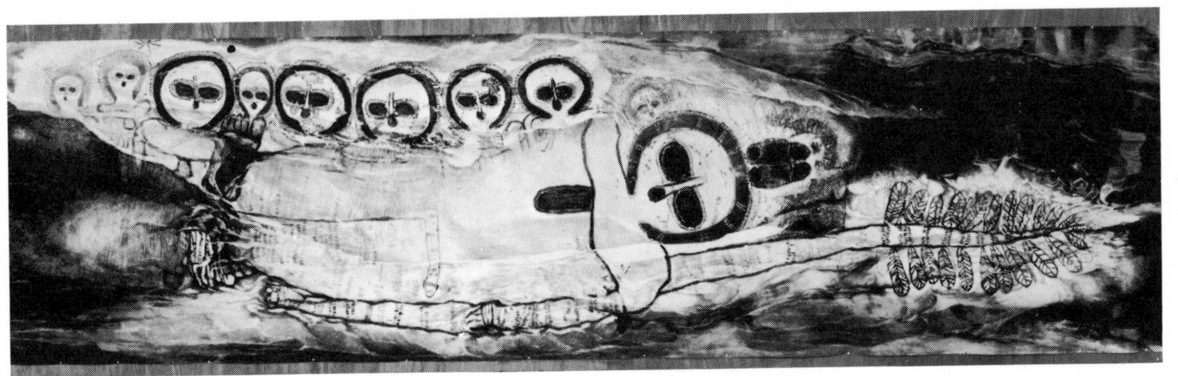

It is interesting that the idea of a personal creator does not crystallize until mankind has reached the stage of primitive farming. The idea of the protective power is archetypal, but it has to move into full consciousness, no longer within the never-never land of the deep unconscious, before the form of a real creator-deity emerges. The god is in some sense the product of a rational intellect. He is reasonable and can be conceived as an old, old man of immense and incredible power. Blake's sublime vision of the Ancient of Days circumscribing the universe is probably the best presentation of the theme. This Creator-God possesses almost invariably an active, male personality; he is no permissive, gentle, dark and feminine person. The People of the Book (Christians, Jews and Muhammedans) picture him as the creator who could walk in the beautiful, ordered Garden of Eden and who talked to our first ancestors in a personal form. At this stage he is the dream figure of the wise elder who is the guide and helper of the soul. Yet he has always been subject to modification by human reason.

The Polynesians' idea of the creator is quite rational. These enterprising navigators knew that all life came through the gift of sex. This holy magic was the means by which the ancestors came into being, and before them their ancestors, so that at the beginning of time there must have been a unity. The giving of life for birth was through the agency of the male acting upon the

Left: The Ancient of Days strikes the first Circle of the Earth, by William Blake. Above: A 17th century church relief in Sweden shows Adam and Eve in the Garden of Eden. Right: Adam and Eve, from a 3rd century AD painting in Syracuse Museum

female. So the creator had to create a feminine side to his worlds. The name of the god of creation was Tangaroa. He was male and a parent of all beings. Some accounts say that he was formless, and manifested himself in human shape when he brought the world into being. Many groups of Polynesians made him a creator, but also an unknowable entity, and some even said that he was a force of life within living beings. The identities are confused, not so much because of the wide dispersal of Polynesian tribes, but because the ancient religion has been superseded for more than two centuries, and memories have included additional elements derived from Christian missionaries.

One legend tells of Tangaroa being enclosed in formless darkness, as if he were within an egg, from which he created male and female first beings which were later forced apart from each other to make earth and sky. From their sexual contact were born all things.

Another version places Tangaroa as a sky god contemplating the limitless ocean. Into it he threw down a stone and created land, and then a seed which grew into a vine but fell and decayed. From the wreck emerged strange maggots which became human beings. But this is probably not the original concept which we may find in a figure brought home from Tahiti by Captain Cook. This is a human shape, covered with little figures apparently budding off the body of the god. His features are also composed of little figures. Within the body cavity there had been a cache of some two hundred smaller figures, of which one survives. This figure had an erect penis, which long ago was broken off by some misguided person who saw corruption in what the original artist saw as the holy symbol of life. The story behind this figure is a myth of the first creator, Tangaroa, himself giving birth to the original ancestors of sea, air, rocks, storms, plants, animals, fishes and humans. It is possible that if the penis had been preserved there would be a pair of figures on the glans, for an important tradition tells of the Lone God creating human life, before he made a feminine force, by masturbating so that the semen on the earth gave rise to male and female ancestors of the chiefly families. Hence the descendants of the chiefs continue a line of human life which stems from the Creator himself. One must note that in this myth Tangaroa had already created an earth by dropping a stone into the ocean, and it is probable that originally the new earth was the first feminine being that was formed to receive the semen of the god.

The Polynesian myth may have derived from south-eastern Asia whence the ancestors sailed into the great ocean in the first millennium BC. There may be a link with the first being, P'an Ku, whose cult came from Siam to southern China not long after the Polynesians had migrated. At the far end of Polynesia, in remote

Above: Tangaroa, the Polynesian creator of all living things

Top left: Hoa Haka Nana Ia, 'Breaking wave', first ancestor of the Easter Islanders.
Top right: A Mochica figure vase from Peru, 3rd century, AD. The bearded man may represent Viracocha

Below: On Easter Island giant statues represent ancestors of tribal lineages

Easter Island, the Polynesian religion was complete, and inscribed wooden tablets show that the sacred chants of the gods were much the same as in Tahiti from where the ancestors had sailed. It is significant, however, that the name of the first ancestor on the island was preserved by the statue on the top of Rano Raraku, the sacred volcano. It was Hoa Haka Nana Ia, 'the breaking of the waves'. Here survives the idea of the wind blowing on the waters and bringing forth life. One does not forget that Tangaroa was also god of the great ocean. But meanwhile the same idea of the coming of life from the sea foam was accepted in far-off Peru. The meaning of the name of the Creator Viracocha was roughly the same.

Viracocha was the breath of life, and yet was described to the invading Spaniards in the sixteenth century as a man, an old man wearing a white gown, and with shining white hair and beard. Perhaps we have his image in the form of a seated old man with a white beard found on modelled Chimu pottery of the fourth or fifth centuries AD, but this is not certain. In Inca times the Creator was too important to have temples except one single building dedicated to his adoration. It was not in Cuzco but some two days' march away. There was also a temple near the site of Lima dedicated to the ancient deity Pachacamac, who was also the Creator. The two deities were thought of as being the same under different names. Basically Pachacamac was a sea god. A

Above: The Inca salutes the sun at the festival of Capacraimi in April

Below: The only drawing extant of the golden wall in the Temple of the Sun in Cuzco

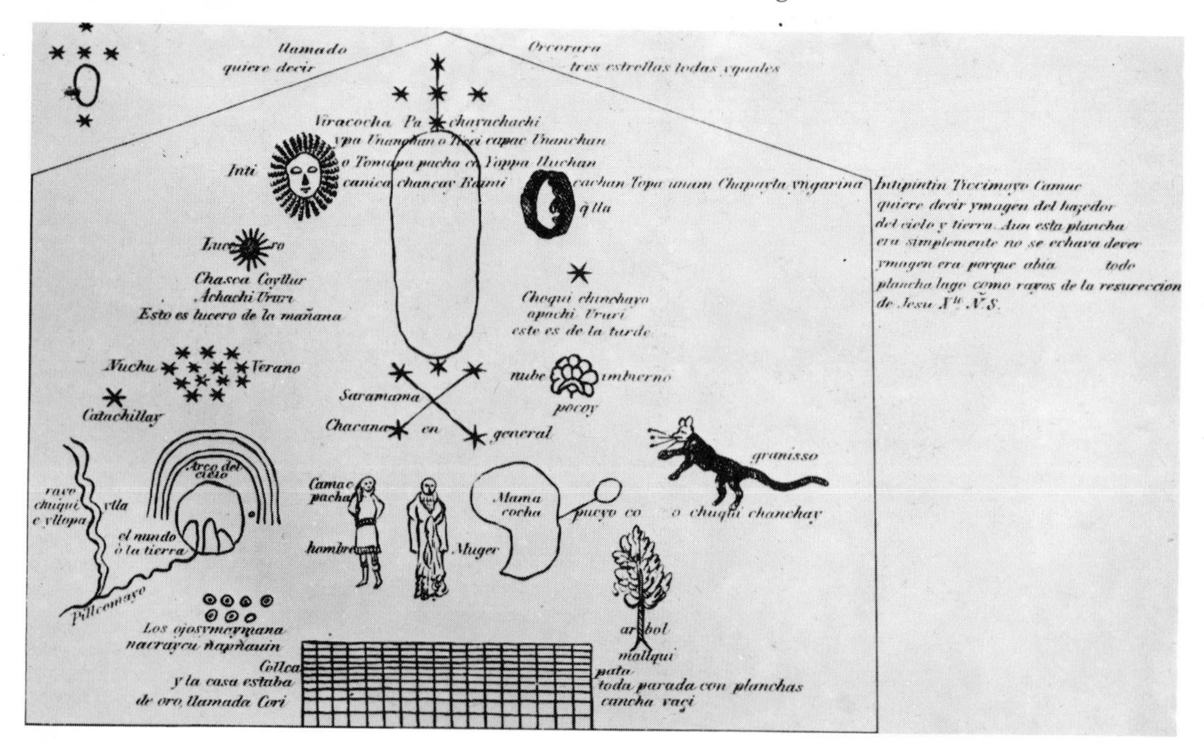

Right: An 18th century reconstruction of the Inca making offerings to the sun.
Below: Stone seats at Kenko, from which the first Inca is said to have descended to Cuzco

textile in the British Museum shows a Creator figure in the midst of a sea full of fish; it is probable that this was a local concept of the god. Viracocha, however, was named after the foam of the sea blown by the winds. This idea is archetypal and belongs to mankind as a whole. In the Inca period it was thought that Viracocha had arisen from the sacred lake Titicaca. He passed over the land, naming places, making mountains and cutting out valleys, and then over the coast of Ecuador he disappeared. One imagines that in earlier times the Creator had emerged from the ocean and caused the land to rise, like the monstrous crocodile in the old English sea shanty. The traverse of the white god sounds like the passage of some immense comet which had remained in the imagery of the Indian tribes for ages uncountable. Viracocha was a god of gods and the Inca worshipped him at the special shrine outside Cuzco where the god was not in conflict with the divine sun, ancestor of the Incas.

In Ccoricancha, the sun temple in Inca Cuzco, the navel of the earth, the first rays of the sun on New Year's Day penetrated the doorway and shone full on the wall of gold, before which the Inca kept his annual vigil. He was alone except for the mummies of his ancestors who had been brought into the temple for this occasion. Each had his niche and golden insignia. These surrounded the current Inca, who on this one occasion had taken off his sacred head ornament to submit himself to his father the sun, as if he were an ordinary man. Then the first rays struck and the temple was filled with golden glowing light.

But what was depicted on that wall? The story of creation. At the top is a group of five stars, symbolizing the four directions and the centre. Left and right are the sun and moon associated with Venus as morning and evening star. In the centre is Viracocha, and below him the Southern Cross as the marker of the pivot of the heavens. Below this are the sacred symbols of lightning and the rainbow overshadowing the earth, which has its mountains and a great river. To their right are the puma and a sacred lake (perhaps Titicaca). The lowest range has the holy places of emergence, the first man and his wife, and the ancestral maize plant. Here we have a sequence of creation, in which time is indicated by the treatment of the Pleiades who mark the beginning of years among all peoples. On the left they are stars; on the right they are under clouds. From Peru the Pleiades can be seen for a short period above the northern horizon in May, and are totally invisible in November. This is the marking of the ancient Celtic year in Europe and in many other places. In Peru they were not a very practical time marker, but perhaps they came from an ancestral tradition before the ancestors of the Indians had moved so far south.

Yet there is Viracocha in the middle of things. He is not himself

A lady worships Brahma, in an illustration in the Khambhavati-Ragini. Far right: A statue of Brahma with his four arms and four heads

there, merely a plain oval of burnished gold in the centre of the golden wall. The statement was clear: the creator was formless and unknowable directly. He was symbolized by the 'Coal Sack', an area of blackness in the Milky Way. But there is a story that at his temple in Cacha there was a great stone image of the god, and other stories relate that in Ccoricancha there was also a golden standing figure of the god.

It is clear that the concept of Viracocha was a dualistic one. On the one hand, the man-like being who walked and created as he went; and on the other, a concept of ineffable power who was beyond human contact. A more primitive society would have found no problem in this duality, but to the Peruvians there was a theological question, and it may well be that the concept of the one invisible source of life from the wind-blown foam of the sea was a philosophic development within the organized colleges of priests in the Inca empire. But an interesting feature is that although Viracocha is regarded as the maker of Peru there is no record of the creation of the earth as a whole.

There may have been a similar hiatus in the stories of creation told among the ancient inhabitants of the Baltic region. At least in the *Prose Edda* the story of the beginning of things told to Gylfi obviously at first is derived from the Bible story, and the All-Father seems to have been equated with God the Father at the time the lawgiver Snorri Sturluson wrote them down in the thirteenth century. But the real story begins when the High One was asked what the creator was doing before the creation. Gylfi was told that there was then nothing: only the open void existed. Then Niflheim was made, the home of mists, in the midst of which was a bubbling cauldron from which flowed eight fierce rivers. First of worlds to come into being was Muspell, the hot southern land, but so great was its terror that none could live there.

The rivers which flowed from Muspell came slowly northwards, cooling as they advanced, and carried a mass of strange material like yeast which finally the northern cold congealed into ice. As more and more flowed it gave rise to a fine drizzle which also froze, and so eventually bridged the northern side of the great void. On the southern side, however, the gap was heated to a sparkling red glow by the heat from Muspell. Then, where the heat met the frost drops of water formed and fell. Among them appeared life, and these began to grow together in the form of a man, who was named Ymir. He was parent of all the wise women, the sorcerers and the giants. Later people were afraid to rank him among the gods because he was parent of the dreaded frost ogres. Ymir the giant fell asleep, and his legs mated and gave birth to the race of frost giants, and under his left arm two growths became the first man and woman.

The tale goes on, saying that the melting frosts became a cow

Aborigines dance to invoke the spirits

who fed Ymir with her milk. She licked away blocks of ice and then revealed a man (here we have a second story of origins), Buri, who married Bestla, daughter of one of the frost giants. They had three sons of whom the eldest was Odin, ruler of heaven and earth.

The three brothers slew Ymir and all the giants except one. They carried Ymir's body to the great depths and made him into our world. His blood was the waters of earth, his flesh was the soil, and his skull was the dome of the heavens. From the sparks from the southern land of fire they made the sun, moon and the planets among the stars. They used the bones of Ymir to shape their world. Then the three first gods went to the seashore and from a tree they made the first man and woman (a third version!). They then built their mighty city Midgard and ruled the earth, awaiting any dangers that the subsequent race of giants might bring against them. Odin All-Father was the parent of gods and men.

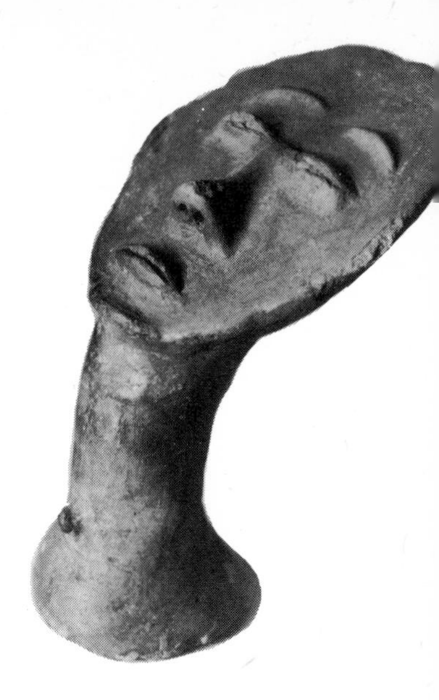

Above: An early 19th century memorial head from an Ashanti grave

The position of Odin in this combination of legends is not unlike that of Zeus in Greek mythology. The Norsemen, however, had a less clear idea of the powers which came before the birth of the standard grouping of gods. The feeling of an all-pervading fate runs through all the religious legends from the northland. Perhaps the contrast between frost and fire had a particularly Icelandic character because the poets could have observed such titanic contrasts.

We find a similar vagueness about the origins of the universe in the Ashanti cult of the sky god Nyame, who was just there as king of a hierarchy of *obosom*, divine powers in the sky. When his story was written down by the great anthropologist R. A. Rattray, the Ashanti had already had some three centuries of occasional contact with European missionaries on the coast, and over a much longer period through trade with Mohammedan Emirates in the Sudan, so some of the pictorial imagery may have come through culture contacts. However, Nyame was typically an African sky god in that he was a ruler surrounded by his circle of lesser gods who formed a palace hierarchy. He was said to have little wish to interfere in the affairs of mankind, but he was never neglected.

Every household in the ancient Ashanti kingdom had its offering table in the open air where a morning offering of a little food and palm wine was made in honour of the protector of all. Usually this was put in an earthenware bowl placed on the triple fork at the end of a section of tree branch. But in some important households the shrine of the god was a brass bowl, a symbol of social importance.

Nyame shared his power with the earth goddess Asase Ya, who was in effect the queen mother of his palace. If she was similar

Far top right: A pottery lamp representing the Earth Mother of the Ashanti, Ghana.
Near top right: Akua ba dolls from Ashanti, Ghana, were carried by girls in the nineteenth century as a charm to make babies beautiful.
Right: The ceremonial stool of an Ashanti queen mother. The central column was thought to contain the souls of her people

to the queen mother of a normal Ashanti kingdom she was also regarded as the spiritual basis of power, the mother of the god who as king and son would be the active face of power in the kingdom. Certainly Nyame was regarded as the patron of Ashanti kingship. In the reign of King Osai Tutu, the Golden Stool was called down from the sky by the priest of Nyame, whose only temple was the most holy spot in Ashanti. At a great ceremony where many animals and some people were slain for the gods, the priest called to the heavens, and a great cloud appeared from which descended a very simple wooden stool, hung with two golden bells. It slowly descended in front of the king. But it was too holy for him to sit on it because it contained the spirit of the Ashanti nation, as protected by the Power Above.

This Golden Stool was a kind of Palladium to the Ashanti nation. During British domination the Stool was safely hidden away, nobody says where, and when a particularly stupid white governor demanded that the Stool should be brought out so that he could sit on it as a sign that he was now the ruler, he was quietly told that it came long ago and no longer existed. This was true, because the Stool was kept in a bag and consisted of some fragments left by the white ants and the two golden bells from heaven. It is now in its proper place in Ashanti.

The Stool reflects the Ashanti feeling that the great King of Heaven was always in touch with his people, though not officiously controlling their affairs.

Some light on the Ashanti attitude to the sky god came to me through the sculptor and writer Namba Roy, who was a Maroon from Jamaica. The Maroons won their freedom from slave raiding in the early eighteenth century when their queen mother, Accompong Nanni, and her aides defeated a British regiment and then signed a treaty of mutual non-aggression. There was a Maroon legend that the Lord of the Sky once used to walk in his garden on earth, but Earth Mother Elohda had decided to make some human beings. She took dough and prepared an oven to bake the little creatures before she gave them life. She had hardly placed them in the oven when she heard the forest stirring and Nyame (or Nyankopong) came by. She hid her work and talked with the god until he went away. Then she returned to her secret task. Alas, some of the little beings were soft and white, poor things; others were just beginning to go a light brown; and others were a beautiful rich brown and just right. Hence the three colours of the human race. But the sky god was angered, and let down the corners of the sky so that the earth could never see him again.

This little tale may well represent an earlier form of Ashanti belief in a period when it was thought that the heavens were somewhere outside the sky dome and not necessarily above.

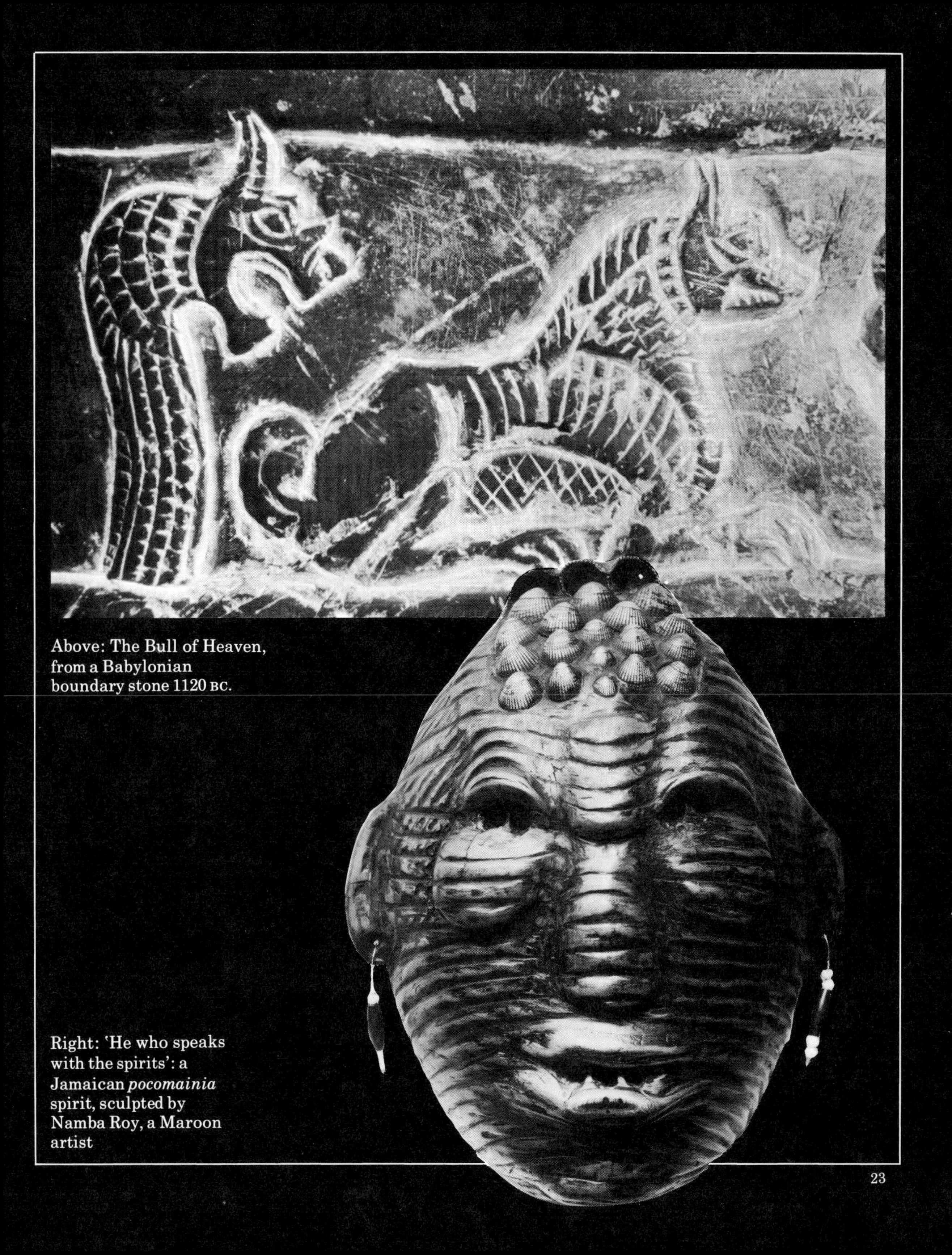

Above: The Bull of Heaven, from a Babylonian boundary stone 1120 BC.

Right: 'He who speaks with the spirits': a Jamaican *pocomainia* spirit, sculpted by Namba Roy, a Maroon artist

On the whole the Ashanti belief in Nyame shows us a distant but kindly being, giving life to the world and receiving adoration and regular offerings from here below. His form and the customs of his court were those of the people on earth. Yet there seems to be no tradition of his ultimate origin.

The most reasoned story of the origins of the gods seems to be the Babylonian creation story, the *Enuma Elish.* But here the beginning is a vaguely personified dark emptiness from which, in a series of stages, emerge gods, and eventually Marduk assumes power as the King of Heaven. The struggle of creation is emphasized in this well-known epic. In some ways its sequential nature is not unlike the story of the origin of the Norse deities. We find a more understandable first cause and a more gentle account of the creation in the earlier Aryan epics and hymns. The simple polytheism of the first Vedic time reflects a pastoral people with many gods but not a great deal of unity among them. Probably the important feature of many gods grouped according to function was a reflection of the nature of tribal life.

It is at a somewhat later period when the newcomers to India had settled down into organized city states—perhaps derived from contact with the defeated peoples of the Indus Valley culture—that ideas of a divine hierarchy were codified. At the same time, when cultural advance made social unity necessary under a leader, it became easier to consider that the heavenly hierarchy must also have a ruler. One must remember that in addition the larger social unit of the state, much larger than the tribe, would include priestly astrologers who would have time to develop philosophy. Certainly there was a strong tendency to philosophy in the Indian mind.

Among the complexities of Hinduism there are many variations of the story of creation, but essentially the story in the Upanishads (of around 1000 BC) is the one which expresses most directly the thought about a supreme being, an uncreated mind who assumed form and brought form and time into existence.

The document relevant to our enquiry is the Brihad-Aranyaka Upanishad. In this, creation has advanced a step, the Brahman is in the form of a man alone in the infinity. He feels fear, but reasons that fear is felt when one is no longer the Only One. He realizes that there is no happiness and that the lone one cannot experience happiness, so he divides himself into two. They are male and female, the first man and wife. He embraces his wife and then through the union of the two comes the birth of the first human beings.

The female half of Brahman is greatly disturbed, for she is created and is therefore in some sense his child. Should she have been embraced by her creator? She determines to hide herself by assuming an animal form, first as a sacred cow; but Brahman

Shiva and his consort Parvati, enthroned on the sacred Mount Kilasa: a Kangra painting of the late 18th century

becomes the bull and she gives birth to the first cattle. And so it is through all forms of life, Brahman as male and female creates and gives birth to all living things. And so Brahman is at once creator and all creation, for everything is of his making.

Afterwards he makes fire by friction with the mouth and hands, as symbols of the fire-stick and the hole which it makes in the hearth-stick. It seems that these are symbols of the human sexual organs. It is said that the fire-hole was smooth and without hair inside. Fire is a god, and is created by Brahman as are all the gods; and he is the container of all and within all. He creates Soma, the seed which is moist, and all water. Thus in the universe is either food or the devourer of food. Agni, fire, is the eater, Soma the food.

And so the creation assumes form and name, the gods exist as created by Brahman, and all things have been made by him. He exists in the highest heaven which he created for the gods, but he is within all that he created, since all creation comes from himself. He has entered all his creation as if he had flowed into every part of every being. In humans he is within every part, the innermost unity, the divine Self of all creation.

In later times the cult of Shiva accounted for the creation. Shiva is a terrible god, the Lord of the Dance. As King of the Beasts he represented all the forces of nature. It appears that he was historically an ancient deity whose image is found in the pre-Aryan civilization of the Indus Valley. He was regarded as having existed before any creation. The making of the world and its eventual destruction was a matter of pleasure for the god, the fruit of his eternal dance. In this guise of the creative dancer he is seen in many figures which represent the beauty and grace of his being.

Another legend derived the high god Brahma from the primeval Brahman. Some say that Brahma was born from the navel of the pre-existent one; that he developed and enclosed himself in a golden egg, which later was broken in half to become the earth and sky under the dominion of Brahma who ruled from his Olympian heights in the heavens. But these stories are many and indicate local developments of folklore, and several schools of devout philosophy. Reason and love had entered the hearts of the mystics, and so mythology became more and more of an inner experience and less and less capable of explanation in material terms.

A deep sense of the overmastering power of the mysterious force which keeps the world and its people in being seems characteristic of the human condition, at least in its unsophisticated natural state. The highest concept among these stories is that of the Hindu faith. The material concepts of Zeus or Jupiter in the more technically advanced classical world are compara-

Above: A Chinese Taoist painting on an 18th century dish depicts the spirits of happiness and long life

tively unimportant. Probably the reason may be found in the different developments of philosophy. In India, the tendency was for religious teaching to grow through introspection and reasoning on a non-material plane. Western thinkers demanded an explanation of the world as a rationally constructed, material entity, and so western philosophy theorized in terms which gradually became more scientific and in some measure materialistic. This, however, is a point that is never reached in mythology. Perhaps the nearest is the point reached in thought in the Far East. The Buddhist finds the gods are temporary manifestations, more durable than humans, but not eternal. In their thought there has been a continuous development of life for untold ages, so that the question of a creation is of little importance, and one sky god is likely to be superseded by another. All is in transition on the path to the state of Nirvana, which is simply nothing of this material universe. The Taoists gave the impression that Tao was before space or time, and that Tao formed a feminine counterpart and so commenced a chain of being. But all was uncertain and formless, because Tao was everywhere and nowhere, was everything and nothing.

Now, whether there is any unifying thread in these different forms of belief is a matter of debate. The variants are many, and cultural contacts between people of different continents are unlikely. It seems on balance that the nature of human beings is to accept the idea of a supernatural being of some kind. This was the simplest answer to the problem of the origin of the earth on which mankind lived. At first the emotion felt was vague and irrational. There was a Power Above, and that was sufficient. Later we find civilization has advanced and that with larger communities and greater leisure a class of philosopher-priests develops: hence the many intellectualizations. Reasoning was limited to the premises of the local folklore. On the basis of the stories of the gods rational eschatologies were constructed. But always this world above the earth was a place far from mankind, distant, little concerned, but full of magical power. If one seeks an externalization of the idea it is to be found in the stars. The mystery of the great celestial globe which encircles the earth always impressed primitive man. In the patterns of the stars, particularly those on the road of the sun and moon (the Zodiac), gods and heroes were seen, but beyond it ever the great mystery —who was up there turning the wheels of fate?

To us it is all different; the starry orb has become deep space, perhaps endless. All the objects within it move to well-defined laws. We end up by getting nowhere, and the final answers are still a matter of debate. But what of our material world with its seasons and extensions in space? How did the ancestors think of them?

Below: The sun's path among the constellations with the signs of the Zodiac among the other star groups

2. The Winter Sleep

Our views of the quiet time of the year are complicated by the Christmas celebrations, and also by the great celebration of November which in Britain is linked with Guy Fawkes. Guy has become a strange mixture of folk hero and the ultimate villain. He was the explosives expert who was in charge of the plan to blow up King James I and his Parliament on 5 November 1605. By a strange coincidence (the conspirators were impeded and forced to change the day several times) the explosion should have happened alongside a national fire festival, on the night of 31 October to 1 November. This festival on the Feast of All Souls is now kept as a day of remembrance for the dead. When the British changed their calendar in 1752 eleven days were removed from that year, so that the true anniversary of the old festival of the dead fell on 11 November. But in more ancient times this festival marked the death of the year. The Celtic peoples, who were basically farmers, held a great festival with bonfires and rolling fire-wheels to mark the death of the old year and the falling of the sun to the depths of winter. It is probable that the burning of prisoners of war mentioned by Caesar took place at this time. In some way the festival was a prayer to Llwy the Long-Handed, the Rising Sun, to come back and spread blessings over the land in the coming year. It was believed that the world of nature went to sleep, only to awake again on 2 February at the snowdrop festival, now the Feast of the Purification.

A legend of the god Pwyll, Lord of the Westering Sun, is preserved in the ancient Welsh book of stories, the *Mabinogion*. As usual, by the time the story came into writing cultural change had softened its outlines, but it remains a powerful myth echoing ancient thought. The main change is that the gods have become princes and kings, though their abodes remain only partly on earth. The structure of an early medieval society has taken over, but the magic remains. This is a normal process in the transition of myth to folktale.

Here is the story: Pwyll, Lord of Dyfed was a great king and a brave warrior. One day he set out to hunt the deer in a valley where the mountains began (one can see the place now near Llantony Abbey). He travelled the forests, and after passing through a dark thicket he came to a beautiful meadow. There, bursting from the woods on the mountain slope, he saw a magnificent hart. It bounded into the open chased by another pack of hounds. They belled in a tone of their own which he had never heard before, and they were brilliant white with no speck on them except that they had red ears. They were so brilliant and strange that he was unable to concentrate on his own pack, which rushed at the new hounds just as they had torn down the stag. Pwyll turned to them and saw his dogs had surrounded it. He strode up to cut its throat.

A modern Guy Fawkes bonfire still symbolizes the conquering of darkness

Suddenly from the wood there rode a nobleman on a dapple grey horse. He upbraided Pwyll at his bad manners, and threatened to disgrace him at every turn throughout his life; but Pwyll had the grace to give a humble apology. His opponent then revealed himself as Arawn, Lord of Annwn (king of the Underworld). The strange king told Pwyll that friendship would be fully restored if Pwyll would undertake a task of defeating a rival lord of the Underworld; but first Pwyll and Arawn must change places. So by great magic each assumed the form of the other, and Pwyll was taken to the cave which was the gateway on the road to Annwn.

In Annwn no one knew that Pwyll was not Arawn. The nobles served him and at the great table in the hall there was conversation. The Queen of Annwn was the most beautiful of women, wise in discourse and elegant in form. There was no man who would not have desired her. But at night when they retired to bed naked, as was the custom in those times, both were silent, and Pwyll turned his back to the back of the beautiful queen. Thus was their relationship for the full space of a year, and yet their friendship during the days never waned.

When the day of adventure was come, Pwyll, fully armed, rode up the path to the outer world, and reached a river, across which was the beautiful meadow. There on the other side was Hafgan who claimed to be Lord of Annwn. The great warriors prepared to strike and rode at each other. As they met in the middle of that cold stream Pwyll swung his sword, slicing his opponent through the shoulder and giving him a terrible blow. Hafgan screamed and pleaded to be given his death blow, but Pwyll remembered that he had been warned that a second blow would restore Hafgan. He refused to slay Hafgan and sent him away: he died before he could find succour. With this achieved Pwyll crossed to the green meadow. There Arawn met him, and after thanking him for restoring the unity of the underworld realm they exchanged appearances. Arawn found his kingdom at peace and full of happiness, though the Queen was happily surprised when at last he gave her pleasure in their great bed. Pwyll returned to his fortress and there heard that in the year which had gone he had been a bringer of peace and prosperity to his people. Thus the western sun and the northern sun-under-the-earth had changed places. This ancient story derived from some earlier concept now lost.

The Celtic concept of the year depended on the sinking of the sun in winter and his subsequent return. It is interesting to find that the other-world was described as being like this world, only rather more glorious. This is close to the idea of Avalon, the Apple Island of the west, which the great departed reached by boat going into the sunset. That way went Arthur the King attended by the dark maidens who are also the blackbirds, harbingers of peaceful death, to some old families of Celtic origin.

Above: A Celtic god as the hunter of the forests, from La Colle, Mont St Jean

Below: A Saxon helmet from Sutton Hoo with a relief of the horned war god and a dragon crest (7th century, AD)

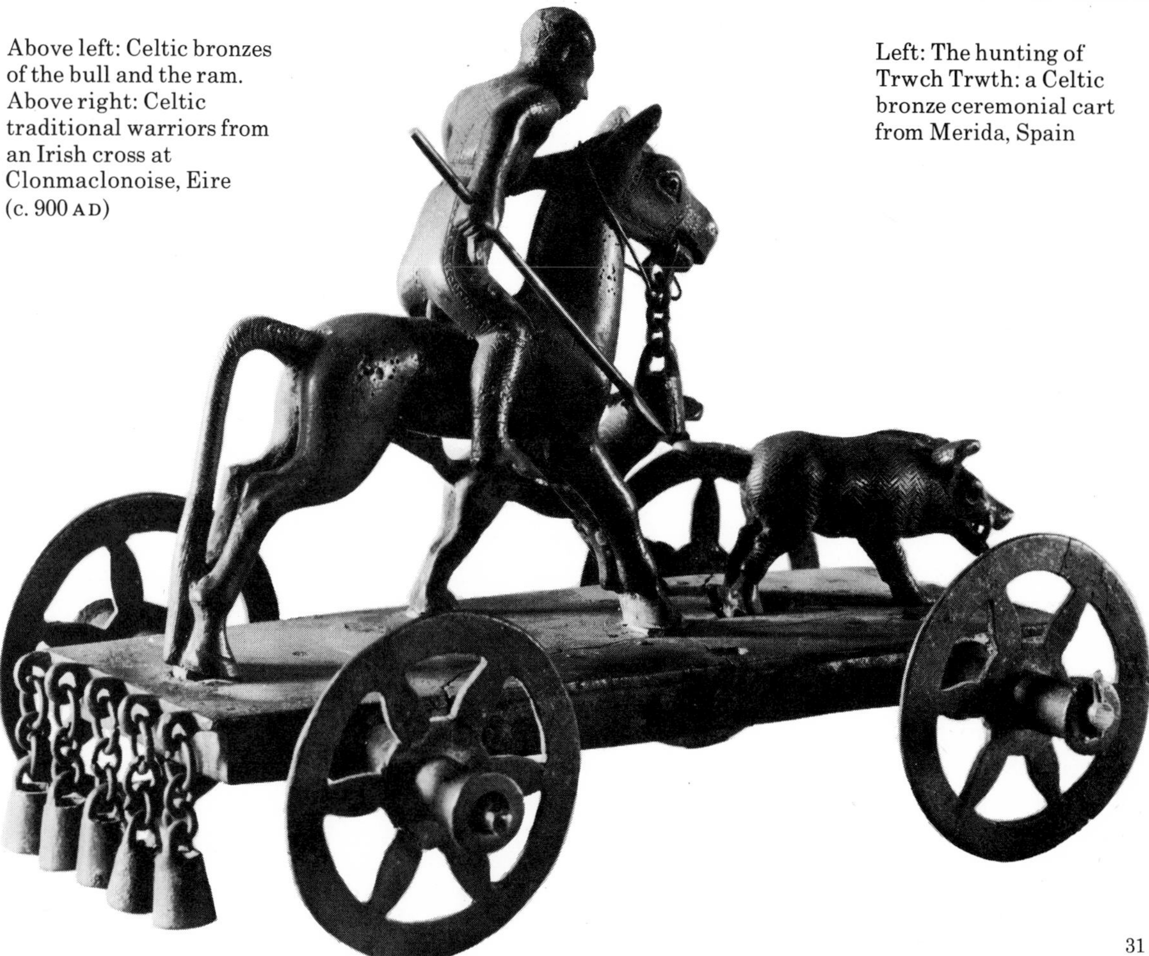

Above left: Celtic bronzes of the bull and the ram. Above right: Celtic traditional warriors from an Irish cross at Clonmaclonoise, Eire (c. 900 AD)

Left: The hunting of Trwch Trwth: a Celtic bronze ceremonial cart from Merida, Spain

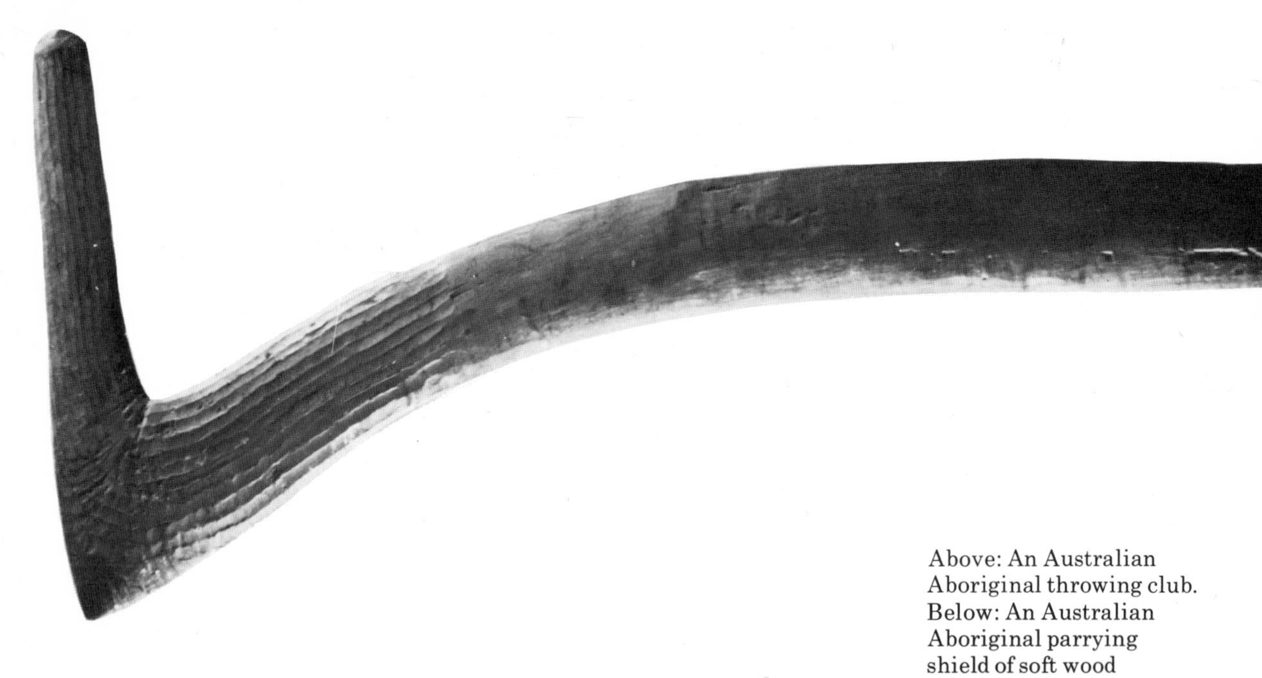

Above: An Australian Aboriginal throwing club.
Below: An Australian Aboriginal parrying shield of soft wood

The idea of the land of the dead being in the west was deep in the Celtic mind, a link with the dark land where the sun descended. It has parallels in Polynesian thought, too, where the souls were said to cross the sea over the trail shown by the sun at setting. Souls, being from the living world, went down with the sun in the west. Their festival was in November, the downturning of life in the fields. Then one hoped that they would enter rest in preparation for life, as symbolized by the sleeping and growing seeds.

But the dark winter days were celebrated also by people without agriculture. There is an Australian aboriginal story from the southeast corner of the continent, near the estuary and hills where Melbourne now stands. This is the region where, when Sun Woman is far in the north, there is cold and people used to wrap themselves in opossum skin robes. Sometimes there was snow when the old one in the sky scratched her skin. (Now we say it is the blast of cold air from Antarctica which brings snow to the southlands.) When the world was new, when the ancestors had appeared from the north like giants, and when sun and her brother moon carried their fire-sticks on the journey through the sky, there were two brothers. They were great hunters, and speared much game from among the animals which were not their totem kin. When the cold days came they, like the rest of the little tribe built themselves huts of boughs and slabs of bark.

They then ate meat raw or sundried, but had no fire to cook it with. They saw that the ball of the sun came down low in winter, and they thought that if they could catch her they would become warm and happy again. So they prepared a strong net, a very strong net, and they searched until they found a very tall gum tree. They climbed the tree and waited till the sun came near, then threw their net and captured her. They rushed down and carried the captive sun into their wurley hut, small like a little dome. 'Ah! Good!' they said. But soon they felt too hot, and there was a sweet odour coming from the kangaroo meat, but there was no holding Sun. She set the wurley on fire and the two men leapt out as fast as they could to see the captive Sun fly on across the sky. But they took some of the burning wood and kept it smouldering, for now they could have fire whenever they wished, and they could roast their meat.

But that was a very sacred story and only told to men who must be initiated and given knowledge of how fire came to earth. As for the fire-sticks, they were cared for by women who always carried a glowing stick ready to light a fire and roast the food when hunters returned home. But the women were never told how the useful fire was first captured by brave men.

Below: The sun carved on a boomerang from Western Australia (mid-19th century)

This myth was directly conditioned by an observation that the sun was lower in the sky in the winter. Ideas of a period of preparation, the ending and beginning of new life seem deeply ingrained in the human psyche. The link, however, with observed astronomical phenomena is not always there. What is more important than the sky is the rhythm of life, both human and agricultural. The connection of the human life of birth, growth and death with the life of the vegetation is important. In the European and North American world the life and death of John Barleycorn is an echo of the vegetation myth. And somewhat similar ideas come from tropical Nigeria. In the Niger Delta region thick forest covered the ground. It was a dangerous world in the old days, for the many rivers and swamps harboured deadly crocodiles and serpents. The forests were the home of the silent leopard, and mysterious illnesses came sweeping from time to time through the villages. In this world, populated by many spirits of nature, mostly inimical, lived the Ibo. They were not, as now, educated traders and capable citizens of a great country rich in oil; in the old times they lived in small clearings in the all-smothering forest. The villages were scattered and independent. There was much strife, so that for safety's sake it was agreed that the markets should be held in selected areas where people did not carry arms. Thus among the old-time Ibo there were many groups and many differing cults, some of which paid homage to a sky god and the sun.

One group, the Umundri, chose a divine king from the members of one of their few leading families, dedicated to the divine ancestor Ndri. When the old Eze Ndri (divine chief) died a new one was chosen under the inspiration of Ndri. He was to have neither brother nor sister, and his parents must have died before he could be consecrated. Although through his social position in the tribe he was entitled to possess the little pendant figure which marked him as immortal, he must die. The Guardian of the Royal Regalia conducts the ceremonies. In the house of the chosen chief a grave is dug and lined with fine planks. The king-to-be is stripped, washed like a corpse, and sprinkled with sweet-scented red camwood powder as if he had died. He is exhorted to go to his grave, from whence he must arise glorified and shining white. (Many Ibo carvings of spirit beings were painted white to show their glorified state.) Then the grave is closed with a wide plank. Earth is scattered on it and his widows sit around and lament his going. Before the tree in which his life was consecrated, animals are sacrificed and the tree cut down. All his contacts with the world of the living have been destroyed.

At the end of the day the grave is opened, and the 'corpse' is removed. His grave clothes are stripped away and he is washed in a lake which has been the home of a spirit power for many ages. Then he is smeared with white clay from head to toe. He has come forth glorious, the white shining one.

The next move is to take the new divine king to the sacred village, Aguku, where, placed upon a sacred mound which was a termite hill, he prays for his people to the Creator and the Ancestors. Henceforward he must wear only white or blue cloth, his legs are graced by copper anklets, and he may only walk barefoot. He then makes a circuit of the whole tribal territory, never eating in public; for the divine beings do not eat, and so he must never be seen to eat. His food is prepared by members of a sacred clan, and they are the only people allowed to touch him. So sacred is he that he is fed by a boy who has not reached puberty, and who belongs to the sacred Adama lineage.

At the far end of his long pilgrimage he reaches Aguleri. There he is seated on a pile of stones (not easily found in that swampy delta country) and given some long thin 'rays' of white clay to eat. These symbolize the feeding of the divine ancestor with light. Now he must create the world anew. A special messenger is detailed to dive into a pool and bring up a ball of white clay, which stands for the world. This is done as soon as the new Eze Ndri has said his blessing over the waters. He is now like the creator, lord of the newly-awakened world. He must now return to the sacred central village at Aguku, never to leave it again. The god has returned to live among his people. For a year he lives secluded in a simple hut where he works great magic for his people. He has to make a palm tree both flower and bear fruit in

Above right: Villages in the Niger valley celebrate the cycle of life. Below right: A detail from an engraved walrus tusk shows the Eskimos' preoccupation with food and hunting

This Nigerian Ibo headdress represents a divine king and his family

one day. This done, the oil is pressed from the fruit, and sent to take part in the sacrifices to keep the land fertile.

At the end of the year of seclusion the Eze Ndri is installed in a new palace of finely carved wood. In the centre is a mound which contains the crowned skull of his predecessor. A ritual combat showing the changes of life in which age defeats youth is performed, and then the ruler is given his regalia, the holy brass mask, and a feathered leather crown. The Eze Ndri then seats himself on the stool on top of the mound. After a while he proceeds from his temple-palace to the town. Great sacrifices are made, human in olden times but now animal. Festival games and banquets are held. Then for twelve days the Eze Ndri sits enthroned to receive representatives from the villages of his kingdom. Finally four mounds are made in front of him, and linked by cords. He blesses them, and by so doing opens the markets of all the land. Life goes on in a normal way again.

Thus the Ibo celebrated life and death in the person of a divine ruler. There is a continual cycle of life—burial—resurrection—giving of fertility—establishment of markets. The resurrection is not in theory a return to the living world but an appearance in a glorified and creative state. Anthropologists have found several links between this ceremony and the rituals of Pharaonic Egypt, not unexpectedly since much influence permeated from Nubia

Above: A western Ibo housepost shows a woman threatened by a leopard.
Right: A clay ancestral shrine from the Ibo of Southern Nigeria

Left: The hunting equipment of the Aborigine: an axe, lances, boomerangs and a shield

through the grasslands of the Sudan and then further south by trade and metalworking contacts to the peoples of the forest. In this case the myth of tribal origin has been re-enacted on a material level of higher potency than the more usual survivals in folk-dance. It is particularly interesting because although the Eze Ndri is a sun god, the ceremony shows no direct connection with the movement of the sun in the sky.

Next, we may direct our search to where there should be some relics of mythology about the winter darkness—Finland. The ancient Finnish collection of poems known as the *Kalevala* tells a story of great magic, when the first magician tries to bring back the sun and moon which had been hidden away by an evil witch-woman. The basic framework is good, simple story telling of a people dependent on their farming and hunting in the wooded land of a thousand lakes. There have, of course, been many influences from outside so that it is probable that the removal of both sun and moon together is a confusion which crept in to make the ancient story more credible. It appears in sections 47, 48 and 49 of this great epic treasury.

The hero of the story is the great magician, the ever-old and ever-mighty Väinämöinen, the son of the daughter of the winds who created our earth. He is assisted by Ilmarinen, who was once the god of the earth and its metals, a great smith of iron, and the ever-changeable Lemminkkäinen, a joyful trickster who helps with a certain magic of his own. The opposition is from Louhi, a mighty feminine power, queen of the dark lands to the far north of Finland, which were called Pohjola. It sounds like a kind of underworld for the dead, but was believed to be the northern end of the earth.

Now Väinämöinen was singing to his magic harp, and his music was wonderful. The moon came from her home in the crooked birch tree, and the sun swept down from his tall fir tree to listen to the music which filled all the world with delight. But old Louhi took her opportunity and crept up to trap them. She persuaded them to come away with her to visit her own mysterious realm of darkness. Once there she led them into a cavern amid the speckled rocks as hard as iron. She sung a charm so that they should never escape until she might come to free them, leading nine white stallions foaled by a single mare. (These may represent the Pleiades around Alcyone at their heliacal rising in April.)

The sky and the whole world of men became dark. Even the heavenly abode of Ukko, the Creator, was without light. Thereupon the Creator took his sword and struck fire from his nails and limbs, and gave it to the maiden of the air to care for until it could be used to make a new sun and moon. The maiden rocked it in a golden cradle and cared for it until it grew large. Then she

Left: A modern Finnish sculpture representing Lemminkäinen.
Below: Ilmarinen forges the magic sword: a scene from the *Kalevala*

picked it up, and tripped. It fell from her arms, down through the spheres of the turning sky and crashed to earth. It caused a terrible fire in the forests, destroying life everywhere it went. Women and children had no protection and were burnt up, and rivers flowed so that a great lake formed. (This sounds like the reaction of the frozen tundra to a huge meteor.)

Väinämöinen and the craftsman Ilmarinen made themselves a boat to seek the fire, now that the sun was gone. They sailed past the estuary of the Neva and met the First Maiden, the lady Ilmatar. She told them of the disasters and directed them to Lake Alue, which had passed through three terrible upheavals in the summertime. Eventually a fish had swallowed the fire spark; then another larger fish had swallowed the first one; this happened four times.

The two heroes took tree bast and wove themselves a net. They cast many times and failed, but they would not give up the search. They found the first seed of flax and planted it in the ash of the fires. It grew and became a fine plant. In a single night it grew like a beautiful tree. They then prepared it by moonlight (a contradiction which hints that the moon was not hidden in some versions of the original poem). With the linen thread they made a new and stronger net. It was so huge that it took hundreds of people to drag it around the lake. The heroes then went into the water to catch the fish, but without success. Then a dwarf of tremendous strength arose from the waters. With prayers to the water spirits he tore up a tree and beat the waters to disturb the fish. Then Väinämöinen drew in the net and found the great fish. It was dangerous to touch it, but the Creator sent his son to cut it open with a magic knife and the fish was sliced open along with the other fish inside. The spark of fire was found but it escaped, singeing the beard of Väinämöinen and seriously burning the smith Ilmarinen. However, it was an injury quickly cured by the Hoarfrost giantess, and the ointments sent by Ukko from his heaven.

With the magic fire recaptured and safely on earth the people called on Ilmarinen to forge a new source of light. The young men and the girls both called for a return of the moon to give light in their darkness. The great smith forged gold and silver to make a sun and moon, but Väinämöinen counselled him that it would be useless. The smith persisted and after mighty labour put the sun on the crooked birch tree and the moon on the tall pine. Nevertheless there was no shining light from them.

Väinämöinen cast lots with sticks to ask the Creator to give him guidance to find where the true luminaries were hidden. The lots gave him the desired information, that the sun and moon were both hidden in a mountain in the land of darkness. He travelled many days and came to the river which divided the two

lands. None could be found to ferry him across. Then he lit a fire and sang magic songs so that the Lady Louhi, the aged goddess of the dark land, heard him. Then he waded into the river and marched through it to assault the country folk of that dark land. He slew the warriors and destroyed many villages. Then, unable to get at the imprisoned sun and moon, he returned to Ilmarinen the smith who forged him many more massive weapons. The smoke of the forge rose high in the air and the ringing hammer strokes reverberated. Louhi heard them. Changing herself into the form of a grey owl she flew to the forge. She questioned Ilmarinen about his work. 'I forge a neck ring to imprison Louhi in the granite mountain,' said he. Finding the threat of doom upon her, especially now that her armies were destroyed, Louhi flew away into the dark. Then suddenly a high-flying dove felt the warmth of the sun and flew down to tell Ilmarinen that sun and moon were both released and rising into the heavens. He told the Old Wise One.

Väinämöinen thereupon sang a chant of praise, calling the sun the golden cuckoo and the moon the silver dove. He prayed for good fortune for the hunters and fishermen now that once again they could see their work.

This Finnish legend, from the *Kalevala*, gives a very ancient story from Northern Europe. It has obviously been added to from time to time, and even rationalized, but it retains most of its heritage from the past as a myth, and lives on today because of its attitude to the world of nature. The story belongs to the Iron Age since we find the magical Ilmarinen is an iron smith; yet the way of the hunters and of the animals is that of late Stone Age times. We have the picture, and probably a very true one, of a hunting society newly introduced to metals from their neighbours.

Above: A late 19th century western Eskimo paddle linking eroticism with the successful hunt

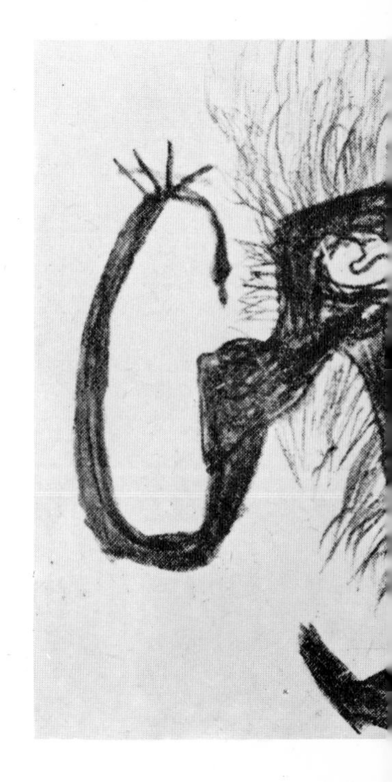

The Eskimos were a people without metals, who lived by hunting. Their life was determined by the division of the year into the time when the sun-girl shone, and when the sun was away hunting and the moon man illuminated the sky. Their preoccupation was with food. In their hard and happy life there was little leisure time. Everyone was occupied with making clothes, weapons, and transport, both sledges and kayaks. In the evenings and in bad weather when they could not move from their homes they told stories of wonder. In every little tribe there was at least one person who was inspired by spirits. When the seizure came on there was a swaying of the world and uncertainty and fear overcame the shaman. He could see the beings of the spirit world, and wondered at their marvellous powers. In our case the shaman, who lived among the Caribou Eskimos of Northern Canada, could never resist asking the spirits what happened to the caribou when the world was covered by snow in the winter. One day he was in trance when his protective spirit, a torngak of great power, told him that his questions should be answered, provided that he did not tell of the way to the place which he should see. He was told to travel alone in a special and secret direction. To make the journey he took snow-shoes and extra boots, for he must go alone, without supernatural help.

So the shaman walked through the snows, around lakes and across the tundra. He found little enough to eat, but managed to catch a few hares and trap a few birds. For two moons he walked and nowhere did he see either caribou or other human beings. Then suddenly the torngak appeared to him again.

The hunter must be still and silent, uttering no sound, and not allowing his natural wishes to kill animals for food to assume form in his mind. He must simply be there, nothing more, until the sun set.

Below: A tournarak, an evil spirit of the western eskimo

Top: An Alaskan Eskimo mask representing the spirit of the winter frost.
Centre: This ivory net-sinker brings good luck to the Eskimo in fishing.
Bottom: A shaman's soul catcher, used among the Indians of British Columbia

Then when the last glow had faded he was told to look around him. He saw as if from a great distance an enormous winter house built of rocks. It was as all Eskimo winter houses are, mostly underground, and all he could see of the outside was its rocky domed roof with grass growing on it. The entrance through the tunnel, which was built to prevent the winds blowing into the house, was bigger than the crawling tunnel of an Eskimo house. This one allowed even the great bull caribou to carry his antlered head high as he walked through. Before the house stood a great bull, huge, so that an ordinary moose could walk under his legs without touching him. Then the hunter was aware of a moving mist, and as he looked he saw that it was swirling to the house, but it was not just mist but all the herds of caribou, in the northland silently moving to the tunnel, through which they entered their underground home for the days when the sun did not shine. Guarding the great house of the caribou the gigantic bull marshalled the migrant herds into their winter home and then lay down guarding the entrance.

The hunter then felt himself turned away. The magic boots the torngak gave him helped him to make the journey back more speedily. But though he had learned where the caribou went in the snow times he never found the direction, nor could he describe the road across the desolate tundra. So it was safe for the spirits to allow him to tell his story.

Thus the hunting peoples of the North rationalized the winter migration of the herds. They thought them to be motivated in the same way as humans, especially in their social reaction to climate.

In every case we have found that people have translated their own way of life as the only way. Their gods have lived and behaved like people to some extent, though much more powerful. When it comes to anomalies one can often postulate some other place of origin. It is as if the people moved but never adjusted their myths. An important case in point is the Inca period of penance and fasting which took place in November, which has its only rational explanation in some link with the northern hemisphere solemnizations of the approach of winter darkness. The Australian aboriginal story of the catching of the sun is simply a matter of local observation of the comparatively low level of the sun in the north during winter there. After all, the aboriginal peoples have been moving into Australia over a period in excess of 25,000 years.

Everywhere there seems to have been a feeling that November marked the ending of a period of activity: the point where life went to sleep and production of new life was at its lowest ebb. We must next turn towards the first awakening of nature.

3. The Rising Sun

On 2 February the old-time Celtic peoples celebrated the awakening of the earth. In the Christian world it is candlemass, the Feast of the Purification. In pagan days it was the snowdrop festival, a festival especially to celebrate young children. Its signal was the appearance of the delicate white snowdrops in the woodlands. But, of course, a vegetation festival was confined to a relatively narrow band of latitude. The world view must be different. Everywhere the star watchers noted that the second quarter of the farmers' year would be the day (our 2 February) on which in the morning Regulus in Leo was setting, and in the evening Sirius was on the eastern horizon. The great event they all welcomed was the way in which the sun had begun to rise in the sky. It was a matter for a mythological celebration in ceremonial and rejoicing in the Middle Earth, the Mediterranean, for there Spring was obviously beginning. Further north there was a feeling of hope that the first melting of the frosts would bring a good year. Mother Earth was awakening. Perhaps some of the philosophical elders thought that in the time of the youth of the year they might remember the lost innocence of their younger days.

Thus in this section we should look forward and see the young rising sun as the forerunner of the summer to come. The region of the world where the sun was most neglected was the Pacific Ocean. The sun was not a destroyer; it did not disappear in winter; it did not even become low in the sky. Hence the shining ball of light was a natural thing, just another of the children of Ta'aroa, like the islands and waves. From the Micronesian islands, whose Polynesian descendants probably left them behind as they gradually pushed further out into the great waters, there is a story of a human sun. The Gilbertese told of a creator called Na Reau who made the first man and woman to live on the beautiful islands. They were forbidden to have children (a garbled echo of a missionary story of Adam and Eve?) but in secret they disobeyed the god, finding that there was delight in sex. Eventually they had three children. But they were not unobserved. The eel swam quietly to the home of Na Reau and told him that the humans had increased their number. The jealous god took his great war club to destroy them.

He arrived in the islands and was met by the first two people who sought his mercy on the grounds that the children were necessary for human life, for one was controller of the fish in the sea, and another was the moon to light them in the dark nights, and the third was the sun, who made work possible all day long. So, seeing that humans were reasonable creatures, the creator left them to follow their own path. This innocent little fable has nothing to do with the seasons, because in Micronesia there are no seasons. Its most interesting point is that it echoes an almost

Gilbertese children in ceremonial dance costume

universal tradition that sun and moon come later after a phase of darkness in which life began. Is this attitude of mind due to a psychological understanding that life and intelligence arose out of the deeps of the unconscious state? We cannot be sure.

The date of the first returning of the sun in northern latitudes is given as 2 February, though this is a theoretical date relating to vegetation changes. It can be determined by the stars, for at that time of the year the two stars of Gemini, the twins, and Procyon set on the western horizon as the sun rises. The modern astronomical model of the universe matters not at all to primitive man. The ancestors looked at the sky and saw the stars telling the seasons and foretelling the appearance of plants and animals all in due season. It is no surprise to find these stars symbolized as people in a Navajo myth, which comes from the North American dry lands around the same latitude as Morocco. Here the constellation Gemini passes overhead at midnight in mid-January. It is prominent enough to figure in myth, and when in February the twin stars seem to reach the edge of the earth at sunrise there is reason for the shaman-astrologer to see a link between earth and sky beings.

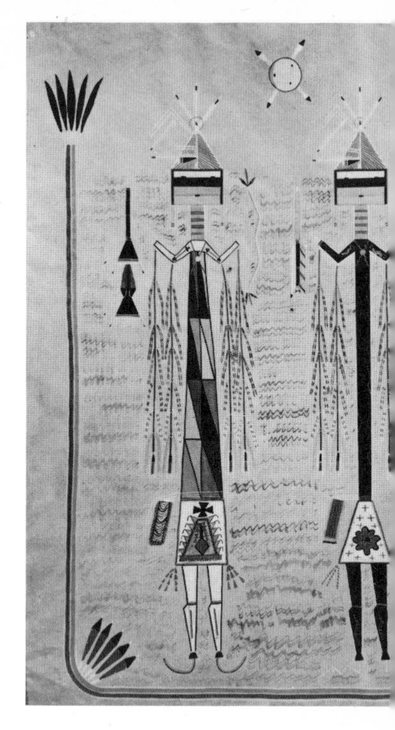

Above: A Navajo painting of four rain spirits with rain pendant from their hands, surrounded by lightning and a rainbow, from the Shooting Chant, a Navajo ceremony lasting several days

Once upon a time, a very real time, when men had been punished by the gods for their neglectful behaviour, First Woman looked at the people and was sorry for them because the plague of demonic monsters was still destroying them. They had been disobedient and wilful like children but she thought that the horrors which had been unleashed upon them were too bad. She wished for a child. Near her mountain in the northwestern quarter of the country she found a girl child lying in the sands. She took the little thing with her into the sacred mountain. Then the child proved that magic was upon her. In four days and in perfectly natural rhythms the girl grew into a beautiful young woman. Estanatlehi was her name. She went walking in the woods on the mountain slope, and there she met a young man of great beauty. For four days they met and lay down to make love to one another, for each was so beautiful. She told First Man and First Woman of her happiness. But they thought it was only imagination, for they found no tracks on the ground. But First Man looked again and saw the one who did not touch the ground: it was the sun.

Estanatlehi persuaded her parents to build a screen near the house; there for four more days she enfolded the sun prince in her body. They were in perfect happiness. Then another magical four days went by and she gave birth to twins. In four days they grew into handsome young men, and in another four days they demanded to see their mysterious father. Then on the fifth day they climbed into the mountains to enquire the way. A stranger met them and told them that the home of the sun was beyond the

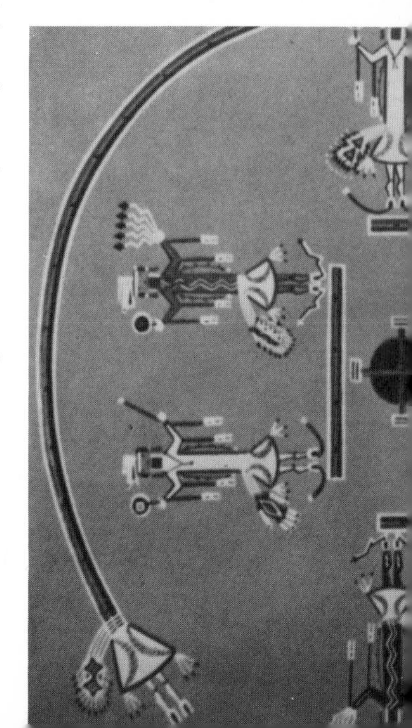

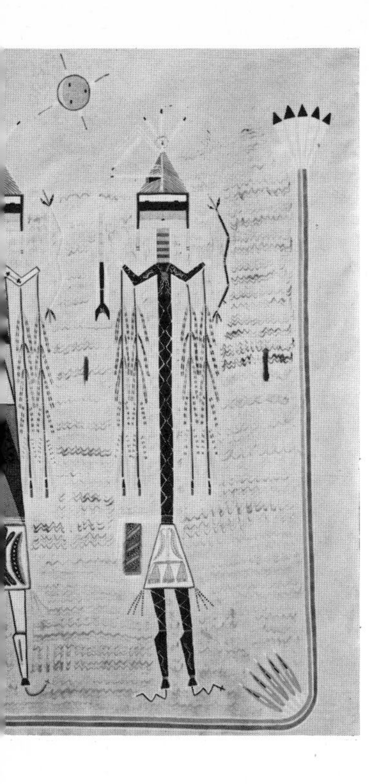

mountain on the edge of the earth, to the east. So they journeyed and went far until they came to the great house of the sun. It was guarded by the Bear and the Serpent (probably stars or constellations, though not those known by the same names by western astronomers). In the house they saw the sun's wife with twin sons. (Perhaps she was Estanatlehi, but not certainly so. They are almost certainly the twin stars Castor and Pollux with Procyon. That would assume that the sun was in his house at the beginning of February.)

The sun's wife warned the visitors that they should go before her husband returned for fear of angering him, but her twin boys welcomed their brothers, and hid them in a skin bundle on a drying frame. When the sun returned he had already been told about the visitors' arrival. So his twins told him the truth. He unrolled the skin which hid them and out fell the twins from earth. He offered them all manner of wealth, in each of the four directions of the world he offered them great treasures, but they refused all honours and power. They had been tested by being thrown against the mountains of the four directions, but had always bounced back unhurt; now that they had scorned treasures the sun asked them their mission. They replied with the story of the suffering of mankind in their struggle to resist the monsters. The sun then gave them a mighty war coat, the knife of victory, a charm for the winds, and a bundle of thunderbolts. Then wrapping them in a great thundercloud he brought them to earth in their own country, to the Eastern mountain which was the home of a terrible giant. The brothers conquered and destroyed him with the help of the sun. Then they destroyed the awesome giant antelope, and the man-eating birds. The ogre that slew people who walked in the mountains was next slain, and finally the people whose glance was deadly lightning were subdued. The tasks of the twins were now finished. They went back to the lodge of the sun to return the magic weapons. The sun was very proud of them and desired to visit Estanatlehi again. He built a palace in the east for First Man and First Woman, and in the west he built a palace for Estanatlehi. Thus every evening when he came down from the sky he could look on the face of his beloved.

Below: Sister Rainbow blesses the spirits of the four directions

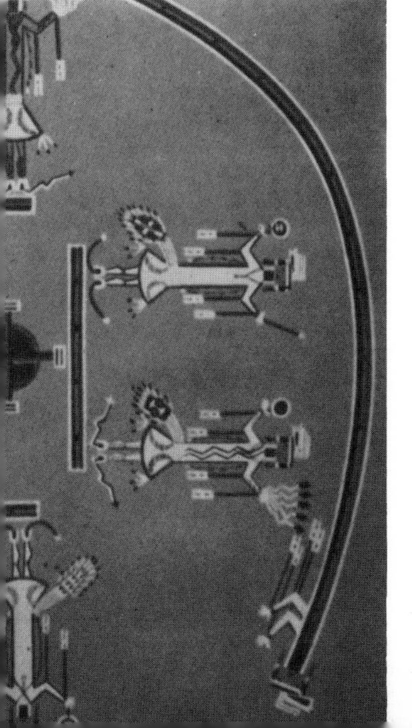

In this myth, which superficially is a long story full of adventure, the positions of the houses represent stars: Castor, Pollux and Procyon, the family at sunset, and possibly Antares and Vega at sunrise, all in February and early in the month. The two twin brothers are planetary spirits, the Morning and Evening Star. They take turns in conquering evil, and sometimes become invisible when they are in the house of the sun. But we must remember that these sky myths represent something apart from just the movements of the heavens; they also reflect an inner world, partly a rhythm of time, partly the magical story of human life and the conquering of its difficulties. But under the ever-bright skies of the Navajo there is little to be seen of the winter sun himself. Perhaps the ancestors long ago before the long forgotten journey southwards elaborated the legend, but to the modern Navajo all these adventures took place in their own beloved land.

The winter darkness and the emergence to herald springtime is to be found beautifully expressed in Japan. The heart of Japan is only latitude 36° north, parallel with Gibraltar and Malta. Yet the story of the Sun Lady is as clear as if it had a circumpolar origin. However, the climate is much more extreme than that of western Europe, and so the stresses of snowtime may well have added to the feeling of darkness when the sun was down to only 58° at midday in winter as against 14° from the vertical in summer (32° and 76° above the horizon).

Now there were once the great waters, and upon the waters there appeared something like an iridescent shape of oil, which floated and moved, flowing freely. Then gods were born, and eight generations of gods came and then hid themselves until Izanagi and Izanami were born. As commanded, they then made the earth solid under heaven. In many adventures they met and coupled, thus creating the many islands in the ocean. At last Izanami gave birth to Fire, but this last birth killed her. Izanagi beheaded the unfortunate child but other deities were born from its blood. Then inconsolable Izanagi descended to the underworld and sought his lost beloved. Alas, he was allowed to see only her decomposing corpse, and, filled with horror, he rushed away pursued by the powers of hell. At last he reached the mouth of the cave that was the entrance to the underworld, threw peaches to the hell hounds who were chasing and so escaped. The gate of the underworld was shut, and so it remains to this day. Then, fouled by his contact with death, Izanagi the god set to cleansing himself. Everything he cleansed brought forth some new life. When he was finally stripped he washed in the ocean and all fishes were born. Then he washed his eyes. From the right eye the beautiful Sun Lady was born, and from the left her sister the Moon, Sukiyomi. Lastly he washed his nose, and the tempestuous and mischievous god Susanoo was born. Then there was peace again. The goddess born as the Sun Lady was the divine and ever-loved Amaterasu.

Thus the world became lovely under the shining glory of Amaterasu and the fitful gentleness of Sukiyomi. All things prospered, until Susanoo decided to leave his realm of the sea and visit his sister Amaterasu. Then befell strange things because Susanoo could not restrain himself from violent play. Amaterasu, expecting difficulties, had assumed warrior's garb.

Izanami and Izanagi stand on the floating Bridge of Heaven as the wagtail approaches them before the emergence of Earth

耕隨筆

伊邪那岐伊邪那美二神
立天浮橋圖

月耕

She carried arrows on her back and held forth her bow humming and ready for action. As a proof of his goodwill Susanoo promised her to make children by magic. He wished for some boys and Amaterasu took his sword, broke it into three pieces and after chewing them blew from her mouth a vapour which turned into three beautiful boys. She then gave five necklaces to Susanoo, who chewed them likewise and breathed a mist which became five girls. Amaterasu claimed them as her children, and the eldest boy became the ancestor of the Emperors of Japan. All the others were ancestors of the most noble clans.

So happy was Susanoo that he took to dancing and became

Amaterasu, the sun goddess, is teased out of her cave by the laughter of the gods

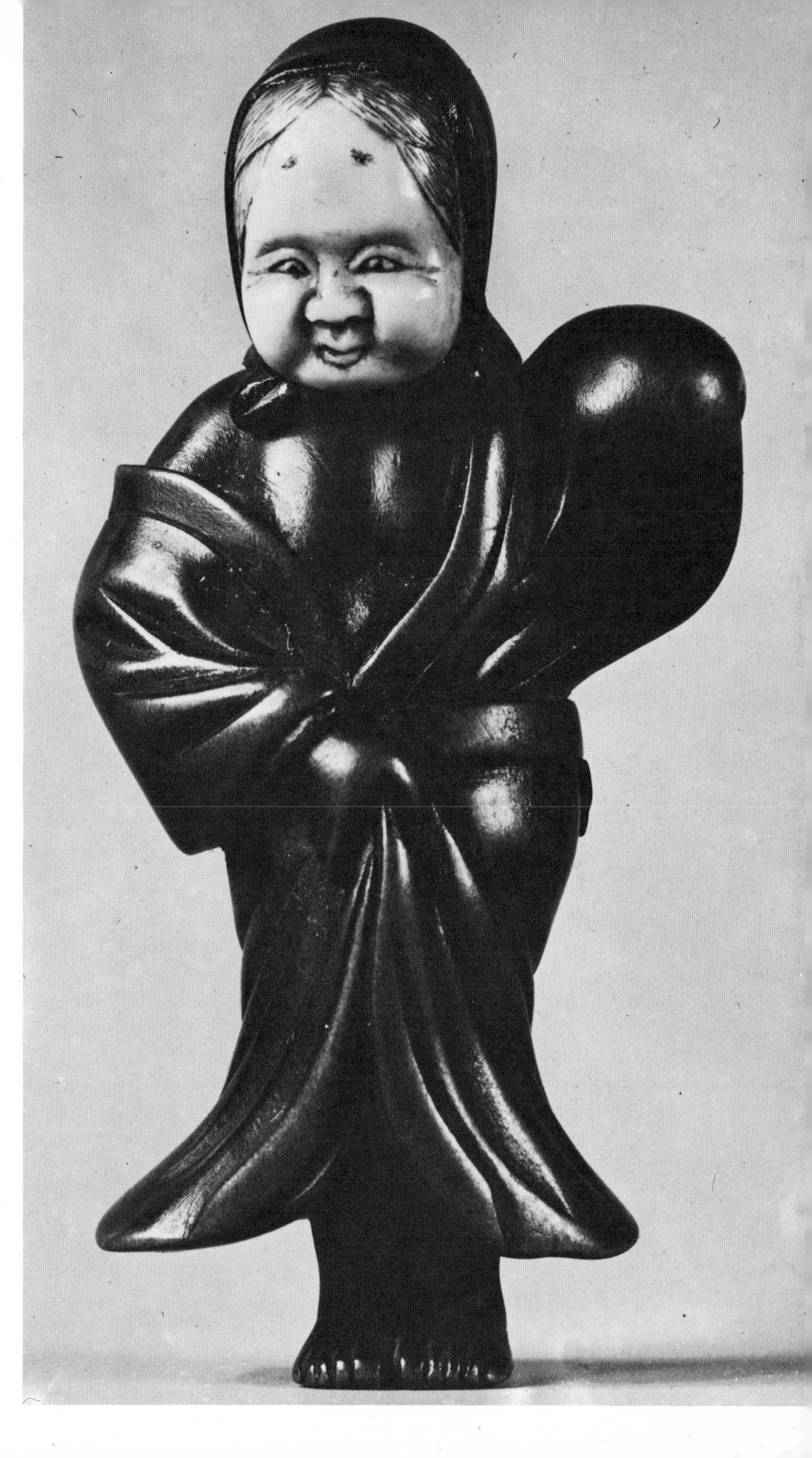

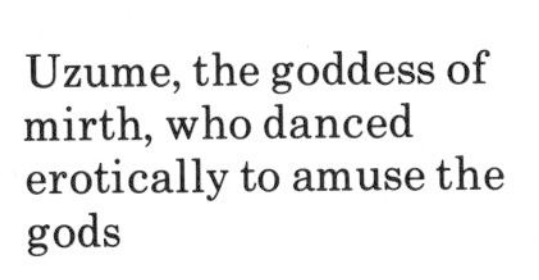

Uzume, the goddess of mirth, who danced erotically to amuse the gods

more and more violent. He destroyed the rice fields in his violence, filled in the water courses, and deposited excrement in the temples made for the ceremonies of the first fruits. Amaterasu tried to excuse her brother, but like the typhoon he could not be brought to rest. One day he tore the roof off the palace where Amaterasu was weaving glorious garments and threw in the carcass of a piebald horse which he had flayed. It was a joke, but it caused the death from shock of one of the maidens of the palace, and so terrified Amaterasu that she fled to shelter in a deep cave. She blocked the entrance with a great rock, and, deprived of her shining presence, the world was left in darkness.

All the agents of evil came out in the darkness to bring trouble to the world and all the gods of good influence gathered to resist them. These gods, an almost infinite number, eight hundred myriads of all the forces of nature, gathered together to decide what to do for the return of Amaterasu, the shining Sun Lady. They called for the advice of the god of memory and accepted what he propounded. First they collected a number of cocks and made them crow by showing lanterns. Thus they symbolized the crowing at dawn which heralded the sun. Then they found necklets of jewels and a beautiful bronze mirror which they hung on a tree before the entrance to the cave, adornments for the morning beautification. Then a large tub was up-ended in front of the cave and the goddess Ama no Uzume put on ornaments of rustling leaves and danced on the tub, pounding with her feet like the pounding of servant girls crushing the rice in the morning. Then she began a striptease to the rhythm, taking her belt off; and the gradual opening of her flowing kimono revealed glimpses of breasts and belly and then it fell away so that all her beauty was revealed. The assembled gods cheered for her and burst into happy laughter as she displayed the home of life and then turned laughing to display other areas of dancing beauty. They made such a noise with their laughter that from within the cave Amaterasu called to ask what the celebration was about. Ama no Uzume replied that they had found a new goddess to give them light and joy. At that she peeped out, and saw the mirror reflecting some of the scene of jollity. She took a step forward and the strongest of the gods dragged her out. Others stretched a rope across the cave so that she could not retreat again. So she stepped forward and once more light and warmth flooded the world. The magical dance of springtime fertility ended and the warmth and love of Amaterasu brought back life after the wintry darkness while she was in the cave.

The violent Susanoo was seized by the other gods, forcibly shaved and then cast out from the heavenly country and thrown to the everyday world.

This beautiful and basically happy myth shows a certain

Osiris with his crook and flail

Above left: In May in the Algarve the Portuguese put stuffed dummies on the roofs, optimistically dressed for a downpour of rain at the beginning of the dry season.
Below left: Citizens of Cadiz at a fiesta celebrate their fruit harvest

community with the ancient festivals of the western European world. One remembers the ancient celebrations of Shrovetide in which the people ate up the last of the fat and fine foods in a wild carnivale (farewell to meat) before the lenten fast. It usually fell in February, and still in many countries is conducted with singing and dancing and comical displays of maskers, and pretty girls who wear anything or nothing according to the circumstances of the moment. No doubt in the past this was the substance of the snowdrop festival in which small children were blessed. It was the return of life to the world of nature, a gay time before the days of short food which heralded the return of the full flowertime of Spring.

In the hot countries around the Mediterranean, particularly in Egypt, the seasonal changes are less marked. The important events for the early people were the bringing of new soil and new life with the Nile floods in July-August and the planting of corn in November. It is strange that the planting of corn should be sad, but just as in England country ballad singers used to lament the death of John Barleycorn, so in old Egypt there were rituals of sorrow at the death of Osiris, the vegetation god. The ripening of corn fell in the period of summer just preceding the Nile floods, but it was February that was associated with the victory of light and the return of brightness to the earth through the defeat of Set by Horus.

Below: A gilt-bronze of Set, the Egyptian opponent of Osiris (19th Dynasty, c. 1300 BC)

Horus is an inexplicable figure at the best. He is all gods at times, and at others a child of prophecy. But he is primarily a solar deity, patron of the Pharaohs, once the lord of all the sky, but later associated with the rising sun, ascending as a hovering falcon, beautiful and terrible. He was opposed by a strange animal-headed deity, Set, who was the patron god of Upper Egypt and also lord of the darkness. (We have a parallel on the hot coast of Peru where the people worshipped the moon and the cool nights and not the divine Sun of the Incas.)

The story of the murder and dismemberment of Osiris belongs elsewhere among myths. But the murder had to be avenged and it fell on Horus to defy and defeat Set. The two were cousins, sons of the sister goddesses Isis and Nephthys, but they were natural opponents. They met and struggled near the junction of Upper and Lower Egypt. There was no quarter, and in the great contest Set tore out one of the eyes of Horus, but Horus knew the magic of Set lay in his fertility, and he seized the penis of the god in a relentless grip and tore off his testicles. The struggle had been fomented by the spirit of Osiris, who told his son Horus of the murderous attack made by Set and asked for revenge. Osiris was involved because the hatred of Set towards the young rising Sun god made him declare that Horus was a bastard and not the offspring of Isis and Osiris.

Left: Osiris as the Lord of the Resurrected Dead (c. 1200 BC)

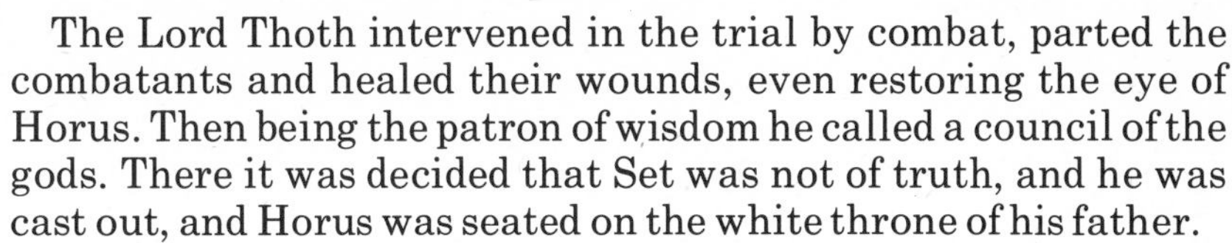

The Lord Thoth intervened in the trial by combat, parted the combatants and healed their wounds, even restoring the eye of Horus. Then being the patron of wisdom he called a council of the gods. There it was decided that Set was not of truth, and he was cast out, and Horus was seated on the white throne of his father.

The struggle reminds one of the Celtic story of the struggle between Gogmagog and Corineus, but it has more to do with cultivation rituals, and in another climate would have been related to early spring. It was a struggle of darkness and light, perhaps of the return of the sun from the burning heats of midsummer. The idea of the sexually powerful Set being deprived of fertility fits in with the ending of the year and the return of light to the world. We cannot be very sure of its calendrical significance because of the Egyptian habit of excluding leap years, thus causing every calendar festival to slip back one day in every four years in a round which would not return to its beginning until 1461 years were completed.

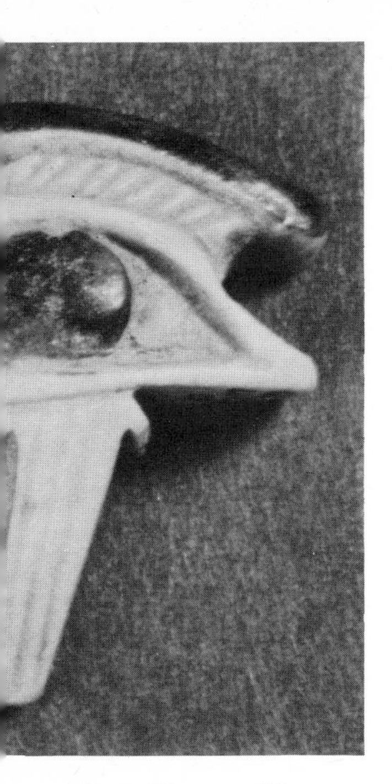

Above: The eye of Horus: an Egyptian charm symbolic of the sun.
Below: An Egyptian stela shows Thoth, or Tehuti, god of wisdom and writing

Certainly the Egyptians had a fixed period festival for the appearance of the Nile floods, but the general moving of feasts through the year must have kept the priests busy with calculations, and the mass of the people in a happy confusion. In later days the mathematically minded Greeks were scandalized, and Ptolemy II tried to arrange a fixed calendar, but there is ample evidence that the Egyptians soon returned to their old habits and continued happily ignoring the barbarians who ruled the country.

Yet we cannot exempt the Greeks from confusions: only they had a legendary event which concerned youth and the sun. The tale of Phaethon's fall was a serious myth, and used to explain the presence of burnt and scarred rocks and rifts on the surface of our planet. One could imagine all manner of explanations for the story of Phaethon. It could refer to a creation story, or to an account of a great comet, or even to a meteor. The crash of Phaethon and the damage to the earth below reminds one of the devastation caused by the spark of fire from the Creator which set the forests on fire in the Finnish *Kalevala*. Or was it originally an experience of an ecstatic who saw something like the miracle at Fatima, in which the sun danced in the sky and was replaced by new forms of light, light in wheels and light falling as snowflakes. This last appearance of unusual phenomena, one might say impossible, was seen by several credible witnesses in this century. But again, Phaethon's story might be a moral tale, or even an account of the apparently erratic behaviour of Venus as Morning Star. It is one of those myths which one has to accept as irrational but which has so great a dramatic impact that it remains in the human mind, an impressive tale about youth and the rising sun and uncertainty.

Phaethon takes control of the sun chariot and terrorizes humanity

We are told that Phaethon was the son of Helios by the nymph Clymene. He was told of his divine parentage and rashly boasted about it. His companions derided him as a dreamer and accused him of inventing a fable. It was Clymene who told her son to approach his divine father and demand some gift which should make it clear to all that he was truly the child of the sun. The young hero set out at night to the end of the earth, and shortly before sunrise entered the celestial hall where his father held court. In a realm of such incredible splendour there was no difficulty in identifying Helios. He was enthroned amid rainbows and the hours, days and the four seasons attended on him. This was such a glorious sight that Phaethon was tongue-tied. Helios, however, sees all things and called his son to him by name. As he did so he screened his unbearable glory so that the mortal boy might approach.

Phaethon told his story and excited the pity of the god, who declared that the lad was truly his son. He declared that he would make all the world realise the divine origin of Phaethon and would give the boy such a gift as would astonish his detractors.

The boy was still hesitant, and to reassure him Helios swore an oath that he would give him any gift that he asked. That sacred oath was a declaration by the Styx, the river which divided death and life. Even the Olympian gods could not break such an oath. At that moment the chariot of the sun was brought in, for it was near time for sunrise. The shining chariot was pulled by four horses of great beauty. They had the gift of flight, but needed the hand of divine wisdom to guide them through their twelve-hour course between sky and earth. Such was their attraction that Phaethon immediately asked his father if he might drive them for just that one day. The oath was irrevocable and Helios could do nothing but keep his word. He explained the dangers of the journey, of the need to keep the middle path through the stars, staying always on the path of the Zodiac. He warned of the dangerous constellations. If this indeed was the February feast, the path would lead from the Lion, on past the Bull, to the final stop with Aquarius the Water-Bearer. Phaethon was warned of the danger which the heavenly creatures could cause him, and that he was neither to approach the starry dome too closely nor to bring the sun too near the earth, which would suffer from its terrible fiery heat. Again Helios begged his human son to accept any other gift and avoid the danger of holding him to the deadly oath. But Phaethon would not deviate from his daring search for glory.

The chariot was ready, the dawn maiden opened the path and Phaethon ascended. The chariot was, as his father had warned him, beyond his strength to control. The horses of the sun soared freely, departing often from their proper course and swaying wildly.

Suddenly they dived and swept near the land, melting snows and causing mountains to erupt as volcanoes. The people of earth were terrified. Many a city burst into flames and its people fled to caves and rivers to pray the great Thunderer, Father of Gods and Men, to save them. But the chariot raced on, drying rivers and lakes and cutting a swathe over the earth where men now see the great deserts. It was on that terrible day that the Ethiopians burned black and their hair twisted into tight knots. Phaethon, terrified, prayed that he might be rescued by his father from the results of his foolish presumption.

But before his father could do anything, great Zeus acted. His thunderbolt fell and struck Phaethon from the chariot. The terrified youth fell to earth, scorched and broken. The remains fell into the river Eridanus. There the nymphs of the river found his fragments and gave them burial. His mother came to lament, ever weeping into the river, and his three sisters lamented so that the gods changed them into elegant poplar trees which at certain seasons weep tears of resin around them. Cygnus, the close friend of Phaethon, begged to be changed into a swan so that he could search the river for any remains. His wish was granted and swans still search at the bottom of the waters.

This strange story has little explanation. It is almost a moral story to remind young people that rashness brings its own downfall. But yet it goes deeper and leads simply to mysteries which are not truly rational.

Around the world the passage from winter to the first presage of returning life was observed by rituals, and where the seasons were not well marked there was still a legend of a promised return from the darkness, yet without the full resurrection of life and fertility. There is usually a theme of gentle development, but it can also be a story of disaster from too rapid a search for ascent. In a way its importance was stressed in the Eleusinian mysteries. The first initiatory ceremonies fell in the month of flowers when the earth was covering herself in a fresh garment of beauty to welcome the *Kore* back after her winter sojourn with Hades. The sacred and ennobling rituals of this early season included public processions and dancing. There were the secret rites in darkened halls and passages under the earth, and sacrifices were made. Publicly, there were sacrifices of pigs. We also know that the postulants were sprinkled with water by the goddess as a mark of their purification. The basis of this first approach to the mysteries was a visit to the underworld to bring the glad tidings of the pending return of the *Kore* to her mourning mother Demeter.

But everyone knew there was a much deeper meaning, one which could never be fully divulged in the true ancient form which it held in the days when Minos ruled in Kaphtor in the midst of the waters. But for all people this mystery of the first sign of spring, this first hope of the return of life, is symbolic of the step towards a richer life in the development of the human soul, a kind of pre-pubertal flowering. Too often the modern world ignores the understanding of individual development and the deep inner need for discovering that life advances by regular stages which are so important that they should be ritualized. Yet there are always forces at work to deceive us. Perhaps civilization itself partakes of the nature of Mercury, the ever-changing smiling messenger of the principle of uncertainty.

Above: An Athenian kore of the late 6th century BC

Right: Zeus casts his thunderbolts (5th century BC)

HOTEL

4. The Trickster Lord of Uncertainty

The disappointments of early spring, the hopes raised by early sunshine and then blighted by the late frosts, probably inspired the curious joking festivals of All Fools' Day in Europe and around the world, the appearance in tribal ceremonies of a scurrilous comic who is considered something important. He is always uncertain in his actions and has an emphatically sexual image. He appeared in the Commedia dell' Arte as Harlequin with a false penis stitched in the appropriate place on his costume; in the Helston Furry dance he was a kind of flopsy dragon who had a penchant for feeling under girls' skirts. Wherever he dances he is a Mercurial character of change and with a spice of idiocy about him. People must laugh at him, and it is notable that serious-minded folk tend to call him the Devil and confuse him with Satan. That is, of course, because they have been deluded into confusing joyousness with sin, and especially condemn sex as something wicked. Fortunately for the human race, the cruelty characteristic of Puritanism is not widespread.

The mythical mischief-maker is an archetype to which we must all face up. He represents something within us which is a true backslider, for he is always an animal-man. Hence in the tales which follow he is irresponsible, sexy and sometimes named for some wild creature. All the same, he can be a lovable fool, who in the end is forgiven for his thefts and lecheries. Many people consider him to be the irresponsible being who made the earth come into being. He is an erratic demiurge, sometimes glorified as the dancing Shiva creating in a wonder of thoughtless delight, or again debased as a curious animal form. Yet the animal seems to be the deeper original. Meanwhile he lives within us all, for he is the principal of uncertainty, the Trickster, well-known to the psychologist because his manifestations are so universal. The more civilized we are the more we tend to ignore his presence and perhaps we try to pretend that he doesn't exist, with usually disastrous consequences. He represents all kinds of instinctive behaviour that is usually not approved by the conscious mind. In the myths of the world he is unmistakable, but his actions vary according to the cultural context of the people telling the story.

He was a favourite of the North American Indians and no ceremony seems to have done without his presence. Among the Pueblo Indians, whose greater festivals must be made into occasions of happiness and laughter rather than religious gloom, the Trickster spirit was embodied in important men of the tribe who painted themselves with black and white stripes, and went around wearing the minimum of clothes, usually worn the wrong way round, and with bare penes, often modelled to make them appear huge. In more recent times with gawping tourists around, the fashion of wearing a false penis has taken over. The whole intention is to make people laugh, and to accept a good deal of

The Furry Dance at Helston survives an ancient May festival. The original ceremony was less respectable

Left: A false-face mask cut from a living tree by the Iroquois of New York State drove away evil influences.
Above: A dance mask from the Haida Indians of British Columbia represents a cannibal spirit

Right: An Etruscan bronze phallic symbol of the 4th century BC with a loop for suspension

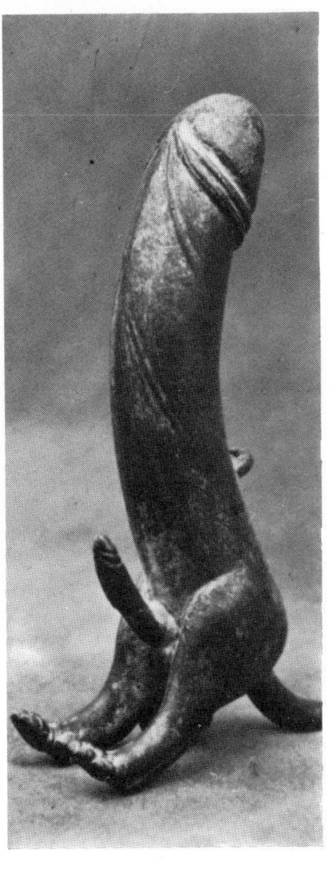

ribald teasing. In this way the participants in the ceremony are kept happy by the Delight-makers.

Sometimes this ambivalent character, the Trickster, was clearly described in a series of tales. The classic form is described in Paul Radin's book on the Trickster where he details the complete surviving myth from the Winnebago. He is at once a being who is a chief, and also an animal. He has familiar conversations with the animals, tricks them and sometimes destroys their children. He is given magic powers, but being unsure tests them and squanders his powers before they can be put to any effective use. His sex life is a disgrace, he deludes young women, deserts his wife, sends his penis to enter girls while bathing, and in the end loses the greater part of that mythological appendage.

His escapades take the form of a series of short stories without much of a connecting theme apart from the generally scurrilous nature of his behaviour. The great theme of his penis is an ancient one and is found about a similar character in several mythologies. It was enormously long, and Trickster used to carry it in a pack on his back. Sometimes he wished to gain pleasure and also to cause trouble and would release it so that it proceeded rather like a homing serpent to find a desirable girl and enter her. It seems that the intrusion was always assumed to give pleasure even if the results later became embarrassing. One day Trickster was proceeding along a woodland trail and he heard a voice from a tree teasing him about his fantastic penis, making fun of him. He could not identify the voice but thought it came from a tree; and when he came closer he heard it coming from a hole in the tree. So he took off his back-pack and uncoiled its contents. He inserted the glans into the hole intending to punish the teaser with an ejaculation in its face. But it kept on teasing and laughing at him because the penis was not long enough. So he kept on inserting the tube, arm-stretch by arm-stretch, until the creature told him that he had no more to stretch into the tree. It was true. Trickster pressed hard but he had reached the end. Then in a rage he saw that the creature had come up from the hole and was still laughing at him. He turned quickly and killed it, smashing it into the ground. But he was now free—his penis was loose. He looked down and found that it was torn to pieces and all that was left to him was the remaining length characteristic of all men since that time. On the underside of the glans one may still see the marks of the chipmunk's teeth.

Trickster tore up the tree and found the broken remains of his former glory. He planted these in the ground, and they became all kinds of root vegetables. So the Trickster created good things for humanity from his own physical deprivation. And the Indians said that the present length of the penis is useful, and no one with a penis like Trickster's old one could really be happy with it.

A Bellacoola Indian mask of Raven: when the dancer pulls a string the mask opens (right) to show the human visage of Raven the Trickster

One meets Trickster here as the curiously emotional and stupid being, not quite human, yet also a creator and bringer of good as well as mischief. Trickster appears in bird guise far away from Winnebago of the Canadian Prairies, in the wild coastline of the Pacific. Here he is a bird-man, the shape-changing Raven. He assumes no small role as a creative demiurge. Raven brought the sun and moon to the people of earth by trickery. He brought fire so that humans could cook their food, but he could never escape from his propensity to play tricks on people, and to enjoy illicit sexual pleasures. He was a thief and a terror to those whom he opposed, but also he was honoured as the symbol of a powerful clan, so we find him constantly changing. On the great totem pole in the British Museum one can see him at the top wearing the ceremonial hat of a great chief, and putting on his bird-skin. In his hands he holds the fire stick, for like the Greek Prometheus he stole fire from heaven, but by trickery.

His story was recited in the old times by learned elders during the winter festivals for the delight of the villagers meeting together in the great wooden house of the chief. The stories included those where the tricky Raven was caught out and

defeated. One was about the beautiful wife of a fisherman who was desired by Raven—after all, Olympian Zeus was equally lascivious, so why not a Red Indian spirit? Raven took human form, and came paddling his canoe down to the village where the fisherman lived. In his headdress he wore a beautiful red feather. No one had ever seen such a lovely ornament before. He walked to the house of the fisherman pretending he was of the same totem and therefore should be given hospitality. Once he was indoors his feather was much admired. He pretended to be surprised. Such feathers, he said, were quite commonplace. They could be found on flocks of fine red birds who lived up a river a few miles down the coast, not a difficult journey to make. Raven wondered why the men were so backward that they had not ventured to find the fine feathers for their adornment. When he left the house the wife begged her husband to go to the place of red feathers. He agreed and after a day or two took his boat and set out on the journey. Raven flew ahead and descended into the valley in his bird form. In those days ravens were beautiful birds of many colours and they had a red crest on their heads. Raven found a fallen tree, rotten with many insects crawling over it. He

This Haida Indian tobacco pipe shows Raven with the fisherman's wife, while the husband is absent with his canoe

changed the whole thing to a flock of beautiful red birds, and a litter of feathers. Then he flew back to the woods just above the village where the beautiful young wife lived. He changed back to a handsome young man and then transformed some more of the rotten wood to feathers. He went to the house, and entered to find the girl pounding cedar roots for fibre. She had cast off her cape and was dressed only in a small apron. In the dim light of the house she was easily persuaded that it was her husband returned with the beautiful feathers. So it was easy for her to caress her visitor, to release her apron and let him caress her vulva and compare the inner lips with the feathers. It was altogether delightful to her, and soon she was wondering how her husband had learnt to give such pleasure. They turned together, admiring each other's physical beauty and repeating intercourse—oblivious of the sound of a paddle and of a canoe being drawn up. Her real husband rushed in, saying that they had been tricked, for the feathers he had brought turned back to rotten wood as soon as he landed. Then he saw Raven. He leapt on him. Taking up the great wooden pounder which the woman had left by the mortar he beat Raven with it as he chased him round the house. The Trickster paid dearly for his pleasures, until at last he saw the smoke hole above him. He returned to his coloured bird form, only to find he was so weak that he fell back. The fisherman retrieved the apparent carcass and threw it into the river to float away.

The drifting bird was a tempting bait to the great fish in that rich river. A halibut saw it and swallowed it, but the fish was caught by men from a village lower down near the sea. They were astonished when they cut it open to see the marvellous raven. But Raven was up to his tricks again. He made himself alive and flew away. Later he returned to the village disguised as an old man, who grew and grew before the warriors till he was a veritable giant, and threatened to destroy them and ruin their boats. He was so frightening that they ran away and left him to work his pleasure. He simply took all their food to be sure of a rich life for his next adventure.

There were many more exploits, usually with a picaresque connotation, but the greatest exploit of Raven was when he took pity on mankind and brought the gift of fire from heaven. He often flew high, even above the mountains, and he saw afar all the tribes of mankind eating raw food, and holding pieces of meat under their armpits to warm it before eating. He was determined to give them the fire which he knew was to be found in the sky. So one day, when it was night above the sky, he flew through a hole in the heavens and going near the tent of the sun he changed himself into a baby boy. Of course, this was all magic, and when the daughter of the skies found him she was hardly surprised that the baby grew into a little toddling boy in four days. He was cared for and not allowed to touch the things in the house, but before long he began to weep and cry to be allowed to play with some of the firewood. There was some concern, but when the sun came home and it was night on earth the women asked him to let the little boy have a stick from the fire to play with. In the end permission was given (on the fourth day, of course), and the child was given an ember to play with like a little torch. All of a sudden he turned into a bird and flew up through the smoke hole in the centre of the roof. Up and up he soared, chased by the sky people, until he saw the little hole in the sky. He dived through where the sky people could not come, and returned to his home, where the stolen ember became the first fire and where people came to him to learn the secret of making fire with two sticks.

In carvings Raven is shown with a little red lump carried in his beak to symbolize his gift of fire. He suffered, however, for his temerity because the soot of the smoke hole in the house of the sun permanently stained his feathers black. That was at least a more humane punishment than the vengeful Greek deities inflicted upon Prometheus.

The Greeks accepted magical Hermes perhaps from the Phrygians, or more probably from the Keftiu who had made civilization flourish in Minoan Crete. His very name is a mystery, but it seems that it means a 'heap of stones'. This referred to a *menhir* standing upright in a pile of stones to mark a boundary. Nobody made him that way, but the stone symbolized his power of guarding all boundaries and of marking all crossroads to protect travellers. Later the *menhir* became a herm, of which two examples stood before every house of substance. Sometimes they bore the head of the god, but always they had his penis carved, in earlier times splendidly erect, but in later times usually quiescent.

Like Raven, Hermes was a shape-changer, a liar, cheat, and thief, a great lover and full of trickery and laughter. His world was filled with his illegitimate children, most of whom became famous heroes. He himself was the original traveller, for not only crossroads but all the ways of the merchants were dedicated to him. The Greeks could not think of him as a creator. For that role they demanded greater spirits, old Chronos and Zeus. But Hermes was the son of Zeus and Maia of the Pleiades. In this he held a position akin to the Babylonian Marduk, but he was no conqueror of the other gods. His realm was always one of movement and magic. As Psychopompos he was responsible for leading the souls down to the other world: perhaps because death was regarded as the unexpected visitor, akin to the changeable nature of Hermes. As well as acting as messenger between earth and underworld he ran at the behest of Zeus as the messenger between the gods, and between gods and men. His sandals were propelled by wings, and often his brimmed hat was also winged. He had a herald's staff, but, more importantly, he carried the *caduceus*, a baton on which two winged serpents entwined. They emphasised his changeability and his sexual prowess. Maybe there was once a legend like that of Raven's exploring penis, but it is not recorded. It seems that Hermes might have been very important in pre-classical Europe, since he was always the darling of the peasantry; and as Mercury he was considered by the Romans to be the equivalent of the high god of the Druids and of Wotan of the Germans. Just why that identification was made is not clear. The other identification of the god with natural phenomena is much clearer, since the little planet Mercury does his curious dance as a faint morning or evening star in quick succession and, while visible, never going very high, neither in the sunrise or sunset. The idea of a small being swinging from above to below and either leading the sun or diving after it fits the nature of the tricky god rather well. It is likely to be a universal belief, since we find that a similar young deity, Piltzintecuhtli, was worshipped by the Mexicans, and in the Aztec codices he is shown as patron of a boy's festival in which a greasy pole had to be climbed. He symbolized in this aspect the chances of fate struggling to victory or slipping back to invisibility.

In the case of Hermes we again meet the duality of identification with the outer world, and with the inner archetypal character—extreme aspects of changeability. The old philosophical statements about the planetary element in the human personality still seem reasonable and are used in language still understood. We can easily accept the idea of the moonstruck lunatic, the jovial person, the saturnine, or, in this present context, the mercurial temperament. In all these confusions of ideas and differing explanation, one feels the presence of winged Mercury,

Right: Shiva dances in a circle of fire. His dance is symbolic of his powers of creativity and destruction, and his unpredictability

Below: The Herm of Dionysus from Tunis

Above: A Greek terracotta from Myrina: Aphrodite stands beside a herm.
Right: Mercury messenger of the gods, literally flies on the winds

Far left: A great phallic statue on the Greek island of Delos is the last word in herms.
Above left: This satirical Etruscan bronze of a faun perpetuates the tradition of Hermes and the Trickster.
Left: A single face of Hermes the god from a double head post found at Ephesus in Turkey

who has a sense of the comedy of human affairs. Now if we return to his Greek name, Hermes, we have a different connotation, for he is also the patron of the alchemical process, the Thrice-powerful, Hermes Trismegistus. Here he has been equated with the Egyptian Thoth, lord of wisdom. The influence of such thought is to be found in the medieval impression that Mercury was patron of science and art. In Rome Mercury was the god of contracts and of merchants, which is why he protected roads. It may be that the Romans also had the idea that contracts were subject to change and trickery.

The original Hermes was the most liable of all the gods to adventure which had unfortunate after-effects. He was witness to the dispute between Hera, Athene and Aphrodite. The dispute was caused by Eris, goddess of discord, who had thrown her apple of discord among the immortals when she was not called to the marriage feast of the nymph Thetis to the hero Peleus. So, bringing the goddesses to the shepherd prince, Paris, son of King Priam of Troy, Hermes carried the apple with him. After a little thought, overwhelmed by the sight of perfect human beauty, Paris awarded the prize to Aphrodite. But alas, Aphrodite rewarded him by an unbreakable oath that he should wed the fairest of mortal women. But Paris was already married. Thus the fates intervened, and the introduction that Hermes made led to the discovery and abduction of Helen, wife of Menelaus, and so to the horrors of the Trojan war and the death of many a hero.

It was appropriate that Hermes should become the guardian of souls, the Psychopompos, the guide who led them to their place in the sad kingdom of Hades. He could also work in the

Above: The child Hermes depicted as a shepherd carrying a ram – a prototype of late Christian representations of the good shepherd

Left: The Judgement of Paris: Hermes brings the three goddesses Athena, Hera and Aphrodite before Paris to decide which is the most beautiful. The artist, Heiron, seems to favour Aphrodite (extreme right)

opposite direction and his natural fortune did not desert him when, after the death of Protesilaos before Troy, he was able to bring the wraith of the dead hero to visit his widow Laodamia. He was so real that she begged him for a caress, but he refused and to underline the refusal his face changed to the visage of a decaying corpse. Then, returning to the semblance of life he exhorted her to aspire to a higher love than earth could give. Hermes returned to conduct his charge again back to the land of the dead, and at that Laodamia herself fell dead and followed the messenger of the gods down to the other world.

Another important function of Hermes as Psychopompos was the annual return of Persephone to earth. He was ordered by the gods to bring back the goddess of springtime to her sorrowing mother Demeter, but before they left the underworld the god Pluto gave her a pomegranate. This was magical and compelled the goddess to return each autumn to her underworld husband. Once again the messenger of the gods was deceived and his message partially negated. This marvellous event in the world of nature was an important phase in the Mysteries of Eleusis. Those who wished took note and were enlightened.

The myth where Hermes, son of Maia and Zeus, comes most clearly into line with primitive mythology is the story of his earliest infancy. Maia is the middle star of the Pleiades, who sets with the sun late in May. Her abode in the sky is not far from that of Taurus the Bull. But in the legend she was a nymph on earth and mother of Hermes. As soon as the little boy was born he was cleaned and put to bed. Nobody watched him, and he simply got out of bed and went cattle-stealing. On his way through the fields he found a tortoise. He took the empty shell and putting a stick in it tied with several strings he made music with it, the first lyre in the world. Then he came to the pasture where Apollo's herd of cattle browsed. He rounded them up and took them to a hiding place where he imagined he would keep them. When Apollo returned, he was astonished to find the herd gone from their accustomed place. He enquired all around and came to the home of Maia. She denied that her baby son could have done such a thing. Zeus, however, who had knowledge of all things accused Hermes of the theft, and led Apollo to his herd. But Hermes, always ready with an appearance of innocence, artlessly presented his irate brother with the newly invented lute. This so charmed Apollo that ever afterwards he was the friend and protector of Hermes. Thereafter there were to be many love affairs and many children for Hermes, but mostly they were rather unhappy. He became the patron of all magicians and scientists. Thoroughly unreliable, he yet had a few true friends and was ever ready to escort souls cheerfully through their frightening voyage to the other world.

Mercury was also patron of magicians, probably because of

their tricky nature. And the Polynesians, particularly the New Zealand Maori, had a demigod with a similar attachment to magicians. His name, Maui-of-a-thousand-tricks, explains his general character. He was not directly evil; there was another, mightier god of darkness and disaster. Maui was also a graceless creature, much beloved by the people because he reflected the common human frustration with the rules of everyday conduct. In Polynesia the institution of the *tapu* preserved social barriers and protected property, but Maui had broken every *tapu* ever known, and was also an arch-thief of quite mercurian quality. The social and sexual traditions of Polynesia were strict, but Maui broke them right and left. He slept with many beautiful ladies and left such a trail of offspring that the semi-sacred *hei tiki* was made in his image . . . at least from his last adventure. It used to be worn by ladies of good family to ensure the continuance of their lineage. Perhaps its odd features, resembling a distorted foetus, refer to the birth of Maui. He was the son of a sea goddess, who looking at his horrible aspect threw him away on a beach. However the name *hei tiki* refers to the male penis, as the maker of new life. That too reflects the spirit of the amorous adventures of Maui.

Maui lived because the sea god, seeing the poor little aban-

Left: A Maori wall panel shows the demigod Maui pulling North Island, New Zealand from the sea (from Rotorua, New Zealand).
Below left: Maori ancestral guardians of the dead at Rotorua. The dead man's skin is depicted by the creases on his legs

doned child on the beach, took pity on him and rescued him. He brought him to the paradise of the ocean and there little Maui learned the story of the gods and of their children, the Polynesians. He became the much-loved independent child, always full of mischief, and able to trick and deceive his elders, usually without really hurting them. He visited the home of the sun and stole some fire to bring back to earth. But, of course, fire was a good servant and a bad master, and it burnt down many houses before it was tamed as people learnt to be careful. In those far-off days the sun moved irregularly, and moved around the world at varying speeds, and always much faster than it does now. There was never time to finish any work because the night fell too soon. It was Maui who plaited a great rope with which he lassoed the sun and slowed its progress. Of course, he was wrong to do so: it was not his position in the formal Polynesian society to do such things. But the unconventional action, like the theft of fire, had the most happy consequences for the human race.

Another impious theft led to Maui's greatest adventure. He dared to enter a burial cave and stole magic power by taking his grandmother's jawbone, to use as a fish hook. He caught many fine fish, but always cast for something better. In the south Pacific he threw out his line, and the jawbone caught something truly gigantic. The godling heaved at his line and nearly sank his boat, but he persisted in a titanic struggle. Eventually his catch was hauled to the surface; it was *te ika a Maui*, or to the white man, North Island of New Zealand. It is said that South Island was his boat.

Below: A Maori canoe baler carved with a mask of Maui. The handle represents his predatory penis

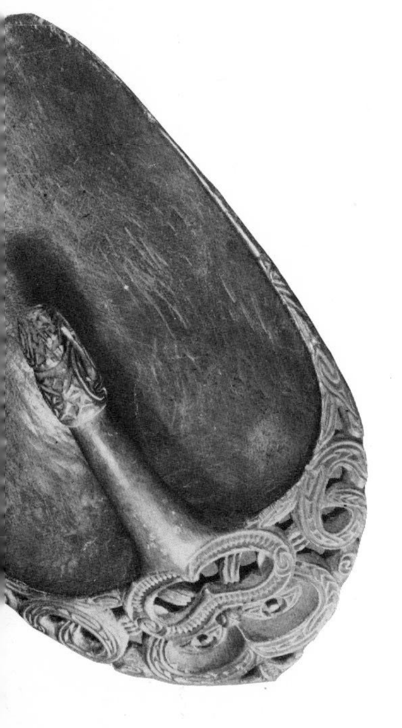

His greatest exploit lead to Maui's death, for he tried to bring back life to those who had died. He determined on a desperate attempt to be reborn, and with this in view he tried to re-enter his mother's womb. It involved all his powers of deception and of silent movement, but just as he was entering the vagina there was a disturbance from the bird which had followed him. Mother Earth turned and contracted herself so that Maui was killed, his head crushed, while seeking life. Thus there was to be no rebirth for humans and they went to the mysterious western land beyond the sunset, which was thought to be the abode of the dead. This final adventure was the culmination of the uncontrolled sexual life of Maui, and in part explained his identification with the penis.

The Polynesian ancestors came from southeast Asia, but the highly developed religions of Asia have little room for the trickster in his primitive form. Yet every group has something of him in it. In Hinduism, there is an aspect of change and unpredictability in the great Shiva, whose dance is inspired by himself alone. He creates and destroys, gives gifts and destroys evil forces. But he is too sublime a personage to be just a development

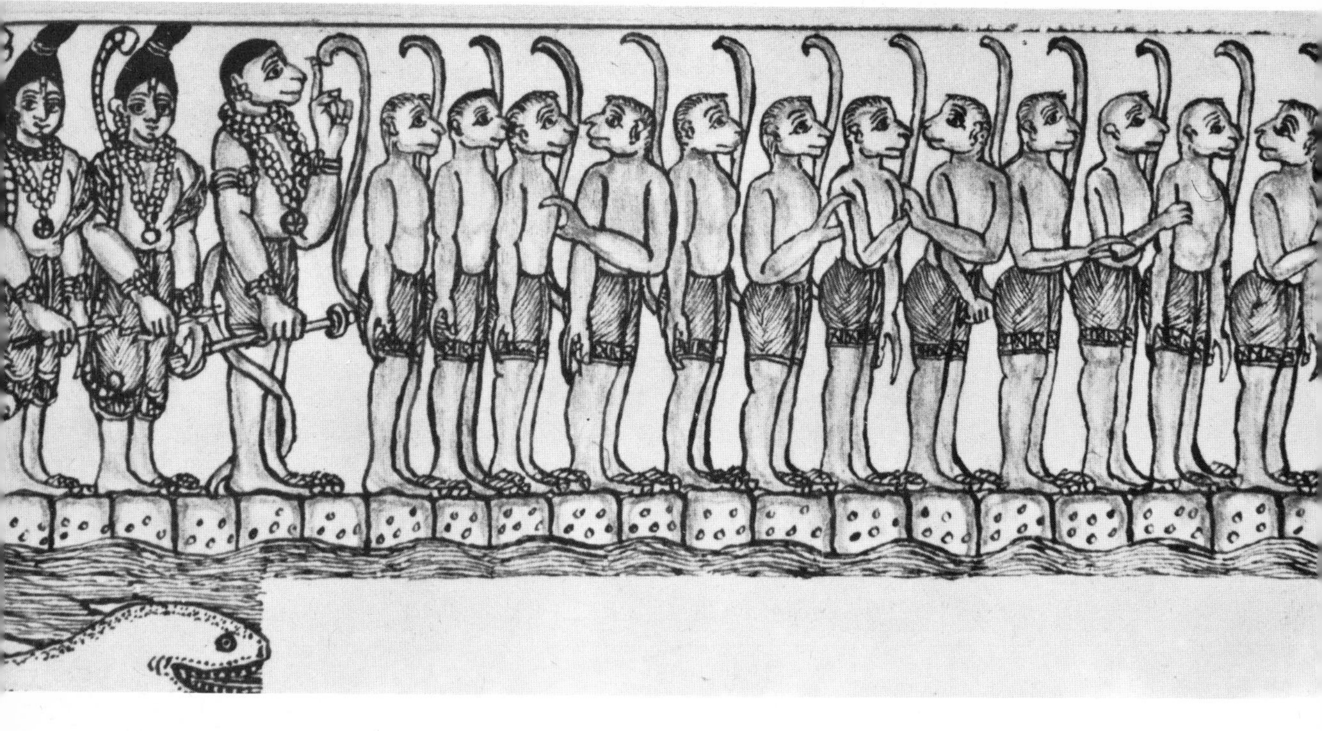

of a primitive religious idea. Perhaps if we knew of the myths of the Indus civilization we should find the character more sharply drawn. Another aspect of friendly gaiety and destructive impulses is to be found in the charming figure of Hanuman, who as leader of the monkeys assisted Rama in his search for Sita. Hanuman, having decided to help the despairing lover, entered into conflict with the forces of the ocean, led his monkeys to build a bridge of rocks across the straits, and finally assaulted the armies of the demonic Ravana who had abducted Sita. In this case Hanuman turned all his influence into defeating evil and darkness and assisting the force of love. He seems a personification of the powers of the animal aspects of human personality brought into play for the service of creative affection.

The clearest personification of the Hermetic personality in high places is found in those tales of Odin All-Father. The Romans were not quite right in equating him with Mercury, because Odin held a position in the assembly of the gods more akin to that of Zeus. Yet there are many similarities which the Romans noted. Odin was tall and beautiful, though grey. He appeared to men wrapped in a grey cloak and wearing a broad-brimmed grey hat which shaded the patch over the eye he had lost in acquiring the knowledge of magic runes. Married to the beautiful Frigg, he yet was continually unfaithful and left many fine children around the world, one of them the ancestor of the

Left: Hanuman invades Sri Lanka with his army of monkeys and the Hindu gods

Right: A Fuseli drawing of Odin at the mouth of the Underworld

Volsungs, and another reputed to be the ancestor of the Saxon kings of England.

One of the benefits Odin brought to mankind was the gift of poetry. It happened that on one of his visits to earth the god saw nine serfs reaping the hay. They had some difficulty, so he asked if he might hone their scythes for them. He gave them such an edge that they wanted to buy the wonderful hone stone. Odin told them they should have it if one could catch it. He flung it into the air, they rushed forward, and as they reached up they swung their scythes and each one died headless in the field. Then Odin went to the house of the farmer, the giant Baugi, who was brother of Suttung who owned the wonderful mead which inspired poetry. Baugi was sad because he had just heard that nine of his serfs had died. Thereupon Odin offered to work for him to bring in the hay more easily than even nine serfs could manage. He gave a false name, Bölverk, and so did not make the giant suspicious. He asked as his wages for one drink from the sacred mead which men said was in the possession of Suttung.

The giant and the disguised god went to Suttung to ask for a draught of mead, but they met with a downright refusal. That night, the false Bölverk suggested that they should bore a hole with an auger through the wall of the cave in which the giant's daughter Gunnlöd sat guarding the sacred mead. They tried and Baugi blew into the hole to clear it, but the dust flew back into

Left: Hanuman is seen here as protector of Rama and Sita, both enthroned in his heart

his face. Bölverk continued to drill and when Baugi blew the dust went right through. But he was suspicious that he was being tricked. But he was slow, and Bölverk changed into a serpent before his eyes and entered the hole. The giant stabbed at him, but he had moved too far in. Within the cave Gunnlöd saw a handsome man before her. He was so charming that she had no hesitation when he asked to sit beside her. He pleased her so much that for three nights they slept together and he gave her much happiness. In return she offered him three draughts of the mead. He accepted, and in one draught emptied the cauldron. At the second he emptied one of the large pots, and at the third he emptied the last pot. Then suddenly he turned into an eagle and flew out of the cave. Gunnlöd set up a howl and her father Suttung saw the eagle flying and realised what had happened. He too turned into an eagle and gave chase. Odin was hard put to escape, but as they wheeled and swooped over the mountains they came to the great wall of Valhalla. Odin in his haste let drop some mead on earth, where it remains ever ready for poets and wise men to sip from. The gods had seen Odin approaching and spread out bowls in the great courtyard. Thereupon Odin disgorged the holy mead, and wisdom and poetry remained with the gods. Suttung, unable to cross the great wall, returned to earth.

These stories of the Trickster, shape-changer, great lover and liar are so characteristic of the pattern of our other legends that we must accept the Roman identification even though Odin in concept was greater than Hermes.

The African versions of the Trickster are many. Here he seems to have had no particular calendrical aspect. He is just himself, a mirror of mankind and totally irresponsible. One form of him has had a most extraordinary evolution which has resulted in him being changed from an insect, Anansi the Spider, into a white rabbit, hero of many children's books. For Anansi, the crafty Spider of Ashanti legend, was taken by the slaves to the West Indies long ago. His tricks and cheating amused them in the long days of subjection, his love affairs must have saddened them under the grim separation imposed by the white masters. But gradually the language came in and Anansi became Nancy boy. Then his friends took him to the United States where he lived in the hutments of the cotton-picking South. There runaway slaves sometimes mixed in with the Indians, and told their stories among the Cherokee who also had many trickster tales. Their version was a white rabbit, a naughty tricksy creature who fitted so well that Anansi became a rabbit and the tales told by the slaves came to centre around Brer Rabbit. Eventually he was ascribed to Uncle Remus, much in the way that another set of fables had long ago been fathered upon an African slave, one Aesop. He was usually the cunning and yet foolish fox in Aesop.

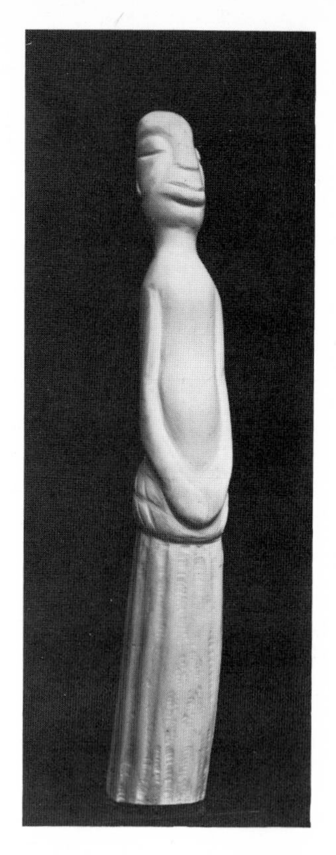

Above: Anansi – the West Indian form of the Trickster – carved by Namba Roy, a Maroon sculptor

Right: A Maori tiki carved in greenstone

Overleaf: above left: Hanuman, the monkey-demon, causes mischief among men.
Below left: Pueblo dancers of New Mexico in a ceremonial spring festival.
Right: Pueblo Eagle dancers of Santa Clara

Above: The Yoruba goddess Ifa carries her magical bowl and divination tray

Left: At a Pueblo festival in Santa Fé, New Mexico, Old Man Gloom is burnt to herald the spring

Uncle Remus also made him an innocent fool for the children of the white masters and he got into print and scampered around the world without being able to reveal the true depths of his nature. But originally Anansi is the typical animal-trickster. He is as foolish and easily tricked as his many victims. In other words, he is a very good reflection of the gullibility of human society.

A more powerful and equally widespread African figure is the Yoruba spirit Eshu (or Elegba). He is one of a group of *orishas*, spirits of life who inspire people with differing moods and qualities of life. These *orishas* are closely akin to the Jungian archetypes who live within us all. In Yoruba society the cult of the *orishas* centred around the Gelede society, whose members sometimes appeared in public. Then they danced in long gowns to disguise themselves, and on top of their heads lay masks, one for each, representing the *orisha* that inspired them. The representative, or bearer, of Eshu had a mask with a long plait of hair from the side growing over the back. It ended in a knob and was adorned with the fruits of the oil palm. For those initiated, this lock of hair was a large curved penis, and the oil-palm fruits were symbols of riches and fertility which were the gift of Eshu.

Those who were inspired by this being accepted his great magic as a blessing, though they felt some fear about his uncertainty. He was the patron of people subject to danger; recently he has been accepted by coalminers in Nigeria, the followers of a dangerous occupation. He comes to people in dreams, and not only to men. Women also love his symbol, the smooth large penis, proud and unpredictable in its energetic dance. It has the gift of new life to lay within them, and that gift is also dangerous. The male devotees recognize this danger: birth is a moment of the balance of life and death for mother and child. Thus Eshu in his own land was at once a terror and a beautiful being of exciting joys.

The cult of Eshu-Elegba spread with the Yoruba traders and slaves from their section of the Nigerian coast. He has danced in the West Indies, found himself loved in Brazil and represented the necessary philosophy of uncertainty in many places. In the civilized world he has not altered his image, and he can inspire people with his unpredictable desires. He is a kind of Cupid, but unashamed, a red driving fire which leads men and women to desire and its marvellous, yet frightening, consummation. As we can see, the power of which he is the symbol is universal.

The Trickster heralds the spring in Europe and North America. Here we must leave him and move on in the year. The true spring is awaiting, the season of flowers and romantic love, the period when birdsong fills the greenwood, and Maia dances among the Pleiades as the sun rises on a May morning.

Left: A young bison, symbol of food for the hunter: a prehistoric cave painting from Altamira in Spain.

Below: Botticelli sums up civilized man's love of springtime with the promise of flowers and fruit in his depiction of Primavera (third from right)

5. Flowering Fertility

Life must have some goal. Even the most primitive peoples saw and welcomed the fulfilment of spring in the return of warmth and the sudden blooming of the wild flowers. Poets and prophets over the centuries have celebrated this time of beauty and strange excitements. But the idea is not universal. In tropical lands there is no winter, and so no spring in the sense that the northern people know it. But these tropical lands are full of life, strange life of forest and river. Here there are rhythms of death, decay and reappearance, more life and new life. The tropical vines flower in their season, and the fruiting trees, perhaps with many seasonal harvests, demonstrate the tremendous reproductive powers of the natural world.

There is no evidence of any single tribe which thought of the earth as male. The tradition from primitive man until the present day is that the earth is female. Our cave-painting ancestors sought out deep caves where, in the womb of the Earth Mother, they painted prayers for new animals to come to give the people food. The Plains Indians of recent days thought that the souls of the animals were kept by the mother under the earth and were released to meet the needs of the hunters. No one would insult the great Mother by slaying more than was needed for his family: the divine gifts were not to be wasted. After the first stirrings of spring there came the full flowering of Life, spring time, the only pretty ring time, when birds do sing, hey ding a ding ding, as Shakespeare wrote, a century after Botticelli painted Primavera scattering her flowers, flowing and beautifully pregnant with life.

Primavera is somehow like the moon. One can picture her flowing through the clouds: the moon whom the Aztecs envisaged as mistress of magic who grew large, and waned, but then gave birth to her own self as the new moon. A myth formed in the sky for all country people of every culture. The moon as well as earth was a lady. She was the lantern of lovers. In the moonlight boy and girl might walk together gently and find a secret love which the older people could not see too clearly. The rhythm of the moon in twenty-nine days is closely similar to the rhythm of fertile young women. Certainly in primitive life there was a link between the life cycle and the cycle of nature.

In the great stretch of the Celtic lands, from the western rocks of Ireland to the mountains of Asia Minor, the moon goddess was an important lady. She was a symbol of feminine independence as she passed over the stars and between the sunset and sunrise. In Britain they called her Rhiannon, and the stories tell of her quiet superiority over mere males who might chase and never catch up with her serene ride. In an old English folk song kept now for the babies to ride on one's knee, we sing, 'Ride a cock-horse to Banbury Cross, to see a fine lady on a white horse. She

Above: A stela from Ephesus shows Cybele between her two lions

has rings on her fingers and bells on her toes, and she shall have music wherever she goes.'

This lady was never meant to walk. Was the music the music of the spheres, or was it the flutes and trumpets of her worshippers? Apuleius gives us a gruesome picture of the worship of the goddess Cybele, the music and the image on the horse, the transvestite priests and their horrible mutilation of fertility in the service of this Earth Goddess, the Great Mother. The utterly masculine confusion is here between earth and moon and life. It appears that the staid Romans were utterly bowled over by the bloody licentiousness of the Cybele cult. They had not been able to see the hidden cruelties involved in the cult of the goddess. For themselves they divided the powers of Luna into Diana, who was cruel enough on occasion, the motherly Juno, the hag-like Hecate, and the queen of the underworld. But for the spring they had special festivals, of which the Floralia was the greatest. This was the happy time of rejoicing and garlands.

In faraway Britain, the Island in the Mists, as travellers called it, there were also Floralia. We have some still; the Helston Floral dance is one, and other dances from Devon and Somerset follow the same Maying pattern where amid dancing and song with garlands of flowers a group of mummers, of whom the greatest is the hobbyhorse in fantastic mask, chase any girls they may meet. Nowadays the horse only demands a kiss, but in ancient times he used to try to drag the girl under the skirts of his costume and pull her skirts around her waist. No doubt there was once a caress of the sexual organs, laid bare for a momentary laughing contact in the name of good luck. The flowers and songs were all part of the dance of fruitfulness, and the curious mask of the horse with its formal pattern may be an echo of the old Welsh Mari Llwyd, the horse-skull ghost. The thought of horse and mare in these ceremonies has some link with Hecate who was patroness of horse and hound. In fact, it is hard to differentiate between the aspects of the Celtic Great Mother as moon, flower maiden and mare. One can see her image still on the hills below the fortress of the Dobunni in the Vale of White Horse, Oxfordshire.

Far left top: Fertility figure from Willendorf, the ideal woman of a hunting community.
Left: Indian sculpture of Yakshini, spirit of life and growth.
Far left bottom: The god Dionysus with egg and cockerel, the symbols of fertility and rebirth

Yet the surviving folk custom of the greatest importance in springtime Britain is the Godiva procession and the Maypole. Both have changed greatly in the last century. The Maypole used to be taller and crowned with flowers, as in Germany. It had none of the streaming ribbons of the modern Maypole dance. It was once the erect pole of fertility, the symbol of the coming summer and the erect penis of Cernunnos of the oak trees. The flowers were beauty and fertility symbols. The ring dance around the pole was a jolly occasion for the young people to hold hands and sing together as they tripped around the garlanded pole. Not all

Above left: The White Horse of Uffington, Celtic symbol of the Moon Goddess, carved in the chalk and religiously cleaned by the local inhabitants for nearly twenty centuries.
Below left: The Cerne Abbas giant probably represents the Celtic god Cernunnos. The square enclosure above his head was formally the site of the local maypole

Above: Erecting the maypole at Barwick-in-Elmet, Yorkshire (Elmet was an ancient forest). The use of poles to lift and ropes to pull echo pre-industrial methods.
Right: The Castleton Garland, a figure representing Jack-in-the-Green, rides in procession

remembered the magical significance of the symbol except as a rather improper joke, but all enjoyed the social occasion and had their individual romantic dreams of marriage and happy families. In some ways this spring festival had replaced the old Carnivale, but the time change was great and the connection never complete. Carnivale had its own sanctions before the solemnity of Lent. Mayday was the joy of flower time.

The Godiva ride remains in many village celebrations, though the heroine is now a folksy character dressed in pink fleshings and wearing a wig of flaxen hair to conceal the contours of her body as she rides side-saddle on a white horse. The horse, which should really be a mare, is ancient, the pink-dressed young lady is a romantic character from Baring-Gould's story about the Lady Godiva of Coventry. Alas for storytellers' romanticism, the real Lady Godgifu was the happily married wife of Earl Leofric, and having had several beautiful children was not really eligible to take the part of the processional Godiva. One hopes that perhaps when she was a teenager she had been honoured by riding as the Spring Maiden. The custom is far more ancient than the days of the great Lady of Coventry. It was the festival of flowering life for all the world around. Probably its patroness was Freya, the Germanic version of the Celtic Rhiannon. Freya had her home with the milk-white cattle in Heligoland and each spring she was taken in her great cart, theoretically drawn by her cats, but in

fact by doomed young men who drew her around the island and then returned her through the woods to her sacred and secret temple. Thereupon they were slain so that none might reveal her secrets. But her procession brought flowering life and ushered in the fruitful part of the year.

In 1972 a few girls in the Godiva processions in England discarded the pink fleshings and really rode in the traditional way, totally naked, but they were few and of course covered up with the long wigs. In olden times she was naked and her hair did not conceal her natural beauty. Her companions were other girls who scattered flowers over the bystanders. In some villages the Godiva was preceded by an old woman painted black on a black horse. The thought behind it was that the Spring Maiden drove away the darkness of winter. She was chosen as the girl with the best reputation for modesty and good behaviour in the village, and to be allowed to ride naked was an honour much envied by other girls. There was a mild sexual element since tradition had it that the Godiva was of such good repute that she would be sure to marry a fine gentleman before the year was out. The Spring Maiden, or the Godiva, was the expression of the natural relationship between the state of the season and the wellbeing of humanity. The freshness of young womanhood and the promise of fruit from the flowers was combined as an expression of living beauty and hope.

Yet mankind was aware of the dangers of life. One sees it

Right: Krishna, shown with a blue face, embraces Radha (in the lower register)

Below: A romantic 19th century impression of the Norse goddess Freya

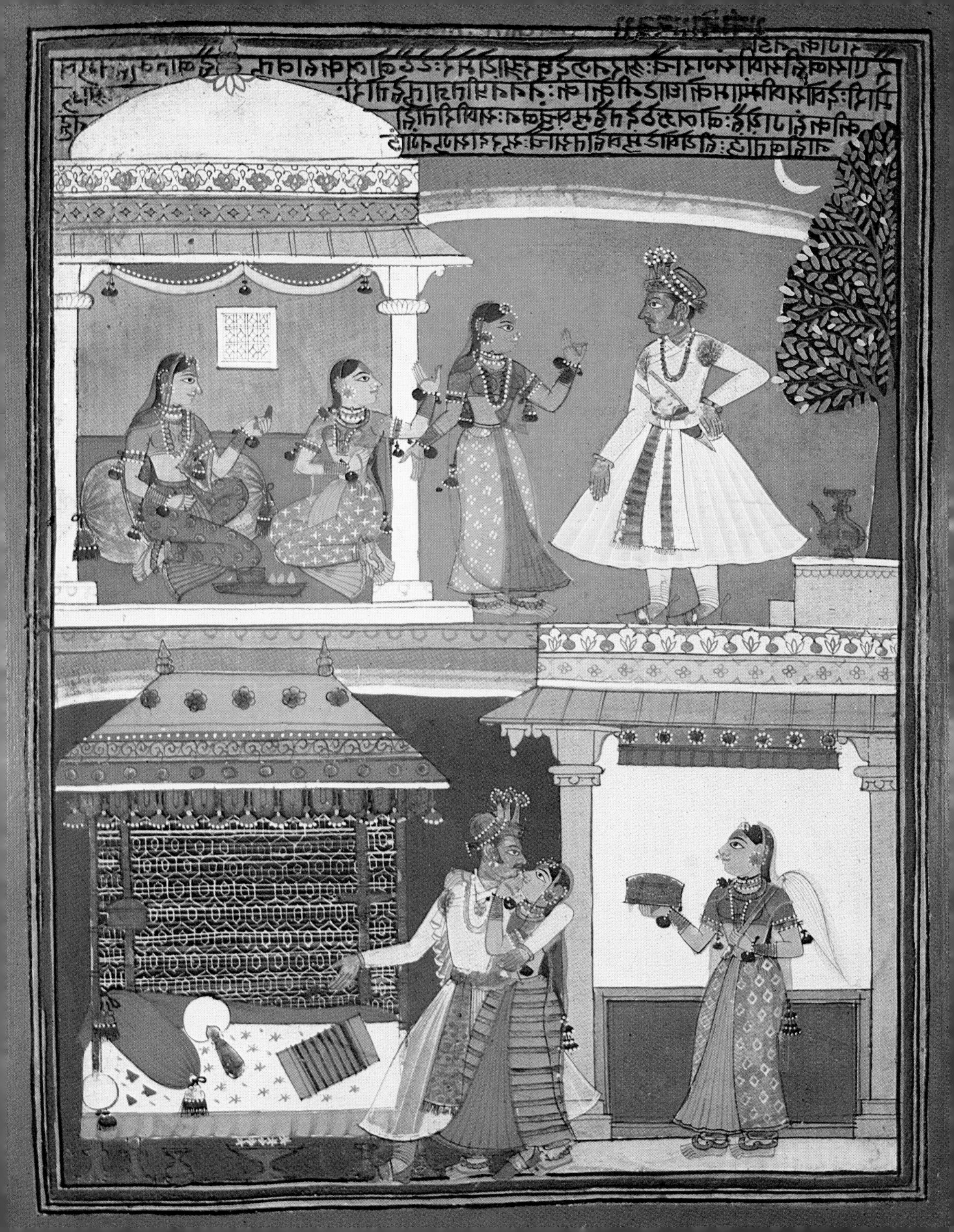

Above left: Malinese Dogon dancers from south of the Sahara have a fertility dance based on the mating of the antelope, whose antlers are represented by their head-dress.
Below far left: Diana the huntress for the Romans symbolized the ideal of chastity, which was carried to a gruesome conclusion in the cult of Cybele, the Great Mother.
Left: An Inca wooden beaker shows Spanish immigrants mixing with Peruvians

Below: A fertility carving from the Torres Straits in which the woman is very much the dominant partner

echoed in the nineteenth-century ballad 'I shall be Queen of the May' in which the maiden dies on the eve of her finely dressed parade as May Queen—a ceremony which replaced the Godiva ritual—because life is mutable, to be taken away as suddenly as the breath of wind may take the blossom from the apple trees.

When one associates the Godiva procession with the Maypole dance the festival also displays links with the hobbyhorse dances. The spring maiden being presented to the sacred penis and the teasing activities of the old mummers were intended in those days of innocent honesty. It all amounted to a statement that flowers were for fruiting. The representatives of the human race demonstrated the holy secret of life and its ecstatic dance of union. Such symbolism occurred all over the world, though not always with such simple beauty as in these old processions and dances. It is a matter for discussion whether the people were the happier for such displays of open sexual magic and wonder. The Puritans frowned upon such things, not because of the jolly, earthy pornography, but because they reminded the people of old times and Romish superstitions. Poor Godiva! She turned slowly into a poor obscure actress in dusty knitted tights who was wheeled out to give a spurious air of naughtiness to the local Carnival, held not at carnival time, nor on May Day, but usually in August. Perhaps she will come back to us, but not until people have learnt to laugh and be joyful about the whole subject of flowers and flirtation.

This happy erotic innocence was once enjoyed by the Polynesians. In their warm islands on the other side of the world, where seasonal change was slight, they celebrated natural fertility in many ways. Their worship was corresponded more to the phases of the moons. Seasons changed only in that the winds altered direction and the fish streamed to other waters. Clothing was worn for ceremonial occasions, and very beautiful it was; but the naked human body was the noblest sight and people were not shy of working without clothes. It was practical for women to wrap their loins in pretty tapa cloth, but men frequently wore nothing but ceremonial tattoo. Marriage was highly respected not only in itself but also in relation to a family's ancestors in the past and continued family in the future. But before marriage sex was never something to be hidden or denied. The enjoyment of caresses and carefree intercourse was the enjoyment of holiness.

In the beginning the creator, alone, created the first beings through masturbation. His semen became the spirits of the lands and seas, of fishes, birds and humans. The greater gods of the first creation lived in the normal way, they built up the world through their children, all born naturally from the magical copulation of male and female powers. The human race was created by the gods as naturally as all living things.

The Maori cult of Hei Tiki: the nephrite figure is at once a personalized penis and a foetus

The first man was named Tiki, and his penis was somehow his being. He was the channel through which life was to come from the gods to the human race. The belief was that life was continuous and the handing down of descent through the penis was something holy, making the sacred organ the object of artistic expression. In many ways it became a Trickster figure, because of its unreliability and its rapacious nature. However, the female vulva was more often considered to be rapacious. In Maori carving it is often armed with teeth.

Tiki was a popular figure in art. He was usually sculptured as a standing male figure, with a somewhat distorted head to echo the form of the *glans penis*, and most commonly with slightly bent legs to suggest the rhythmic dancing movement of his activity. In New Zealand, coldest of the Polynesian lands, a different art style developed and Tiki became a sacred neck ornament. He is now usually known from the jade pendants worn by the Maori and the finer ones found in the museums of the world. Some of the more ancient tikis are massive, of hard nephrite, and weigh up to four pounds.

The early European visitors to New Zealand became acquainted with the tiki as a neck ornament worn by people of noble descent. As a badge of social importance it was often confiscated from rebellious chiefs or taken by soldiers from the bodies of slain noblemen. The story spread that it was a charm connected with childbirth, and the European mind, given to seeking realism in art, translated it into a more or less realistic picture of a foetus.

But the tiki was in fact a symbol of the charming god of sexual enjoyment, with his head on one side and his body curled up ready to spring into activity when desired. In ancient times it was worn only by women of chiefly rank. The inheritance went to the eldest grand-daughter. The chieftainess died, and after the appropriate time the little girl was led to the burial cave and removed the precious symbol from the bones to wear it herself. It was important socially because it showed that she was of direct descent from the gods, and that her family was separated from the great ones by fewer generations than were the families of lesser members of the tribal society. Later it was worn as a charm symbolizing the force of life by chiefs, especially when going to battle. However, ancient traditions slowly disappeared and the tiki became an ornament. Small ones were worn by many people, and there was even a busy trade a little less than a century ago in pretty small green tikis made in Bohemian glass. Beliefs changed and the old gods were becoming a part of the past. People began to adopt the white man's attitude to sex, not perhaps to the licentiousness but to the hypocritical tendency to regard the sex organs as unclean and intercourse as a sad failing of human nature. So the old identification of the greenstone pendant with the force of life was exchanged for the idea that it was in some way a lucky charm. The change in less than two centuries was akin to the change in the meaning of the joyful maypole in Europe. Life went on, but shyly, and in a Freudian context of something shovelled into the dustbin of the mind.

The Polynesians were so accustomed to a tropical environment with but minimal seasonal change that they celebrated no special spring festival, even in chilly New Zealand. In tropical Africa, however, on the southern borders of the Sahara we find a true spring fertility festival, though the seasons are simply storm and dry. The Bambara and several culturally-related people in the republic of Mali had a long tradition of a fertility dance based on the mating dance of the antelopes. When the natural forces release the emotional switch, the antelopes become sexually excited. They pretend to fight, leap high and rhythmically in front of their intended mates and in general indulge in a form of rather strenuous play.

The human reaction is different. Instead of being instinctively affected by atmospheric conditions and the need to procreate, the people try sympathetic magic. They need more life, not only for themselves but for their cattle and the crops around their villages. In 1973 a terrible drought slowly drove life away from the advancing edge of the desert. Everything possible was to be done to defeat the forces of drought and sterility: the rains encouraged, the fertility of the land strengthened. The people called on the spirit world where the forces of nature exist to help.

To encourage life and promote fertility, the young men, as the active human forces of fertility, prefer to dance. They prepare caps which are surmounted by abstract forms of antelopes. There are male shapes, and female shapes with their mates on their backs. The small heads and elaborate openwork necks have made these beautiful objects collectors' items. Although these are objects of beauty looked at by connoisseurs or kept in cabinets, they are really symbols of power. They have magic, and the magic depends upon human offerings of strength and energy. The young men dancers must open their minds to achieve contact with the world of unknowing. They dance.

The dance is preceded by meeting, talking, thinking and singing. The drums talk. Rattles, harps, whistles and dancing and singing with all the ecstatic rhythmic feeling of Africa make an atmosphere. The dancers are prepared by being painted and decorated. They are equipped with the antelope caps. They then dance by leaping up and down. On and on, endlessly repeating the mating ceremonial of the antelopes. They dance, by the fire at night, on the dusty soil by day. The people sing and beat the rhythm, the girls dance and encourage the dancers to go on and

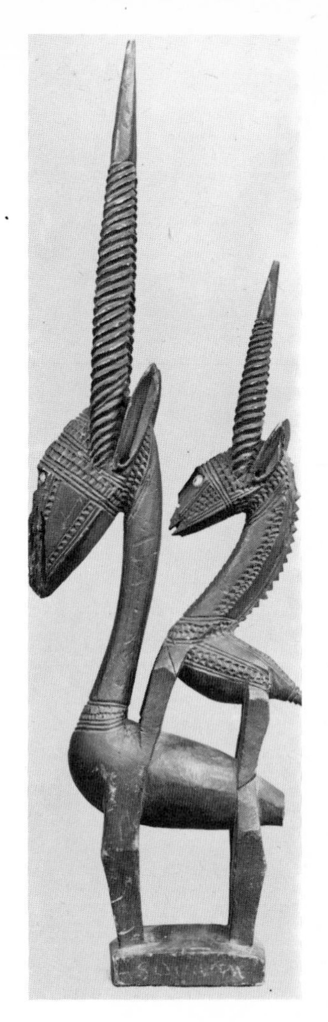

Above: Guro head crests from Mali promote fertility; this one represents an antelope and her mate.
Above right: The Inca blesses the maize by participating in the first planting, which took place during the August moon.
Right: An Inca drinking vessel features the digging stick for planting maize and the vase for the fermented maize beer, chicha

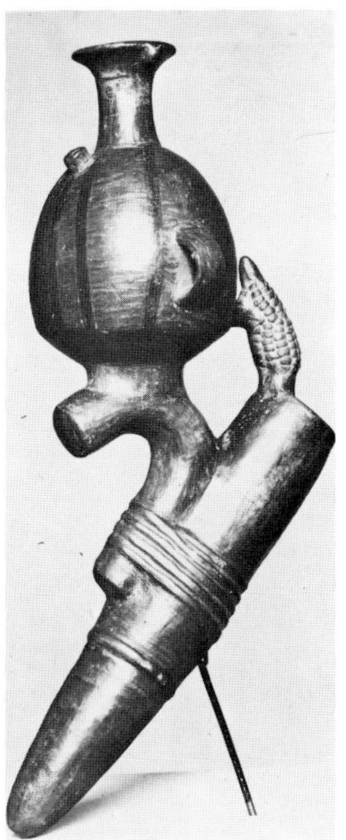

on. The dance may continue for days. The dancers have some rest, but they go on to the point of exhaustion. This point is slow to reach a climax because if the rhythm is right and the dancer heeds his posture a dreamy happiness of near-trance enables the body to continue the dance without extreme fatigue.

The action of the dance and the words sung are based on years of tradition. The people have been acting a scene from the life they share with their ancestors and their descendants. They show the need for life and fertility.

The idea of suffering and working with a true ecstatic enthusiasm is not simply restricted to Africa. It has parallels throughout the world and in many different religions: for example, the processions in Europe at Rogationtide when the fields are blessed. In some places, choirboys are still taken round the boundaries of the parish and at special boundary marks some of them are whipped, 'so that they will remember the spot exactly for next time'. It echoes something, probably more ancient than the need to remember the shape of a field. It is interesting that the African ceremony described has a fertility objective but without direct sexual activity by the participants. One wonders if certain palaeolithic scratched figures near the entrance to some of the French caves may be related to such an animal fertility ritual. The figures represent men and women copulating in animal fashion. They are not great works of art, and they can hardly represent normal palaeolithic practice. One must assume that it represents a ritual, probably designed to increase the numbers of game animals. Yet it is interesting that such paintings are not found deep in the caves, but outside. Was it a ceremony or naughty dance performed with much laughter, while the shaman went secretly about his magical work depicting the desired animals in the womb of mother earth?

An example of a similar custom comes to us from Peru where a legend of Inca times tells of the reprehensible behaviour of the coastal people. (The Inca were Puritan in attitude.) Why the coastal tribes of northern Peru were so interested in sex, in all forms of eccentricity, is not clear. As they lived in intensively cultivated river valleys nestling between areas of irredeemable desert, it is possible that they were practising some form of population control. Certainly the towns of the Chimú, as the coastal people were called, were luxurious and exceedingly rich. They may, of course, have decided to amuse themselves at leisure without considering the feelings of the Inca up in the mountains. Yet they cannot have been an effete race since they made a brave showing in the final battles to keep out the Inca armies.

It appears that, after the conquest, the Incas allowed some customs to continue, or else the memory of them was strong enough to be retold as information given to Spanish missionaries some thirty years later. At the great planting festival young people used to gather at the temple of Pachacamac to call fertility on the land. According to custom they were the people drafted to be married in that season. They were all happy and stark naked, and lined up hand-in-hand on the field before the temple pyramid. At a signal they raced in pairs to the temple and up the steep and long external staircase. The first pair to reach the top lay down and, in front of all the people, copulated. The event was a matter for great rejoicing. Their practical coupling was a reminder to the forces of nature that the land must have life, that fertility was what was needed of the gods. No doubt the other young couples were prepared to enact the ceremony at home, but they well knew that the ideas of nakedness and sex were important to the world, that without this factor life would not go on. Nature and humanity were united.

The Chimú people, however, had a moral story of the gods, and they told Father Calancha, a Spanish missionary, the legend of the Evening Star, who was a male. It seems that the lord of the mountains, a fierce god with overlapping canine teeth and a dreadful scowl, had two pretty wives. One day he was away hunting and the Evening Star came quietly up to the mountains. On the way he met the two wives, made himself very agreeable to them, and persuaded them to slip out of their long gowns to have intercourse. They enjoyed him quite naturally, but suddenly the lord of the mountains came down from above and found them. He bound up the women, and the Evening Star was tied up naked as he was and thrown hurtling through the sky down into the Pacific Ocean. It is said that because he was so lascivious he was tied in a bundle with two of the most lascivious of animals, monkeys, and all drowned together.

The legend not only showed that wives should obey their husbands and that adulterers would be punished, but it has a cosmic meaning: that the Evening Star could never reach the heights of heaven, for he was tempted and after a short while he fell. Therein we find the movement of Venus as Evening Star put in the framework of a Peruvian social story. An interesting feature of the story is that it is illustrated on pottery vases from the same area but of the Mochica culture, more than a thousand years earlier in time. The tale would link some ritual of sex and expiation with the Venus calendar and not with the solar spring festivals. Perhaps that is why it did not result in any birth or fertility magic.

The other Chimú coupling for the spring has an echo in Egypt. In spring, Pharaoh must have intercourse in a temple with the high priestess on a sacred bed of newly sprouting wheat. It was witnessed only by the temple priests and priestesses, however, and not by the populace, though later a symbol was shown to the

Left: An Aboriginal painting from Groote Island off Australia shows a creation myth of a woman who was fertilized by the Morning Star (bottom right and centre).
Above: 'Lady Precious Green' (Chalchihuitlicue) sings a spirit song (denoted by feathers) as she causes the vessels of rain to fall upon an offering. As water goddess she gave fertility to the maize.
Above right: The Mexican goddess Tlazolteotl gives birth to herself, as the old moon gives birth to the new.
Below right: The spirits of the maize: a Mochica vase from the Peruvian coast, 7th-9th century AD

people to show that the act was successfully consummated.

Far to the north, in Mexico, the Aztecs had a festival called Xilomaniztli, to celebrate the appearance of the young green cobs on the maize plants. They made the usual horrid offerings of human life, but they also linked life to this stage of their beloved maize by giving the young god a feminine form. On this festival the young ladies became girls again. They went to the fields and danced back with their hair unbound and their breasts bared as if they were young teenagers. Their function in the ceremony was to bring back a few of the green ears, the *xilotes*, which might be eaten as a sign that the maize was growing and food would soon be in the granaries once more. They also showed that their bodies were beautiful and that their firm breasts were ripening for the time when they should give nourishment to children. There was no great sexuality about it, but just an enactment of fact. The Aztecs, however, deliberately avoided any sign of happiness in sex. It might seduce their warriors from the joys of combat.

Among the ancient Slavs a male spring deity, Yarilo, was worshipped with dances, but these were of an openly erotic nature. The god was thought of as a white man in white garments riding on a white horse, and, like the Celtic moon goddess, his feet were unshod. He wore a chaplet of flowers and was for a time adored by young women. Even into the nineteenth century girls of Byelorussia celebrated the festival by electing one of their number as a kind of May Queen and dressing her in the white clothes of the god to receive gifts of flowers. They then danced in a huge ring around the fields recently sown with spring wheat. But by midsummer the god was finished with; he was made up in an image of straw and burnt at a festival not unlike a funeral wake in which drunkenness was the order of the day. The intoxicated girls, weeping copiously, lamented the death of the god in a form of overture to the autumn festivals.

All these ceremonies of life and flowering happiness lacked a deeper mythology. They seem to have been practical affairs, rather like the practical farmers who took part in them. The reason was not only the absolute realism of the agricultural life, but the nature of the archetypal sexual behaviour involved. The depth of real sexual contact and its bringing of peace cannot be clearly expressed through its material manifestation. The link between ploughing the earth and the stroking of the open vulva before full penetration was magically quite clear; but the activity was material and left unrevealed the deeper philosophy, though often there was a link between the joys of planting and the sorrows of harvest death, as in the tragic history of John Barleycorn.

In modern witchcraft there are a few survivals of the old May

Krishna reveals himself to Radha and the Gopis

festival, but they tend to be revivalist and to reflect the many inhibitions of our non-natural society. The old dance of a naked coven in the wildwood in which the couples who came to dance turned back to back and stimulated the opposite partners to obtain the power for projection belongs to a different world from the civilized society of today. The final consummation between all or any of the group in a happy tumbling behind the bushes took place after the ceremony. It was a lowering of the immense tension which had been aroused. Alas, we hear occasionally of the release becoming part of the ceremony, and simple sex replacing the great effort of the ancient magic. But at least the May moon is not totally forgotten.

The philosophical attitudes to life and love in the beauty of late spring were probably in the minds of priests and shamans of many races. They had a rich, magical interpretation in ancient Egypt, and were enshrined in poetry as well as pictures. But the elements in which they transcend the normal pattern of living are found in civilizations with a well-defined religious teaching, administered by a priestly organization. A fine example known to Jew and Gentile alike is that ancient poem, the Song of Solomon. It has been likened to the love of the soul for God, and vice versa. In spirit that is true, but it is also a hymn to beauty, of the quality of the woman of perfection. It is full of the imagery of the agricultural community: the pomegranates, the ripe grapes and melons. The reality has been used as a way of uplift, but that has not prevented small boys of half a century ago learning something about women on a much more material plane. The ancient poem has given us an experience on many layers of understanding, so that all may obtain something from it according to their degree of insight.

Similar is the Hindu story of Krishna and the Gopis. It may be a story of a naughty romp by a hero, or it may be treated academically as an echo of a piece of discreditable folklore from a prehistoric past. But the fact remains that the story has inspired art and has many meanings for those who seek. It is embedded in a long history of a divine being, a myth in itself, but also part of a series of myths about a being who is of the greatest importance to the religious system of India.

Krishna is the eighth *avatar* of the great creative being Vishnu. When necessary, in order to restore true belief Vishnu would appear as a living being on earth. As Krishna, 'the black one' (generally painted blue), he was born a warrior nobleman. As an infant he was rescued from an attempt by the local king to destroy all the small children in the district. The young deity was then cared for by a small farmer and his wife in the area of Brindaban. He grew up a charming child, being helpful and kind, but always full of harmless mischief. He loved dancing and was often found playing on his flute. One day eight girls, the cowhands on the farm, came down to the river, left the cows drinking and stripped naked, except for their ornaments, to take a pleasant bath in the stream. While they played and splashed around, Krishna slipped quietly from his hiding place and stole their clothes. When they came out they were mystified and angry, until they heard the sound of a flute coming from a tree. And there was Krishna in all his beauty laughing at them. He came down and taught them many things of the dance of life and accepted their love and returned it. Eventually the beautiful Radha became his favourite, though not his eternal, consort.

The whole story is a charming pastorale with mythological echoes from the heart of all mankind. One could say that the dark Krishna is the creative inner being who gives love and life. The Gopis are the feminine personality seeking someone to give it pleasure and receive its adoration. But this is a divine story and is as deep as the story of Solomon and his Song. It gives us an eternal picture of beauty and love; and also the spirit of joyful trickery and teasing by which love comes in many unexpected forms. The link with the year is not apparent but one notices that the Gopis were of the age of May Queens in other societies.

The festivals of late spring, of the flowering of the year, mark the passage of the year. They can be compared to the passage through life. But time moves on and midsummer approaches, the time of the stillness of the sun.

Krishna dances with the
Gopis in an embroidery of
the 19th century

6. The Midsummer Heat

The solstice, when the sun was balanced high in its yearly climb before it descended towards autumn, was of great importance to the nations of the northern hemisphere. For the farmers it was a quiet time, and the Vikings said it was the time for *sumerleding*, for loading their ships with plunder. Men were not needed on the farms and could go raiding far and wide, to the great joy of their womenfolk if they came back with jewels, cloth and perhaps a slave or two. But the wise men saw it as a religious matter, for here the sun was opposed by darkness, and the struggle would go against the sun. It was a time of change, when great powers struggled in the skies. Orion was the companion of the sun, and the night sky was dominated by Vega Lyra. Orion with his club, to the Druids the figure of Gogmagog battling against Corineus. Once, mariners might see on the coast of Vectis (Isle of Wight) the figures of the struggling Celtic Gods, and further west they were to be seen again on Plymouth Hoe. Now they are swept away into the sea.

In many places the High Sun was celebrated, and the warriors who were nearly always dedicated to the sun paraded their glory, only half-aware that the victory of one meant death in defeat for the other. And yet, within the heart, there was a similar ascendancy which all thinking people knew must be followed by descent in endless rhythmic cycle as life went on. The Chinese philosophers aptly summarized the concept in their everchanging Yin-Yang symbol. All things are mutable, and in the hour of glory one must think of the quiet and inevitable advance of the shadows. But glory must have its hour, so important to all human societies.

Left: The sun god from the stone gateway of Tiahuanaco, Bolivia, carries a dart and a spear thrower.
Below: The Pharoah Akhenaten makes offerings to the solar disc

The sun has always been the symbol of the glorious warrior, ascending and shining far, yet spreading its destructive heat in the midsummer. The concept is almost always masculine, though the Egyptians put the Lady Sekhmet on her divine throne as a reflection of the sudden blows of sunstroke, like the assault of a lioness. The goddess was not the sun as such; she was one form of solar power, and amazingly beautiful. The sun had a personality as Rē apart from its peculiar godly powers. It could be interpreted as a symbol of the Jungian Self, the united basic personality. So also in Aztec Mexico the sun was a unified being, Tonatiuh, Lord of Fate, but also had many individual aspects. The most dominant was the demiurge, Tezcatlipoca ('Smoking Mirror', the scrying mirror of the magician), who represented the sun in the four directions of the universe. His most important role was as the blue Tezcatlipoca, the high-flying sun in the south who was overhead in Mexico on the days close to midsummer.

It is irrational to divide the sun up into separate gods, each with an individual myth. But that is the way the human spirit works, presenting ideas which are incompatible, yet which have

PRIMER CAPITVLO D. LOS Í
ARMAS PROPIAS

a meaning which cannot be expressed in words. The Mexicans, who kept records in pictures, were adept at this, and their manuscripts are as fascinating as dreams.

The sun in the south was Huitzilopochtli, which means 'blue hummingbird on the left'. He was the war god of the Aztec nation, their expression of the ideal warrior. The god in his total form as Smoking Mirror had drawn the earth-alligator from the waters of chaos. She tore off his foot as she emerged. Yet this creator was at the same time a demonic being of whom people went in fear. He was the Trickster, and yet his power went further, as we know from the tradition that he was always at the shoulder of every human being, whispering ideas which would lead the mind to contemplate pride and glory as the only desirable end. He was also the archetypal tempter. But he was so successful that the nation of the Aztecs accepted him as protector of the warriors and as the leader of strife and victory.

The midsummer festival in Mexico was Tecuilhuitontli—the little festival of princes. In itself it was an inversion. The great festival of the god was in midwinter, but at midsummer there was a sacrifice of a woman who impersonated the Salt Goddess. The people prayed for the rains to come after the long spring drought, and the woman was part of a grand series of days of processions and dances. Everything was offered so that the high sun should bring about change and veil his face with storm clouds. There was a corresponding change in the rite and the usual offering of a male human heart was reversed and a woman's was offered instead. The ceremony with its blood-drenched consummation was very beautiful and an occasion of joy, even to the victim who would be admitted to the heavens. It reinforced the belief that the sun was escorted into the sky by the souls of sacrificed warriors, but was then gently lowered in the west in the care of heroic women, those who had died in childbirth. Here at midsummer was the moment when the change occurred.

No myth in words commemorates this occasion, just the date and the ceremony, which is also pictured in the pages of the *Codex Borbonicus*. Here the goddess is shown prepared for sacrifice surrounded by the four aspects of the rain god, while on one side Huitzilopochtli and his dark assistant Ixtlilton dance. It is clear that, as the assistants who hold the limbs of the victim-goddess and the rain gods who dance around her are unarmed, the sacrificing priest must be Huitzilopochtli himself.

The changing of the year, then, is a time of preparation. As the noonday sun must move towards sunset, so the midsummer sun must prepare for the descent towards midwinter, towards the ceremonies which will bring rejuvenation and a return to the ever-higher ascent. The ceremonial is the myth and the myth is the ceremonial, enacted as a kind of picture writing, to which one

A coat of arms assumed by the Incas after the Spanish conquest has a sun and moon, the morning star and the place of Inca origins

A modern carving of Odin riding the eight-legged horse Sleipnir

must add the verbal explanation if one wishes for words. That is the essential nature of myth. The pictures and the symbolic actions come from the interior world which we all contain, and many of them have similar expressions though they come from extremes of climates and societies.

The sun god is especially relevant because there is a tendency to associate one's own inner personality with the sun. It is a worldwide trait, and one which astrologers take as the key point for casting a horoscope. Where is one's sun among the constellations? That determines the configuration of fate of the newly born. This sun, however, is not really the rising and setting centre of radiance in the sky, but an altogether less material concept. The personal sun passed through one day which is the whole lifetime, at least so the poets and mythmakers seem to tell us. We must not follow the heresy of Akhenaten and worship the material solar disc, the giver of light and warmth, but we must remember that Amun, the Hidden One, is the power behind the sun who keeps the balance of life and creation beyond material things. Just as in the Christian tradition Christ is often referred to as the Sun of Righteousness.

But all sun figures must have their eclipses, and hence the old Germanic tale of the slaying of Baldur. The protagonists are the sun spirit, Baldur, who is not the sun itself, and Loki, an evil power, who is a Trickster but is without the friendly joking

Above right: Chinese philosophers ponder the rhythm of life in the Yin-Yang symbol.
Below right: The Roman god Mithras kills the universal bull of creation

Far left: Akhenaten sits in the sun which he heretically worships for its material benefits.
Left: Isis, the sister and wife of Osiris

aspects of the real Trickster figure. The general meaning of the legend is that even the best are beset with evil. Midsummer was the time for bonfire festivals and dances in old Europe, especially in the Celtic band. New fire was kindled, and young people danced around bonfires and leapt through them hand in hand to bring them good fortune. This may be the last echo of the legend of the slaying of Baldur and his burning in the great boat. But Baldur will rise again, though at Ragnarok when the ancient world and the gods would meet their end.

Loki was an ancient god, son of giants, but living in Valhalla with the other gods under the rule of All-Father Odin. He had by a giantess in the underworld three notable children: the wolf Fenrir who was cheated and bound by the gods until the day of destruction, when he should revenge himself on Odin; the great serpent of Midgard, who encircled the whole earth like a dragon beneath the sea; and the strange princess, half-black and half-flesh-coloured, whose name was Hel, guardian of the land of the dead. Loki was never heard to tell the truth; he was one full of deceits and double-dealing, whose whole aim was to cause trouble.

Baldur was the son of Odin. He was ever beautiful, and in his heavenly home he ruled the hall of truth and justice. Never did he give a false judgement and never did anyone suffer from his hand.

Below: Thor hooks the serpent Midgard (from Altuna Church, Uppland, Sweden).
Right: The wolf Fenrir bursts free for Götterdammerung, the destruction of the gods

He was fair of skin, and golden hair adorned him. He shone with light like the sun itself. All those of Valhalla loved him as the embodiment of light and goodness of heart. All, that is, except the evil-thinking Loki.

Now Baldur went riding in the forests with his companions, and in the dark woods he was assaulted by fear. He was distressed. Then came dreams and omens of dread. Baldur felt that he was to die and must leave the heavenly halls. Perturbed by his obvious sickness and worries his mother Frigg, the Lady of Heaven, sought out all living things, and going from one to another she asked all birds, fishes, animals, small plants and trees for a sacred oath that they would never do harm to Baldur her shining son. Each declared to the goddess that it loved Baldur and would never harm him. All things she consulted save only that soft and gentle lover of trees, the mistletoe, which could harm no one.

The gods thought their beloved brother must be safe, and made a sport of testing it by throwing things at him. It became a regular exercise in which stones, sticks, spears and arrows were cast at Baldur, and he simply turned round and smiled as the missiles fell on him. It seemed that he was totally immune from any danger. Baldur had come to forget his frightening dreams and felt secure in the protection his mother had arranged for him.

However, Baldur had a brother, the gentle Höd, who was blind. It was as if Höd was the night to Baldur's day. Brother never struck brother, and though Höd knew this was only a playful sport he had not joined in the throwing of missiles. But one day he was to be asked to do so by Loki.

Loki the deceiver assumed an impenetrable disguise; he went as a woman to visit the home of Frigg. They conversed in a friendly way, and the woman asked Frigg how it was that Baldur was invulnerable. Then without fear Frigg told the story. Asked if there was anything which was too weak to be of any danger to Baldur she considered for a moment and said it was the mistletoe. After more conversation the woman hurried away, and resuming his proper form Loki descended to the underworld where the weapon-making dwarfs lived. They asked him about the upper world, and he said he had made a wager that no arrow could be made from mistletoe. He showed them a piece of the soft stem. They laughed and promptly shaped it so that it looked like a pointed wooden shaft. It seemed a joke to them.

Loki returned to the home of the gods. Taking Höd to one side he asked him if he would like to join in the sport with his brother, and throw something. Höd explained that his sight did not exist and he could not find where to throw. Loki thereupon took his hand and directed the bow. The arrow flew and it ran right through Baldur so that he fell dead on the spot.

Above: A memorial stone from Gotland shows Odin and the Norse gods above a ship manned by heroes.

Right: Queen Asa's skuta, or ship, from her burial mound at Oseburg, Norway

Silent sorrow struck the gods. When they could speak Frigg asked for someone to go down to the underworld to seek out Baldur and bring him back to earth. Hermod, his younger brother, volunteered and took Odin's eight-legged horse Sleipnir to make the terrifying journey. Meanwhile, the body was to be given a great funeral, so the gods gathered to lay it in a great ship with a high-curved prow. It could not be moved at first, so Odin sent for the giantess Hyrokkin. She came riding her wolf, and put it in charge of eight warriors. They could not hold it until they clubbed it senseless. Then the ogress pushed the ship, and the weight was so great that the rollers beneath it burst into flames as it passed over them. At last it floated, and the gods entered and made their farewell speeches. The last to enter was Odin who stooped over the dead Baldur and whispered a mystery of words in his ear. No one ever knew what was said, but when the day of doom came Baldur was returned to life to enlighten the new world.

As the gods stood on the shore and wept, Baldur's wife Nanna, the Moon Lady, fell dead and she was placed beside her husband's body. The giantess blew hard and the east wind sprang up. Odin cast the flaming torch and the ship sailed towards the west like a new sunset.

Meanwhile, Hermod found his way to the mouth of the underworld, crossed the river of death and entered the great halls of the Lady Hel. Seeking his brother he went around the hall, and then

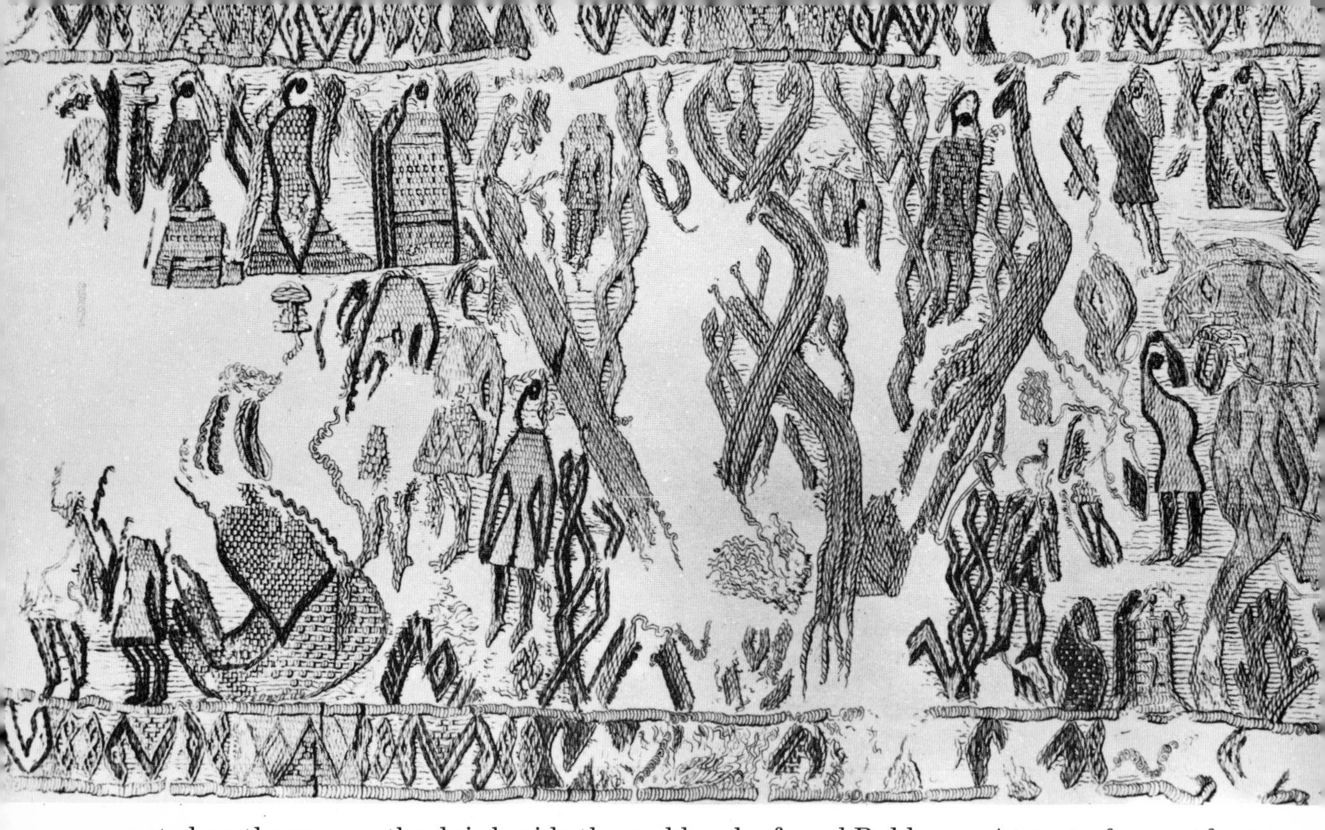

A tapestry fragment from the Oseburg ship burial depicting Norse gods and mythological creatures

seated on thrones on the dais beside the goddess he found Baldur and Nanna. They were yet white and drawn from their experience of death, but there was a new kind of life within them. Hermod told Hel of the shrunken face the need the gods had of the return of Baldur. He recounted the message of Frigg, the great mother of gods and men. But Hel, daughter of Loki, responded but slowly. She said that if all creatures on earth asked for the return of Baldur she would restore him to the upper world. Thereupon Hermod returned with the joyful message, to tell them that Baldur was safe and might well return to give glory to Valhalla.

The gods searched the world, the sky, the air, the sea, and the land. Everywhere all living beings joined in the petition to the Lady Hel for the return of Baldur. They eventually came to a cave. There sat the giantess Thrökk, and the messengers asked her to join the rest of the world in weeping for the dead Baldur. But she said Thrökk would weep only dry tears, for Odin's son had been no use to her alive or dead. So with her single refusal the pledge to Hel could not be kept, and Baldur and Nanna remained in the underworld of Hel. Only in the day of the Götterdammerung would they be released, to shine on a new universe ruled by new gods.

Thus the doom-ridden divinities of the north were forced to await their fate. There was no escaping from the universal power of death while their world was in being. But not all worlds were so grim. The religion of that time had come from the East, from where the gods, the Aesir, had come over the great plains to the Baltic and the mountain lands of the north. Further away, beyond even the great city of the Varangians, were other mountains and plains, where at a great distance of time the Aryan-speaking herdsmen formed a philosophy in which a god of light had become a supreme deity. One hears a vague mention in the story of how Father Abraham met one Melkizedek, the priest of the Most High God, and sacrificed with him, for the inner belief of both was in the One. Later, that belief was to be found among the worshippers of the sun and holy fire in ancient Persia.

The concept of Ahuramazda may be very ancient in highland Persia, but in the seventh century BC a prophet arose, Zarathustra, who channelled the rather scattered beliefs in the spirit of light and goodness into a monotheistic religion. The concept of light was a generalized matter, the light in the universe being both external and within the soul. Such a concept is more widely held than one would think, it appears in many primitive societies where the movements of the sun are not of primary importance. Zarathustra codified the theology of his time into a series of statements about the nature of this universal

A Syrian king, Assurnasirpal, and angels make offerings to the god Assur, who is in the form adopted by the later Zoroastrians for Ahuramazda

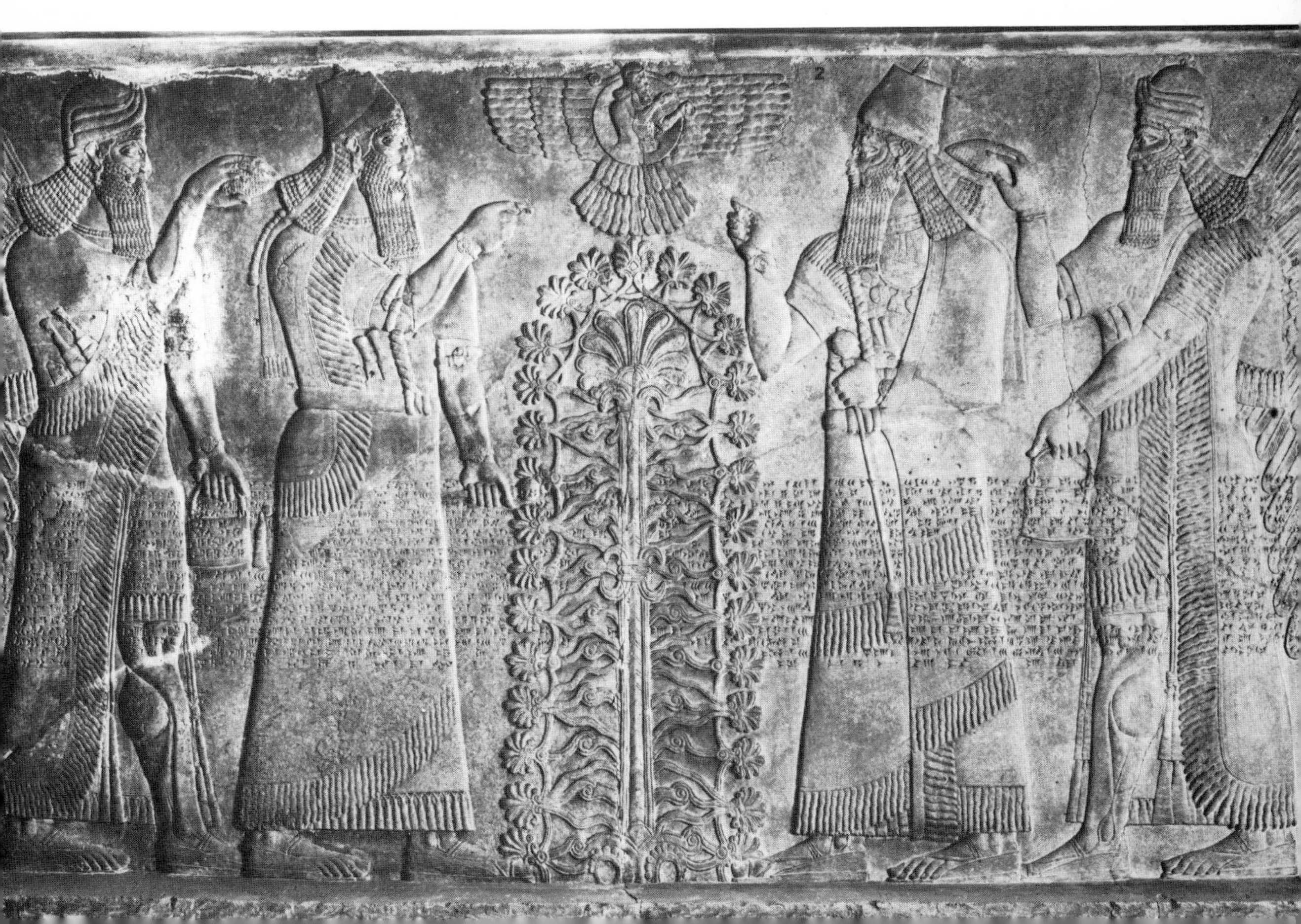

redeeming light. He encountered the usual fate of the religious reformer, was opposed, discredited and hounded to take refuge in a distant region until his lonely death. But his concept of a deity of light eventually triumphed.

Ahuramazda was the product of a spiritual development before creation took its solid form. From the great emptiness he was brought into being. He was a creator of everything, therefore he was creator of the dark, well as of the light, and was correspondingly dangerous. The teaching of Zarathustra was that the unity was also a duality in which the bright spirit was equal to the dark one, but yet destined to overcome. These spiritual powers were the two spirits of the One Ahuramazda. In later times they were seen as a duality of Ahuramazda and Ahriman, light and shadow. But the essence of life was the seeking out of light. The sun was the symbol of light and was often used as an essential representation of divinity. One may see him hovering over the Persian Cyrus on the inscribed rock of Bisitun (Behistun) as a Chaldean form with gown and robe leaning from the winged disc of the sun sign. Here he had usurped the form shown in earlier times by the Assyrian protective gods, who look from the skies giving blessings to the great kings. The idea of protective divine light is universal in Persia and northern Iraq.

From the belief in Ahuramazda flowered many other concepts. The idea of the dangerous character of time unended developed here and as *aion* penetrated the western world. This was part of the religion of Mithras so prevalent in the Roman Army. The bull from which the material universe was created is an idea shared with the followers of Zarathustra. The concept of protective powers set in a hierarchy are akin to the group of divinities who formed a kind of spiritual committee around Ahuramazda. These

The god Mithras slays the bull from whose blood the world was created

An 18th century Bavarian maple-wood carving of the three Magi visiting Bethlehem

beliefs spread, and in the later classical world great respect was paid to the wisdom of the Zoroastrian astrologer-priests. They were the magi who lived an austere and blameless life in the service of light. Just as they saw a unity in the universal light and the daily sun, so they gave an impossibility to the scientifically minded Christians of modern times. Their Star of Bethlehem went before them and was not star nor planet nor comet. It could not be: they were following that light which they knew as the Sun of Righteousness. In their symbolic gifts they showed the depth of the prophetic insight which they pinned on their astrological knowledge. Their belief that the lie was the spirit of all evil led them to tell the truth to King Herod which had such a dreadful outcome in the massacre of small children. Later their beliefs, derived originally from astrology and the sun, expanded into the Manichaean system evolved by the prophet Manes, and which included much Christian belief. At one time Manichaean churches extended from Provence (the Albigenses) to China. The cultus of the light-dark duality, and of the spiritual light which was also the sun had a great influence upon human development. Its original myths are lost to us, but they are obviously related to the creation stories and sun worship which developed in ancient Chaldea and from the Persian mountains.

The thought of the change of light to darkness and the everlasting rotation of days and years was universal indeed. It is obvious to the northern nations with their marked summer and winter, but elsewhere it is never absent. Even in Egypt, the land of eternal summer, contrasts were seen in the stars, particularly in the position of the beautiful jewel of rainbows, Sirius, who was linked with the Lady Isis. When she set with the sun in July the

Right: A bronze sow with her litter is associated with the worship of Isis

Nile rose and covered the land, bringing new life and fertility. So the Egyptians celebrated the equivalent of spring just after midsummer. To them life was a constant movement of periods of flood and of drought, lean years and fat years, and in life a sequence of death and resurrection.

In a sense the Pharaoh was the essence of Egypt. In his health and vigour all the life of the country found its focus. He was an earthly god, living in his great house. Once a year, when the sacred bed in the form of Osiris grew green with sprouting corn, the Pharaoh as symbol of life had ceremonial intercourse with a priestess to bring fertility to his land—the king of the land was the awakener of life. The rhythm of the harvest was a matter of sun and soil, but the rhythm of Pharaoh was within one life. What if age or weakness prevented him from bringing fertility to the land? The watching priests would know from the form of his penis, the divine priestess would feel the quality of his ejaculation in her body. Always the great giver of life must have life and show its power.

The festivals were fixed to the Egyptian calendar. The life of the Pharaoh was guaranteed by the gods at a great festival held every thirty years. Its object was to ensure that the life and strength of the divine king should be reborn and continue. This Sed festival was an ancient ritual and some authorities suspect that once upon a time it marked the end of a chieftain's reign, and life, before another was chosen to succeed him. It is consonant with practices of other primitive peoples, but even from the first dynasty it seems that it was a rejuvenation of the one man. He was the sun on earth, the son of the sun god Rē. So to him the myth of resurrection in Osiris was applied. The myth was chanted, it was written down, and its potency in resurrecting the mummified dead was applied in action to the living Pharaoh.

Osiris had been slain, dismembered and hidden away. His

Left: This relief from Luxor shows a Pharaoh giving offerings to the fertility god Min

sister Isis had sought out the body and gathered the scattered limbs together. The body was wrapped in linen bandages and placed in the tomb. But in the other world Osiris was alive and ruled from the white throne, the throne of light and righteousness. The drama of death and resurrection was an annual ceremony, and yet eternal. The main part of the ceremonies consisted of the procession of the king to a grave, his wrapping in the bandages of a mummy, and his display on a throne at the head of a flight of steps. He was seated under a canopy, holding the crook and flail of Osiris, which were symbols of the kingship, for Pharaoh must be the shepherd of his people and the one who brought grain to the threshing floor. This was ideally shown by Osiris who was god of vegetation and whose death was being magically applied to the living king. At the festival the queen acted the part of Isis and represented her search for her dead brother by shooting arrows toward each of the four directions of the universe. Then before the king a dedicated priest was taken as the slain Osiris, buried in a cowskin in a foetal position, perhaps like the dead in a predynastic cemetery. The priest was in magical sympathy with Pharaoh. Gradually the creature awoke, struggled and stretched and then leapt forth a newly-born living being. Pharaoh similarly stood erect, shedding the mortuary garments as he did so. He was alive, new born, like the risen Osiris, and for another thirty years he would remain fruitful. In the nature of events there were few Pharaohs who could have been subjected to this rejuvenation more than once. Many never achieved sufficient years.

The Sed festival was rather uncertainly tied to the month of July, but with a constantly slipping calendar it is not clear whether it was ever at the optimum magical time. But in Egypt it had to be within the general period of the yearly renewal of the land. Further south under the equator there were other sun kings who were regarded by their peoples as the link between the nation and nature. The best-known of them are the kings of Uganda, the Kabakas, who up to a century ago were still traditional despotic rulers wielding a power hardly less divine than that of an Egyptian Pharaoh. Unlike the Pharaoh and many West African divine kings who had multiple souls, the Kabaka of Uganda had two souls. One, which was the equivalent to the Egyptian *Ka* or double, was attached to the umbilical cord and kept in a special shrine; and the other, the Kabaka's waking personality, was attached to his jawbone and also enshrined after his death. Early in the present century the then Kabaka allowed the ancient bead-encrusted relics to be taken to England, where they reside in the Museum of Ethnology of Cambridge University. These relics include the magic ancestral bundles of the ancient war god of Uganda, Kibuka, who was thought to be

Egyptian painting of the resurrected Osiris: the eyes on either side are those of Horus, the sun and the moon

Overleaf:
The last of a line of divine kings, Frederick Edward Mutesa II, Kabaka of Uganda

the brother of the good power above, Mukasa, who hurt no man and gave gifts of prosperity and good food to his people. Kibuka's sacred umbilical cord, jawbone and penis have been preserved in sacred bundles for some centuries.

The traditional royal burial in Uganda two centuries ago was as horrific as the ancient ritual burials in Ur of the Chaldees. In the Busiro district of Kampala the royal burial temples were erected. Each Kabaka must be buried separately, since it was believed that such great men would never live peaceably together even after death. The souls were too powerful.

On the death of a Kabaka the body was sent to be cleaned and dried. Then it was laid on a bier in a huge conical hut thatched to the ground. Surrounding it was a double palisade. Just outside the burial house the royal wives were clubbed to death. Then between the fences of the palisade men were marched, who were to be royal servants in the other world. In fact they acted the part the little *ushabti* figures were intended for in Egypt. But here in Busiro the men were smashed down with clubs. Their bodies were not buried. Guards kept away vultures and jackals so that the flesh could rot naturally. All was left to fall to pieces. But five months after the death a group of three chiefs cut their way into the side of the burial hut and removed the jawbone of the dead Kabaka. This jawbone was buried in an anthill until it was beautifully clean, then decorated and placed in a wooden box which was wrapped into a sacred conical bundle, to which was added the smaller bundle containing the carefully preserved navel-string of the same king at his birth. His double dwelt with the navel string; his earthly personality dwelt with the jawbone.

There was a national festival to build a temple for the sacred relics. The dowager queen, who had not been sacrificed, assumed the role of guardian of the relics, and officers of the old court took up residence around her. This guard was kept in perpetuity. Among the officials was the prophet, who from time to time fell into a trance and opened communication with the soul of the ancient Kabaka. He was entranced by a draught of beer and milk taken from the skull of the dead king which had been removed along with the jawbone. Thus communication was always open and the great Kabaka still had some interest in the welfare of his people.

The Kabaka was plainly the important being with his sun-like personality, and the two phases of birth and death were marked by the preserved relics. The rising and setting of the semi-divine life was commemorated and made more powerful in influence by the horrific ritual of the burial slaughter. The whole ceremony was accepted by the people as something holy. It was a continued myth from the time of the first Kabaka who was the war god, Kibuka, brother of the creator. As he was buried, so must be all

his successors. Now all the ceremonies have gone, and the last legal Kabaka died in Britain a man much beloved but without power.

The idea of a sun king is an important one all around the world. Perhaps the most perfect example was the Sapa Inca in Peru. But all societies have the idea of royal divinity at some stage in their evolution. It was widely observed in the island world of Polynesia, where the chiefs were often descended from the spirit of light, the Power Above. There was the usual duality of the struggle between light and darkness and between ever-active life and the stillness of death. This cult of the divine descent was also a vital factor in the development of class-conscious and socially-divided cultures. In any given island group chiefs of divine descent organized raids against the followers of other chiefs. Such group struggle seemed to be endemic among the divinely descended tribal chiefs of the Marquesas Islands. In Polynesia descent is usually thought to be from the culture-hero god Tane, lord of light and of the sun. In the Marquesas, however, the ancestor was named Atea, who in other groups of islands was thought to have been the parent of Tane. Possibly the ancestors who arrived in the Marquesas Islands long ago had not preserved the stories of Tane, or perhaps were there before the theology crystallized. The earliest carbon 14 dating for a settlement on Nukuhiva is 300 BC, a long time ago by Pacific standards. In subsequent times there were changes in culture and an expansion of population, which in Nukuhiva led to the populating of some of the drier valleys and constant war between tribes dwelling in them. It is described in all its savagery in Herman Melville's book *Typee.* Every tribe was headed by a sacred chief who could claim direct physical descent from the god Atea. Even as late as the first quarter of the twentieth century many native legends persisted and were recorded.

The girl was named Tahia noho uu. She was daughter of Hina te ii by Tuapu. Everything about this girl was sweet-scented, and all the young men talked of her beauty. Tuapu heard the stories of the beautiful girl, not knowing that it was his daughter, so he hunted her in the darkness and lay with her. But his wife found out the truth and frightened him. So the girl Tahia noho uu was secluded in half of the house, a sacred being behind a curtain. The girl was so wonderful that she needed no food and obtained all her nourishment from the wind. She grew in beauty. Her colour was so brilliant that if one broke a coconut and put it beside her she was as white as the white flesh of the nut.

One time two of her uncles were going to visit at Nukuhiva. She asked them if they would seek a handsome young man as a husband for her. She gave them half a coconut and begged them to seek until they found a young man with a skin to match it.

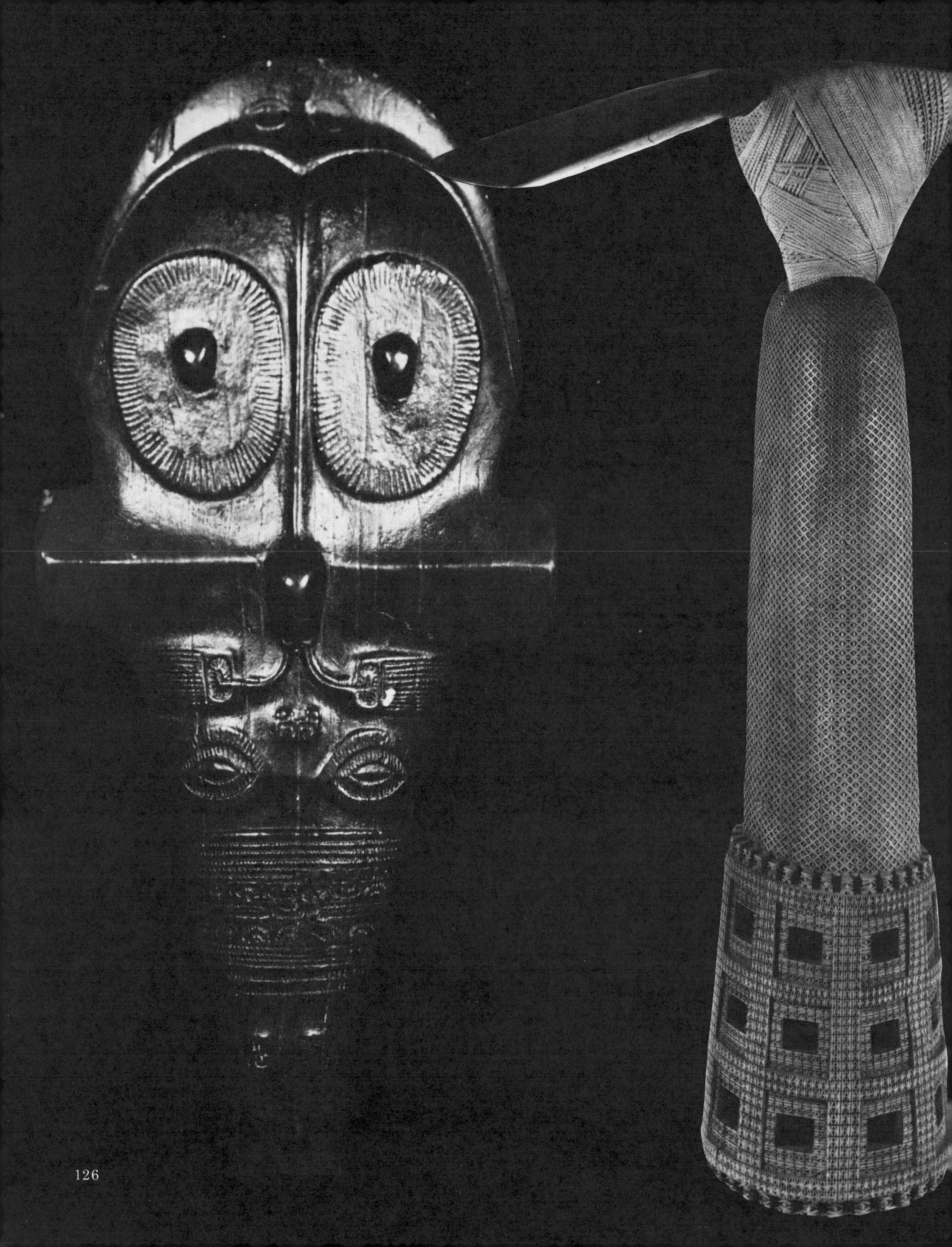

The uncles went to the chief and he said he would like to go to Nukuhiva with them. They decided to go on the fifteenth day of the moon (full moon).

They sailed, and the girl brought up a wind which drove the boat to Nukuhiva in a single night. When they had landed they were invited to a party where the people of Nukuhiva were being tattooed. They stayed feasting and talking until the company all lay on their mats to sleep. They had seen no one with the lightning brilliance of the beautiful Tahia noho uu, but towards morning there was a flash of light and they saw a young man shining white and like their niece. Then they took the half coconut and laid it beside his arm. The colour was the same. There was beauty that astonished the men. So they gave him a box that Tahia noho uu had wrapped up to be taken with them. The box was filled with perfumes. Before that hour there had been no scent of flowers, no sweet perfume of love in all the island. Then the young man and the uncles went to one side. They sat down and painted themselves, put on tapa loin wraps and plumes of fine dark feathers, for that morning was the beginning of a festival. Twice the beautiful shining youth danced, once up and once down the dancing ground. The island chief sat talking with the uncles and all was well.

Then they had to prepare to return to their home at Atuona. They persuaded a bird who sings at dawn to signal to them two hours after midnight, so they set sail with a west wind early in the morning to see the sun rise. Then in the calm they took their paddles. Only twice they made strokes, and the canoe glided up the strand at Atuona. The young man arose and opened his mantle, and the people saw a lightning flash, so brilliant was he. They came to the house, and were welcomed by two women; each was white and beautiful. First the mother came to him and they rubbed noses in welcome. Then she showed the other half coconut and his skin exactly matched it in beauty. Then he went to his wife.

The story continues into another legend of life and death, which we shall come to later. Here the sun in the form of young people seems to be an echo of the earlier mythology in which the gods were on earth in far distant days. They are a symbol of opposites and of their union in order to create new things. The initiative of seeking out the other partner comes from the girl who has a wider knowledge and greater powers than any other character in the story. It could be that she is the moon and he a being of light who may also have included the sun. But Polynesian stories often deal with other wonders, and frequently include a visit to the underworld. We must go to the opposite of the sky and the powers above, and seek out the road to the powers below, to the wonderful world of death.

Far left: A war club from the Marquesas Islands shows a trophy head taken from a slain enemy.
Left: A stone-bladed adze dedicated to the spirit of the god Tane, as patron of creative artists

7. The Powers Below

In the world there are six directions for each person: sunrise, high sun, sunset, no sun, and up and down. The downward direction is ascribed to the hidden world where the sun travels at night. In many places this hidden world could be entered by travelling westwards until the place is found where the sun goes down. In other places one must travel down through deep systems of caves. This is the secret land where the ancestors have their being. It may smell of death and be full of living skeletons, or it may be a beautiful summerland. Some people saw it as a place of terror and retribution for those who had broken *tapu*; others as a more glorious land than this. Still others knew of more than one land of the dead, for there were lands above the sky as well as below the earth. People could not go there without the most potent magic. It is a far way, a long way to that land where the spirits are clothed in light and sing the eternal praises. It is a troublous way to the dusty lands of the Greek underworld. But all men know that at least once they must travel there, by whatever path their tribal custom dictates.

Some people feared the journey to what they believed to be a dim and dusty land, where the rustling shades were clad in owls' feathers; others looked towards a pleasant land like home, only better. And few returned. Everywhere there was the myth of the one who returned from the jaws of death and in this chapter we find the tales that were told about them.

First we must return to the Marquesas Islands in the tropical Pacific, back to the land where Kena had found beauty. Kena was a young chief who had a powerful spell which would work miraculous things when he recited it. Kena had a young wife, but her father had quarrelled with Kena because the young man had made him look a fool. So Kena ran away, and his young wife went after him, ever seeking and never finding until she threw herself over a cliff and was dead. But Kena continued running away.

As he came to Vevau he heard the songs of a festival where the young men were being tattooed. He wished to be even more beautiful, so he recited his charm so that the people there should welcome him and admit him to the sacred ritual. Because of his magic he was able to take a whole series of designs on his skin without becoming ill: usually the operation resulted in unpleasant festering. After the work was completed and the other young men had healed their skins a great feast was called. There Kena was displayed, his body covered with beautiful designs, so handsome that the young women were filled with love and sought to touch and fondle him. But he eluded them, and returned to the Taaoa valley.

Kena was now a man, fully initiated and of the highest social rank. He decided to visit his favourite cousin, the chieftainess Tefioatinaku. She was beautiful and gay, and decided that she

A Maori chief with highly tattooed head: the design emphasizes his social rank, and after death assures that he comes into the company of his ancestors

Villagers gather at a funeral feast on the Marquesas Islands, at which a pig is sacrificed to help the soul on its journey.
Below: A bay in the Marquesas, islands that have inspired many myths

must lie with her beautifully-tattooed cousin, so in her house, secluded from the ordinary people, they revealed all their beauty to each other, and joined in natural admiration (which can only be expressed in the intimate union of sex). For some time they lived together and were happy; but she was already the wife of a chief, who came to hear of the liaison. Afraid to slay Kena, he worked magic and sent two evil spirits to kill Tefioatinaku. They entered her mouth, and when she lay with Kena he heard her whisper that she desired some fruit from outside, and Tefioatinaku left him. He heard a noise in the cave where they lay together, but it seemed nothing. Then there it was again, the sound of voices calling; but the girl said it was nothing, and he should just visit his home now. He went, and as he came to his house his grandmother came out with the news that a messenger had reported Tefioatinaku dead. Kena was deeply shocked. He took ornaments and fine tapa for the burial. But there was no peace in his heart, so he determined to seek for his lover in the land of the dead.

Now Tefioatinaku's mother was a medium. She took a leaf and put some spring water in it. Then she dived into the water and entered Havaii, the underworld. On her return she told Kena she had seen Tefioatinaku in the care of the chieftainess of the underworld. Kena tried to dive in the pool, but only broke through the leaf and hurt himself. So, sadly, he set out to find the way for himself, for he must have the beautiful young chieftainess back on earth as his wife.

Kena took his canoe and journeyed to the east. He met a friend, Otiu, and they continued their journeying by canoe. There were many adventures and Kena acted as the Trickster, often giving trouble to people and on his journey to Rarotonga even causing death by drowning. But still they pressed onward, eastward. They came to an island where the chief invited them ashore, saying he was Kena's uncle. His first messengers were killed, but eventually he came himself to bring Kena ashore. They feasted, and the chief tried to make Kena drunk so that he could kill him and eat him. But the sacred charm came to Kena's aid and he understood the plot. To test him his 'uncle' questioned him, but Kena turned quickly and broke all the old man's teeth, at which his uncle admitted that in this place Kena was already in the first house of the underworld.

Next Kena went to the beach to watch some girls diving and swimming from a rock. They were very lovely and he desired them. But suddenly they came together and sang a verse of a chant, and they and the rock went down through the sea. Kena then sang his own chant and the rock reappeared. He rested awhile and then descended through the sea. In this second underworld Kena and his companion stayed three days making love until the chieftainess of the land discovered them. In anger she ordered them to be tied up, and sat watching the preparation of the fire pits in which they would be roasted before being eaten. But Kena chanted the family geneaology, and the chieftainess discovered that he was her cousin. He would not be separated from his friend, so they were happily released and treated well. On the third day they were told to take their canoe and depart for the rocky land which was the third underworld.

There in the mountainous coastal area there was another unhappy love affair which led to the suicide of the lady concerned. But Kena pressed on to the fourth Havaii.

At the entrance to this hidden land of spirits Kena lost his companion who was slain by the two rocks which crushed travellers who could not leap through them with great speed. Kena marched on alone. At length he came to the village by the house of the goddess Te upo O Tono Fiti, and there was the beautiful Tefioatinaku. When the goddess heard the story she no longer wished to keep the beautiful girl with her. She bathed Tefioatinaku, wrapped a tapa round her loins and gave her a headdress. Then she put her spirit in a basket, which was tied in a cloth. She warned Kena that on no account must he open the basket on the journey, neither must he be parted from the form of Tefioatinaku. On the journey, as the goddess had warned him, the spirit pleaded pitifully to be released, but he was unrelenting, until he had returned to the earth, to his own village. But when he was in the house he undid the basket. The soul entered the form of Tefioatinaku, and at once she disappeared. Kena had to make the long pilgrimage and the short return all over again. But this time he kept the soul basket with him for nine days before he tried to embrace the form. Then at last the basket opened and the soul went into the form which he clasped in his arms, and he found that his Tefioatinaku had returned to him. And as all the dream stories say, they lived happily ever after.

It is fascinating that the story from the Marquesas is so similar to, though happier than, the story of Orpheus and Eurydice from classical Greece. It also has parallels with the story of the Mexican way of death, though the Mexican legend of a return concerns prophecy from a journey made by the spirit in a local time frame. This story tells of a much-loved aunt of the great Montezuma II, High Chief of the Aztecs. The elderly Princess Papantzin (Butterfly) was playing with some children as she sat on a block of carved stone beside the pool in the courtyard. Flowers and scented trees were there, and the bright butterflies floated lazily under the sun. Suddenly the Princess leaned over and fell asleep. The children went on playing, but she did not move, and then they saw she was not breathing. So they ran screaming into the palace and told the great Chief. He came and

A carving of a Quetzal bird, symbol of the breath of life, one aspect of Quetzalcoatl, from Teotihuacan, Mexico

discovered that the kindly aunt was dead. It was a great sorrow. He ordered that the body should be laid in a box and covered over with cloths and flowers until on the fourth day there would be a cremation befitting a noble lady.

On the morning of the fourth day, the children crept out to take a farewell glance at their friend. But there she was sitting up, looking very sad, but alive. Was it a ghost? No: she spoke to them and called for her nephew. So the great Montezuma came out and was happy at being able to greet her. But she wept, and then told him of the vision which had been with her. She had arisen from the palace, walked on the clouds, and flew and flew through the volcanoes and on to the hot country and the land of vanilla spices where the eastern sea washed the land of the Totonacs. And there she saw terror. Out on the seas she saw great wooden houses with wings, flying towards the shore. In them were ugly men with beards, hard-faced like moving rocks, and they were covered in hard stone. They landed and a town was burning. Then she saw them coming over the mountains, these godlike men with lightnings in their hands. Lastly she had seen the great city of Cactus Rock (now Mexico City) in flames and destruction everywhere. Of her nephew, she saw a dead body being dragged to the burning grounds. The spirits of the gods had sent her back to earth to tell her nephew the dreadful news.

This took place at least four years before the message came true. Montezuma thought the gods were announcing the return of Quetzalcoatl to Mexico, and the punishment meant for the descendants of those who had driven him away five centuries before. He was badly frightened and made great offerings to the gods. But for the last years of his reign he was sensitive and nervous, sure that the god would return and take Mexico away from the Aztecs. They did, in the form of Hernando Cortes and his Spaniards in their grey steel armour. When it was all over, the Princess Papantzin wept. But she lived another ten years to see the new Mexico City arising on the ruins of the old. Then once more she died and found her peace.

The journey of the Princess through time was not expected by the Mexican priests. She had been seized upon by a greater power. They would have said she had not really died because she had not been taken on any of the four ways of death. But yet she had truly seen.

The four ways of death for the Aztecs depended on the circumstances under which one died. They were often to be read in the magic books of fate, but most people did not understand that death was walking beside them at any given moment. His skeleton image was in the temples and they knew the stories. But they went on with their normal ways accepting any possible fate with the usual Indian stoicism.

The paradise of the sun and the rain: the god Tlaloc (in the middle register) receives strength from his heavenly incarnation and presides over the joyful spirits in the other world

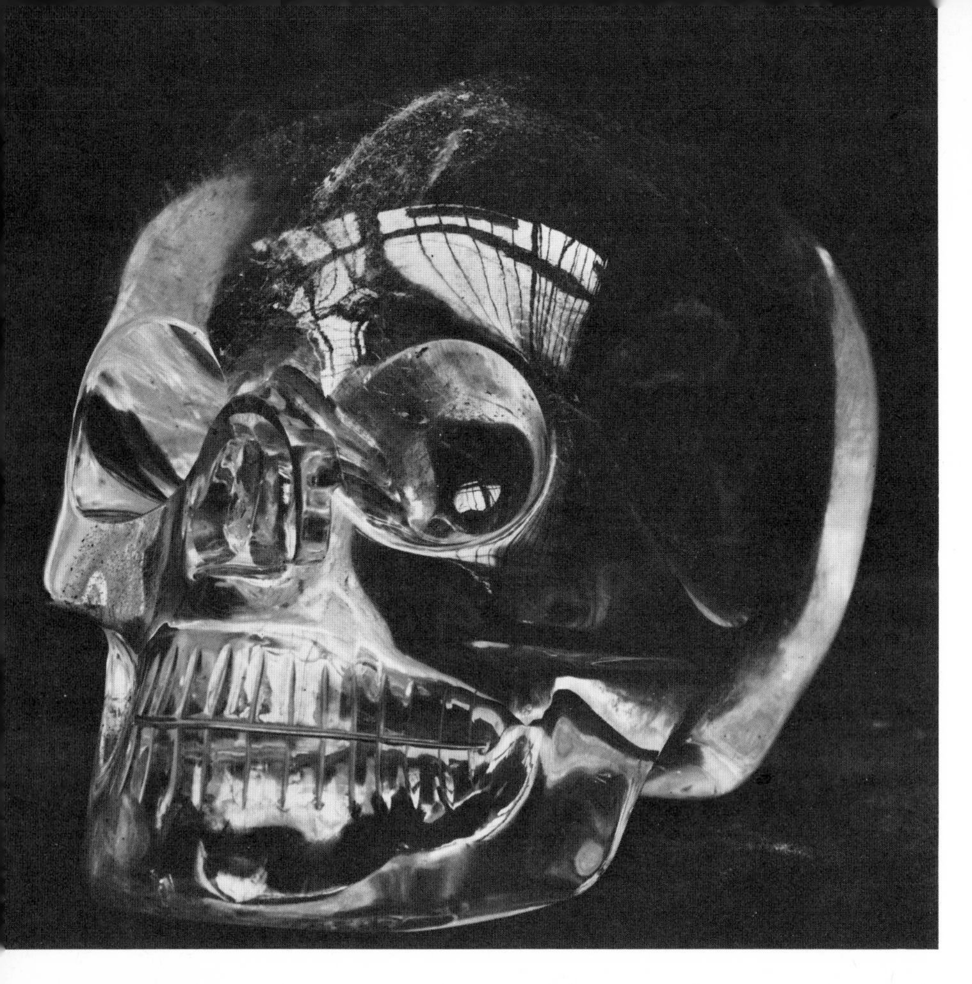

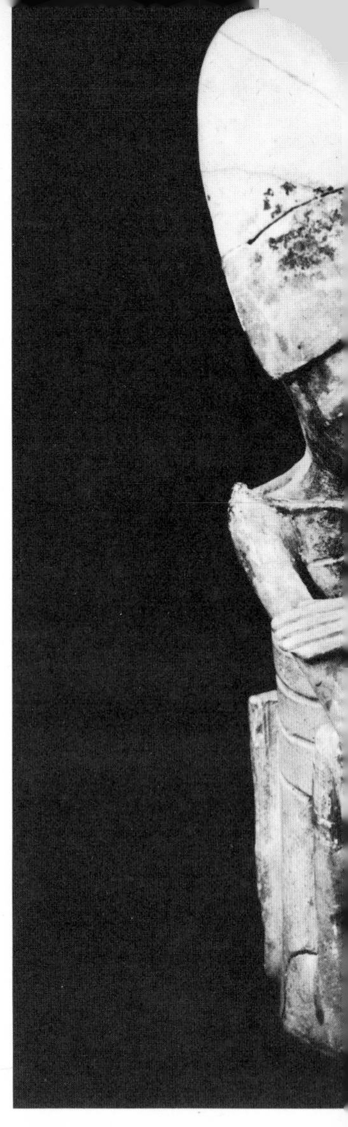

Left: This skull in rock crystal represents the Mexican death god Mictlantecuhtli.
Centre: A pottery figure of Mictlantecuhtli, the lord of the land of the dead.
Right: A Mexican rain spirit (Tlaloque) bearing a vase of fertilizing rain to spill on the fields

Of all deaths the most honourable was to be a warrior sacrificed to the gods. As the heart was torn from the body, the soul assumed the form of an eagle and went to join the great feasting and dancing to everlasting music in the heaven of the sun. There they would send out a glorious company every morning and lift the sun into the sky. They stayed with him until they met their equally honoured sisters at the zenith. These were the beautiful souls of heroic women who had died in childbirth. Then the ladies took the sun to the western sky and gently lowered him to the horizon in the evening. There was yet another heaven for the souls of young babies who had died. They were cradled among the leaves of the milk tree which gave them nourishing mother's milk, until it was time for them to be sent back to our earth to be born once again. The third way of death was for those who had been drowned, suffered from dropsy, or had been struck by lightning. They went to the earthly paradise in the west, to the house of the rain god, Tlaloc. Here they lived in a land of flowers and jewel trees. In the house of the rains they were surrounded by beautiful jade and turquoise, and the air was full of drizzle and

mist (for parched Mexicans a great delight) and dancing rainbows.

The fourth way was to the land of the dead where most people arrived. This was a hard place to reach—the journey took four years. The soul descended through the wind of knives where the flesh was cut from the bones; over a terrible chasm which had to be crossed on a rope narrow as a knife edge; then down again past the clashing rocks which could crush one eternally if one did not jump through fast enough. If, however, one took a red dog on the journey there would be no danger. Finally the halls of the death god Mictlantecuhtli were reached. The residents were not unhappy. The skeleton souls danced and sang and enjoyed feasting. Eventually, before they gently faded out, some of them would be thrown into the central fire, whence like sparks of light they soared up to the Supreme God who might decide to send them to earth again.

So was the way, no less difficult for ordinary people in Mexico than in other parts of the world, although in some ways it was less miserable in the end than the gloom and dust of the lands of the dead belonging to more civilized peoples. The Greeks had their kingdom ruled by Hades and Persephone. They were mighty gods and beautiful indeed, though dark. To them, as to the underworld queen in Polynesia, came all souls, and they alone could grant the boon of release. Persephone, after all, came back to earth each spring and returned in the autumn to be with her husband through the long dark days of winter. The Grecian beliefs are embodied in a variety of stories which leave the impression that again there were many ways of death and many paths to the underworld. In time the beliefs found their way to Rome, and then they were more formal, for here the traditions of the wise Etruscans met with Greek and Cretan, and perhaps even Celtic beliefs. Roman philosophers began to see an ordered system in the land of the dead. Many of the heroes had entered the deep caverns on the way to Avernus, and returned too, but for the Romans the descent was most significantly essayed by their ancestor Aeneas when he was permitted to visit his father, the Trojan Anchises, in the other world. The inspiring story was consolidated by the poet Virgil in the *Aeneid.* So with Virgil let us go, as Dante Alighieri did, on that journey of unexpected facility to the depths beyond Avernus.

The Trojan Aeneas had reached the cave of the Sibyl at Cumae. He had witnessed her trance, and the wild ecstatic dance when Apollo seized her and gave his message of hope to the Trojans. But then Aeneas had asked for himself a special gift, that he should be allowed to descend to the otherworld so that he might once more converse with his father, the wise Anchises. The Sibyl gave her answer, which innocently began with the words '*facilis descensus Averno*' ('it is easy to go down to the birdless lake . . .'). However simple was the descent to the land of the dead where Pluto was lord, hard indeed was it to find the way back to the sunlit earth again. She warned Aeneas of the dangers but promised him help. He must go through the darkness of the forests, and in a thicket near the lake he would find a tree in the windless air on which grew a bough of pure gold, with pliant stem and clustered leaves. Each time a living person grasped the bough Fate would either make it immoveable, or else allow it to be plucked. This bough must be taken as a gift to Proserpine (alias Persephone) who would otherwise allow no return from the home of her husband Pluto.

But first Aeneas must find the body of his helmsman who had been swept overboard in a storm. This was done, for the body had been washed ashore nearby. Aeneas and the Trojans built a great funeral pyre of holm oak and rowan and burnt the body. Then they prayed as they built a mound over the ashes. Aeneas prayed to be shown the way to the mysterious Golden Bough. His mother Venus sent a pair of doves to lead him to the forested valley

Persephone feasts with her husband Pluto during her season in the Underworld

where lay the sulphurous steaming lake Avernus. He followed them, and saw them land and open a little space among the leaves where he could see the sudden gleam of gold. There in the thicket he reached up and took the Golden Bough for Proserpine. It tinkled in the wind like faery music. He brought it with him to the hundred-mouthed cave of the Sibyl. There he found his crew celebrating the funeral feast of the departed helmsman, Misenus. (The site is commemorated as Cape Misenum.)

He then returned to Avernus for his great journey. Four black bulls, a black lamb and a cow were offered and the bodies sacrificially burnt. After a while the earth roared and trembled. A cave opened, and alone the Sibyl and Aeneas entered into the mysterious world with the moving shades of the hounds of the underworld. They went down the rocky trail in darkness, boldly bearing sword and the Golden Bough. The way opened out into a series of caves housing all the fabulous monsters of myth, then passed under the mysterious elm tree and onwards to the steep bank leading to the bubbling slough on the shores of Acheron, the river of death. There they met the old, ragged Charon in his skin boat. He was terrifying, a monstrous old man who stormed and ranted. But the Golden Bough pacified him, though the weight of the living Aeneas nearly sank the boat, meant only for souls. Leaving the legion of waiting souls behind them they entered a deeper passage guarded by the baying and snarling triple-headed Cerberus. But the Sibyl made a sweet drugged posset which she threw to the hungry raging hound. He swallowed it, and soon all was quiet as the monster slept. Aeneas leapt to the cave mouth and over the raging stream to enter ever deeper passages. He came to the land of weeping children who had been denied their full lifespan, and to the forest of unjustly condemned souls. Here he met the shade of Dido who had died for love when he left her. But she would take no notice of him. Sadly, he went on yet deeper to the lands of sorrow, until he came to the vast plains inhabited by those who had died in the wars. His Trojan presence scared the Greeks. He took no notice but continued, lamenting some he knew well from the days of battle before Troy. Then still deeper he went, till he saw a great fortress surrounded by a burning river of lava. This was the prison for evil souls who were there to be tormented by Tisiphone with her scourge of iron. The Sibyl told him of their crimes. Yet he must press on through all this terror and fire. From the land of flames they came to a gateway, mighty and silent. There they planted the Golden Bough, for offerings were left here for the goddess. Then they entered the gateway and before them lay a land of flowering beauty. Here were fields and groves of lovely trees. The whole place was radiant with light and its inhabitants were the souls of the good who had been benefactors of mankind. Over a hill they walked, and then Aeneas met his father. He would have embraced him, but the soul had no substance and they had to be content with conversing with each other, as so often they had done on earth.

Here in this happy land there was no time, only peace of heart and knowledge of all times. Aeneas questioned his father about the purpose of the fates which had led him to Italy. In reply he was shown a great gathering of men, his more distant ancestors, and also his descendants far into the future. Here were the heroes and the Etruscan kings of Rome, the great consuls and wise leaders, and on through time until he came to a delicate young man with dark hair, who was under the protection of an older, wiser man, and clothed in the robe of adoption. If he had the courage this young man would bring peace to the city on the seven hills and have dominion over lands which even far-travelled Aeneas had never seen. He was clad in brilliant armour but yet was sad: he had a duty to overcome a grim fate.

Then Aeneas was shown many wonderful places in the Elysian fields. But his time faded, and the Sibyl brought him to sleep before the gate of ivory, next to the one of horn, which led the way back to earth. He fell asleep happy at the joy of his father. When he awoke he had been carried to the beach near Cape Misenum. With his companions he prepared to set out to seek his fate in this new land of Italy. In due course, after more than a thousand years had glided golden across the land, his dream was fulfilled and Caesar Augustus came to rule.

There is much in Virgil's story which ties in with Etruscan and indeed Celtic thought. In particular, the tree lore is Celtic in character. The thought of a division of fate for souls according to the quality of their deeds was not new, but Virgil had made it so clear, that many of the early Christians thought he had been given the grace to tell of heaven and hell in their terms, and in the Middle Ages he was regarded as a great and benevolent necromancer. Hence it was easy for Dante to take him for a guide through the Inferno and Paradise, though he knew that Virgil, being a heathen at the time of his death some fifteen years before the Crucifixion, could not enter the highest Heaven, where the beloved Beata Beatrice led the maker of words.

In the cases of the higher cultures we have stories which reflect the ideas behind the ceremonies connected with death and the timing of rituals in the period just after death. But in some ancient cultures and among modern primitives the legends are not available. Myths might have come down, for instance, from the late neolithic when long barrows were used for group interments. But one can have no certainty which myths have come from what period. The ritual seems clear to the extent that a mound was erected over a chambered construction. It must have taken

The late Neolithic chamber-tomb within the West Kennet long barrow, built about 2000 BC

a great deal of time and energy. But the results are strange—no great charnel house has been discovered even when it seems that the tomb may have been used over two or three centuries. The West Kennett long barrow had a population of a little more than thirty bodies. But we can be sure that the community was a simple agricultural tribe which could command the labour of perhaps a hundred men. Were the burials in the chambered tomb only those of tribal leaders? Or were the bodies removed from the barrow after a certain time? There is no written evidence to answer these questions. Celts and Norsemen, however, had traditions that spirits lived in the barrows, and that the fairy kingdom was entered through them, a kingdom under the earth, which like the Elysian Fields was illuminated by a clear but unearthly light.

The world of primitive farmers in a neolithic context can be examined in New Guinea, though of course no real connection can be postulated between modern Papuans and neolithic Europeans. In the Highland areas of New Guinea most recently opened up to outsiders, there have been studied several forms of burial assuming the journey to another land. In one area, some spot on a hillside which was perhaps attractive to the dead person is chosen. The body, dressed and painted, is staked in position sitting in the open. From a distance it is watched from time to time. Eventually the bones are exposed, and then they fall apart and nothing is left. The thought is that now the person has gone, their name need no more be *tapu*, and all concern for them is over.

In another mountainous area bodies were placed in a burial cave. Ceremonies were held from time to time, but after a few years the bones were sought out, taken away and thrown into the river. The owner had simply gone away. Nevertheless the tribe built an elaborately decorated ghost-house in which the elders met and ceremonies were held to induce the ancestors to give help to people on earth. There is a kind of natural dualism about this which is not far distant from the attitude of highly civilized societies towards death. The dear departed have passed on, yet we hope they are watching over our welfare in some way. It is the essence of spiritualist belief.

Apart from complete materialism the most coldly scientific attitude towards death is to be found in Buddhist philosophy. The belief is that the personality leaves a vestigial trace of actions and opinions which remain to form part of a following incarnation. After many incarnations all need for return to the material universe is dissipated, and there is an absence of existence in material or humanly comprehensible terms. It seems that in the early teaching the idea of having attained nothingness—nirvana—may never have been absolute, but that nirvana

Above: A Carving representing the fertility of the ancestor from Asmat, New Guinea

may refer to an incomprehensible but yet real state of existence, beyond the confines of our kind of universe. Probably the most important portrayal of this is to be found in the story of the passing into Parinirvana of the Lord Buddha. There was nothing strange about death for the Buddha, or for the monks surrounding him. It had always been his teaching that once he had achieved enlightenment all material things must pass away. The attachment to material things was an attachment to nothing, and it led to the loss of the truth.

Having reached the Sala grove of the Mallas he asked Ananda his cousin to lay a mat that he might lie down and rest. The monks were frightened. They thought their leader would die and leave them without leadership. He said, 'What I have taught as doctrine and discipline will be the teacher when I have gone away.' Then three times he said, 'It may be that there is some slight doubt in the mind of one or another of you about the Buddha, the teaching, the monastic life. Do not be sorry afterwards that you have not asked while we were face to face.'

Then assured by the silence of the five hundred monks that all was well with their faith, he said, 'Then, monks, I tell you now: All things may pass away, but try to accomplish your aim [to attain nirvana] with diligence.' Then he quietly died.

The Buddha had passed from the whole of the spheres of the material existence. His followers hoped that by following the path of selflessness they might also attain this supreme victory over all the senses. In this belief there was no heaven and hell, for such conditions were temporary and due solely to the confusion and incompleteness of human understanding.

But the supreme example of the Buddha in seeking the ultimate freedom from the chains of this world had a curious parallel among the simple tribal pastoralists in the great plains of the tropical Nile. In that vast land of swamp and grass the Nuer tribesmen kept their herds. They thought of death as something horrible and took care to say little about the common fate of mankind. When one died it was thought that the inner personality went to the Creator and that was enough. The body was hurriedly buried with its back to the village, facing the forests. They told the ghost to go away and stay away, and they hoped that it would do so and not return to bother the living. Sufficient immortality was found in the transmission of the name of the departed man to his descendants. Perhaps he might be a ghost for a while, followed by peace and disappearance from the world. No great journey of the dead here, and no contact with them was desired. In a simple way the beliefs of the primitive tribesmen had points of similarity with the deep and elevating philosophy of the Indian Prince Sakya Muni, who through many sufferings found the way of non-material existence.

Left: Memorial skulls from Asmat, New Guinea, keep the ancestors in touch with the living

8. High Summer

In the pattern of time there is a swaying of light and darkness, the midsummer heat wanes, and the sun begins to decline inevitably, but through a glorious period in which the richness of the summer is most appreciated. It is the period before harvest, a restful time for enjoyment of the beauty of the world. Many peoples have thought of the Sun as a power of terror, especially in tropical and desert lands where heat is regarded as an enemy, and the cool of the night is the time of refreshment. But in the temperate zones the sun is an autumn delight. People wear less clothing and feel more alive; even in the far north the Eskimo can sometimes escape from the gloom and expose the skin to mosquitos and sun. Often the sun, or the god who is the incarnation of light, ascends to the heavens and brings back marvellous gifts, just as the Mexican god Quetzalcoatl did in his form as lord of the Morning Star. It is, however, the annual ascent and descent of the sun which is important in conditioning these myths, which reflect the yearly round rather than simple daily astronomical observation. They are also easily linked with the theme of human life and, in particular, the glory of full growth and adult power. Are we not glorious like the sun when we have beaten records, mated happily and achieved social success?

A full example of the god who ascends to the highest heaven, and then, descending, brings back gifts to mankind is to be found in the Maori story of Tane. Tane was the power of light and life; in effect he was the power behind the sun. It is true that they had a rather unimportant solar deity named Ra (not to be confused with the Egyptian Re, pronounced ray). But in the important

A wall of the so-called temple of Quetzalcoatl in Teotihuacan, in which masks of the feathered serpents alternate with masks of the rain god Tlaloc

Opposite page: At a reconstruction of the Inca sun festival, the Inca precedes the burnished disc representing the sun

myths it is Tane who is the great god of the sky.

This story was highly *tapu* because it dealt with Io the Changeless, the high god who was never talked of outside the *wharewananga*, the house of teaching. So only high-grade initiates, those who would be powerful priests, were allowed to hear his name. This sacred quality of Io was absolute, but he wished that the three baskets of sacred stones containing all occult knowledge should be placed on earth so that the people who were to come should not remain in ignorance of the secret of life.

It happened that Io sent his messengers to seek out his firstborn children by Earth Mother. They sought out this first generation of the gods. One of them asked the evil power, Whiro, who said he would make the journey to the heavens, but others sought out Tane and he also offered to ascend to the house above. The messengers asked Tane to come immediately with them but he refused. This was the season of storms and their actions were so uncertain that he would be unsafe if he ascended in the whirlwinds. Yet he promised that in high summer he would traverse the winds and ascend to carry out the will of Io.

In the high summer, when the air was quiet and the sky open, Tane called on the clouds assembled around the edges of the sky. He pleaded with them, and they came from their cloud houses to lift him up to the second heaven, the house of the winds. Then again Tane called and twenty-three winds assembled to aid him.

Above: A carving from a Maori house gable shows a spirit of fertility and life above an ancestor.
Right: This Maori house is supported by carvings of the ancestors, with a protective god figure at the top

Above left: The Peruvian fertility goddess in the centre of the gold plate is surrounded by various cereals, including maize and sweet potatoes. The sections represent the sowing calendar.
Below left: The face of Quetzalcoatl, made of turquoise with eyes and teeth of white shell.

They gathered all their powers and lifted him whirling higher and higher until they came to the tenth layer of the heavens. They were happy and playful winds, but now they had a very serious duty. Before he could go any further Tane had to be purified. He was carried to the latrine of the tenth heaven, and there he was forced to kneel and bite the beam on which people sat while excreting. As he did so there was a great dance and the priestly spirits came to take away the contaminated *tapus* of the earthly condition. Thus purified, Tane was told that he might go still higher, but that he must return to this place so that once more he should be purged of the holiness of the highest heavens before he returned to earth. So great was the power of this holiness that it would have destroyed any earth creature that touched it. Meanwhile he must be washed clean and neither eat nor drink until his return.

The ascent to the highest heaven was perilous. Tane was surrounded by a horde of disruptive spirits led by the dark shadow, the evil one, Whiro. There was a mighty struggle, but the winds surrounded Tane and whirled with such force that they formed a cone of destruction which shattered the enemy spirits as soon as they came near. Whiro was left defeated and his plan magically to obtain the blood of Tane failed. This struggle took place in the land of the pale-haired spirits who were ancestors of the most noble families among the Maori.

But Tane must go still one stage above to the great hall of Io. From the hall where he had rested Tane ascended by a hole in the roof and found himself in the home of Io. He was taken by the spirits of heaven to the sacred sea of Orongo, bathed and spiritually purified, and only then was he led to the presence of Io. Then he was asked whether he was alone, and he replied that he was there simply himself, alone, but that Whiro was also striving to come. But Io reassured him that the winds had prevented Whiro from bringing evil any higher. Then Tane was taken across the sacred open spaces to the place where the spirits waited with a great welcome for him. He was praised and given his titles and names, so that all the future chants to be made on earth should give him his proper honours. Then he was taken to the sacred house, Rangiatea. In it were stored the three bundles of knowledge, all the moons, suns and stars of the twelve heavens and all secret knowledge. He was given the three baskets: the *kete tuauri*, which contained all knowledge of the first parents, Rangi and Papa, who became sky and earth, and of the works to be done by the children of Papa in all future ages; the *kete tuatea*, the basket of all evils, of dissension and struggle, of all the evil deeds ever to be performed by humans and the objects of the natural world; and the *kete aronui*, which held all love and human kindness, all good deeds and all helpful things among the

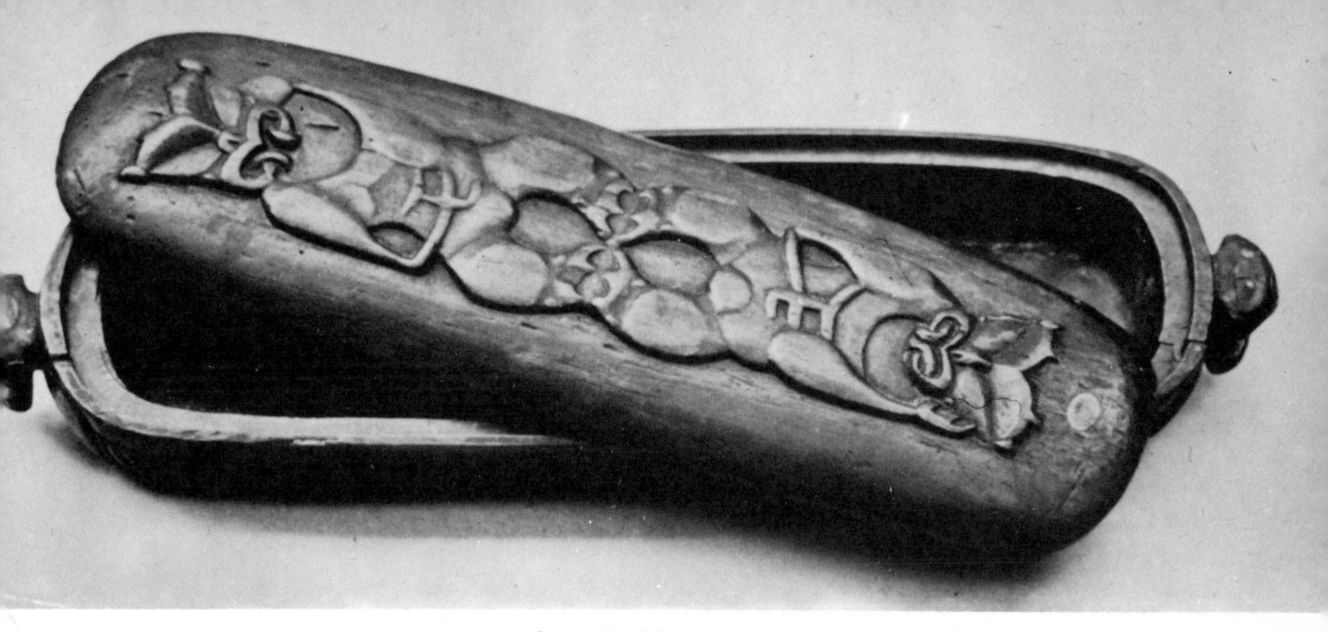

A carved wooden casket in which Maori chiefs preserved their *huia* feathers, symbols of authority

resources of earth. The stones which contained all these forms of knowledge were taken down to earth. They were to be kept in the houses of secret learning and were to be passed down through the generations of learned teachers, never to be revealed openly but always kept within the circle of knowledge.

But first Tane must be returned to earth. The spirits of the highest heaven brought him down to the place of the winds. He had once more to be purified in the ancient ritual of biting the beam, and was cleansed of the holiness of heaven. But no sooner had he been escorted into the air than once more the demon hordes of Whiro the evil one attacked. This time the good winds were aided by their elder cousins, and they captured some of the army of dark Whiro. Tane brought them back to earth, but mankind was not so pleased: among other winged creatures and lizards they included the sandfly and mosquito.

When the returning Tane reached the heaven of the clouds he sent up a high column of thundercloud to show he was coming with the gifts from on high. His people recognized the sign and sounded the great trumpets. All assembled to meet him, and then he went straight to the house of teaching so that the sacred baskets could be purified for entry into earth life.

The ceremonies were spoiled by the appearance of Whiro, who demanded savagely that he should have charge of the holy baskets. But Tane withstood him, and recited the evils that Whiro had brought upon the earth. The children of Earth Mother joined in the chanting and Whiro flew away. Later he would return to spin evil again and again, but Tane would always struggle with him, struggle against darkness, and triumph over it. Every time he descended he would yet rise again, light triumphant!

The journey to the upper world to bring back gifts for mankind sounds like a harvest myth, and in warm and ever-fruitful Polynesia it could only have such a meaning in its most southerly outpost, New Zealand, whence the story of Tane came, though it was told long after the official worship of the old gods had ceased. In Britain the ancient stories of the gods and the legends have been lost for longer periods. The stories have been turned round as they drifted through time. The confusions contain echoes of a duality and a struggle, perhaps like that between Tane and Whiro. For in these northern islands the contrast of the seasons is marked and the movements of the sun are much more apparent. So the struggle of the sun is important, though it has become embodied in many forms, such as nursery rhymes like 'The Lion and the Unicorn were fighting for the crown: when one went up the other went down,' and in the stories of Lugh and Balor. For Londoners the tale became the legend of Gog and Magog. When Brutus came to England with the Trojan survivors he met and defeated a race of giants (a reaction to the gigantic megalithic monuments of the island), of whom the last survivors were Gog and Magog. These heroes were captured and given work as guardians of the gates of Llundein. Their images were carried in procession. Until the fire of 1666 the images were made of wicker, some twenty feet high, covered with painted pasteboard, but now they are great wooden figures only nine feet tall. But Gog and Magog (son of Gog) were also thought to have once fought each other. In the thirteenth century Geoffrey of Monmouth in his *Gesta Britannorum* tells instead of the giants Gogmagog and Corineus who struggled, and one threw the other into the sea. The struggle was over a magic maiden but little is said about her. However, the story of Lugh and Balor seems to echo much the same myth of father against son. We find further north and west in Britain that Lugh, the culture-hero of the Celts, the shining intelligence among the gods, was the hero. His struggle was with his father over the beautiful Etain. The story survives in Sussex in a strange form about two giants. One lay on the hillside at Wilmington and asked his companion on the next hill to throw over a stone to awaken him in the morning. His friend threw the stone. Alas it landed right in the middle of the forehead and killed him. All that the stone thrower could do was to cut a furrow around the shape of his friend to show later ages what a great giant had been there. So the Long Man of Wilmington came to be marked on the hillside.

In the northern counties and in Ireland (where Lugh, bringer of light and wisdom, is replaced by St Patrick) the story was told of a great and terrible giant, Black Crum, who had an eye in the middle of his forehead. The beam of this light destroyed those on whom it shone. But the hero begged from the giant a mighty bull.

Gog and Magog, traditional guardians of London, originally derived from Celtic deities

Top left: Two Celtic bronze figures representing young bulls as fertility objects.
Bottom left: A Pictish carving on the theme of the devouring monstrous dragon.
Above: A Celtic divine bull, found under Notre Dame cathedral, Paris

The giant gave the bull, a wild creature, in the hope that it would kill his visitor, but it grew tame and was slain for a feast. The giant demanded its return and the saint brought the bull to life again with a prayer.

Etain was the daughter of the giant. She was a shape-changing serpent woman who must lead her lovers into deep caves to the land of death. In England the festival of the defeat of the giant was celebrated at the very beginning of August by fights between shepherd boys who built earthen mounds from which they conducted friendly battles. But this was really a struggle between dark and light for the harvest fruits, wild bilberries and the first wheat ears to be reaped. The original story was of great gods who were involved with a goddess who represented the fruitful earth, as in the Demeter-Persephone myth.

It seems that Balor was a form of the creator and also a combined god of darkness and light. He is opposed in his love for the Corn Maiden by the young sun, Lugh or Llwy, who struggles and overcomes the one-eyed giant. Some say he was slain by a sling stone, others by the thrust of a bronze spear into his baleful eye. The desired goddess escaped by a cave to return to the underworld, perhaps at the burial feast for Balor. Then the golden-haired Lugh, as a substitute for her, reaped the first corn. The festival included the sacrifice of bulls and the ceremonial gathering of bilberries which were the first wild fruits to ripen. The tribal chief or village headman then reaped the first ears of corn. Some were buried with prayers for the return of corn in the coming year. The weather was watched for omens of future fruitfulness. Then a great festival gathering was held in which the first wheat cakes were prepared and shared out as a kind of sacramental thanksgiving. Rain on that day, 1 August, was considered a lucky omen. So the struggle of light and dark, of the old and the new sun, and the death and glory of the corn were all celebrated. The festival continued over many, many years and then was gradually forgotten, but echoes of it still remain in harvest-home celebrations.

Lost gods and their fragmented legends litter our world. They serve to remind us that we inherit much from ancient folk who were not great technicians, but children of nature. Even where there was human sacrifice to the tribal gods (and the reaping of the grain was often such an occasion), the element of thanks to the gods and happiness under their blessing was always dominant. The echoes in modern times are no longer clear, since mankind has tried to reject his ancient beliefs and failed to make contact with substitutes which are valid to his inner personality. But what of still simpler people than the Iron Age Celts? How did the sun stand in the eyes of the hunters?

For the Bushmen of southern Africa life was once easy. The

Left: A Bushman at a waterhole, with a woman looking on: a Rhodesian Bushman painting.
Below: Bushmen, men and women, dance for the mantis spirits
Right: A Bushman painting of an elephant monster (from Natal).
Below right: The spirit of a dead woman sends rain

clans had plenty of room for hunting without much risk of war with each other. The land was full of meat, immense herds of antelope and deer as well as rock rabbits and edible lizards. Wild fruits were plentiful, and there were woods and hills where game was easily stalked. Even wild honey was around and water was plentiful. It is all changed now, but the hunters' paradise is still to be found in the stories written down by the early Boer farmers. The Bushmen of course fell foul of their new neighbours, for they had no notion of cattle farming and shot cows for meat. The

farmers thought of the little savages as lower than wild animals, and most horrible atrocities were committed by both parties to the misunderstanding. Many Bushmen were rounded up and sent to the penal colony on Robben Island. There Dr W. H. I. Bleek met them, learned their languages, and recorded their stories—the stories of a palaeolithic people only recently separated from their natural life. It is all so different from the usual fate of myths distorted and partially lost as civilization progresses with its gift of self-sufficiency and restriction.

Bushman attitudes to the sun were not like those of the farmers and they were compounded by being in a warm land without significant solar movement over the seasons. So sun is a material creature, and to them it seemed very near. Here is one of their stories which Dr Bleek recorded in their strange clicking speech. In the original it is as prolix and repetitive as it must have been when the little brown people told it to one another in the cave shelters after a successful day's hunting.

The sun was once a man, an early Bushman, who was still not one of the people who lived there before the Bushmen came. He lived in a comfortable valley and spent much of his time sleeping. From under one armpit there came a bright light. It lit up all the valley round his resting place, but the rest of the land was grey as on a very cloudy day. When the sun moved his arm the light changed. If he lifted it there was bright light; if he lowered it all became grey. Then when he slept at night the light became weaker and reddish. This was not good for the other Bushmen who needed more light for hunting and working. The mothers wanted light to look after their little children and to help their eyes when they prepared skin clothing.

There were two women, so old that their hair was white. They were talking together about the sun. One of them had no children, and she asked the mother of six boys if they should be told perhaps that the sun might be thrown up in the sky. These women wanted the sun up there so that his warmth should dry the wild Bushman rice that they had gathered. So the wise old woman went to the children. She asked them if they would try to throw the sun's armpit up into the sky so that it should shine and spread light and warmth over the people and the land. Then it would shine over the whole sky and they would all be happier.

The children were told to wait for the sun to lie down, when the people would become cold. Then they should tread silently until they could all grab hold of him, swing him in their arms and then with a mighty heave throw him into the sky. Their mother told them that when they threw the sun upwards they must speak to him, tell him that he was to shine every day, to pass through the sky, giving light and warmth to his people. The children said it should be so. Then leaving the ancient woman with white hair,

Left: A reconstruction of an Inca festival: the supreme Inca is carried in procession into Cuzco

Above: The Inca penitential festival was performed every January, as portrayed in the book of Huaman Poma de Ayala

they silently walked to where the sun would lay himself to rest. They waited and watched. When he had settled down they crept up close. There was the sun under his armpit shining brilliantly, but down onto the ground. The six boys approached closer, the elder telling the others to do as he said. They leapt onto the sleeper, and each took hold of him firmly, they lifted him, and with a mighty swing they threw him up into the sky. The old women saw the sun in the sky and knew that the boys had done well. They waited a while and then the youngsters returned, rejoicing. 'We threw him aloft, we told him that he should altogether become the sun, not his armpit only, that he should be hot because we were cold. We said, "Grandfather, remain aloft, become the hot sun to dry the Bushman rice, that you can make the whole earth light, that the whole earth may become hot in the summertime and that you shall always make warmth. Take away the darkness, as you come so make the darkness go away."' And now the sun comes and the darkness is sent away, then the darkness returns but the moon comes out and brightens the darkness so that the darkness departs. When the darkness is driven away the moon sets. It is the sun that comes out and drives away the darkness; he takes his sharp knife (a flaked stone) and stabs the moon. He cuts away the moon, but it pleads with the sun that he should at least leave its backbone for the people. The sun agrees and leaves the backbone, but the moon limps away slowly and returns home for a while, and the sun leaves him alone. Then the moon revives; he comes again following the sun. At first he is only a backbone, but he grows, he becomes complete, his belly fills with meat and he feels no more like an empty shoe. He walks in the night.

Then the Bushmen are happy and sing. The sun is here, all the earth is bright, the people walk while the earth is light, they see the bushes, they can find other people, they see the meat which they are eating, they see the springbok and in the summer they hunt it, they see the ostrich in the summer and they hunt it. They steal up upon the gemsbok and the kudu. The sun is bright over the whole land and people may go to visit one another. They lie down in little houses of bushes. They lie down until the springbok comes. They hunt in the summer when the sun is shining.

In total contrast to the life of the family groups of the Bushmen was the highly organized social life of Peru under the Incas. But Peruvian life was more dependent upon the sun than that of most people. The Sapa Inca was the child of the sun and the worship of the whole empire was centred upon the Sun Temple, Ccoricancha (the House of Gold) in the sacred city of Cuzco. The Sapa Inca was himself a sacred symbol, a direct descendant of Inti the sun god—at least until the half-breed usurper Atahualpa overthrew the true Inca and so opened the way for the easy conquest of Peru under Pizarro. But the empire's organization under the true Incas depended upon the myth of the divine sending of the Incas to rule the world.

The empire was made to observe the festivals of the sun. It was a somewhat erratic system since the calendar was actually based upon the rhythms of the moon. Being great grain producers, they naturally held a harvest festival when the maize was gathered in. This was in the month Aymoray (our May) when the sun was far away to the north, and it was not yet certain that he would return in the direction of Peru after the June solstice.

The best account we have of the Inca ceremony at the maize harvest comes from the Spaniard, Cristobál de Molina. It would not have the total grandeur of the previous era when the truly consecrated Inca Huascar was alive. Yet even under the domination of the Spaniards the unhappy puppet Inca Manco managed a splendid ceremony. This one took place in April, and was the welcoming of the sun, the feast of Intip Raimi. The festival lasted for eight days, and was begun by the Inca, seated on a special throne in the courtyard of Ccoricancha. Around were images of all the Inca gods under canopies of tropical feathers. Leading to the courtyard were two rows of the great nobles of the Empire, all in splendid clothing, great capes hung with pendants of gold and silver, and feather crowns on their heads. As the first light dawned the Inca arose and commenced a chant in honour of the sun. As the sun rose he chanted somewhat louder, and all the nobles followed suit. Then he returned to his throne and received delegations of the people of Cuzco (none except citizens of Cuzco were allowed to reside in the city during the great festival). Then

Right: An Inca mummy of a lady wearing a feather tunic, from the Valley of Chillon, Santa Rosa, central coast of Peru

Another reconstruction of an Inca festival, in which a young princess pours a libation to the sun

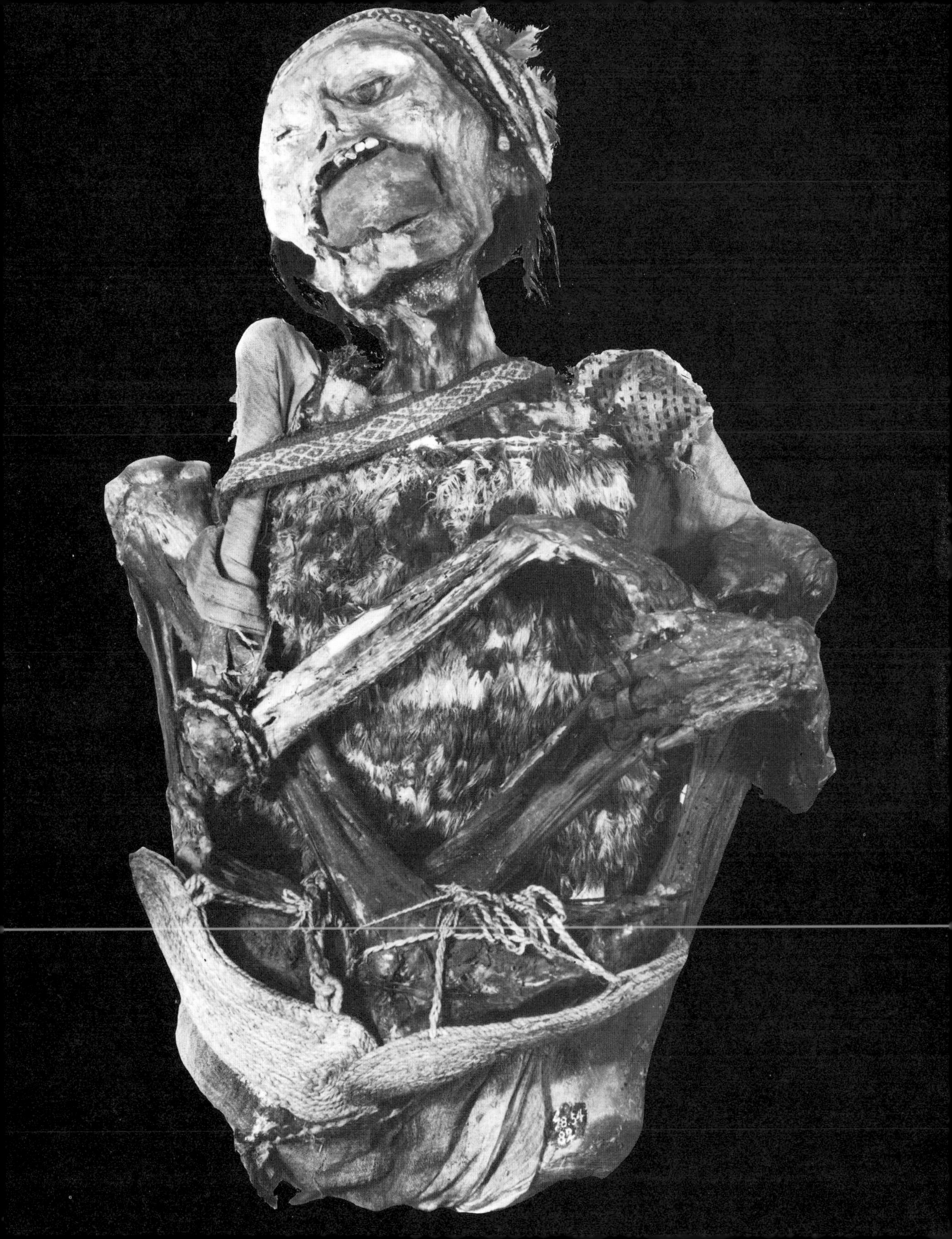

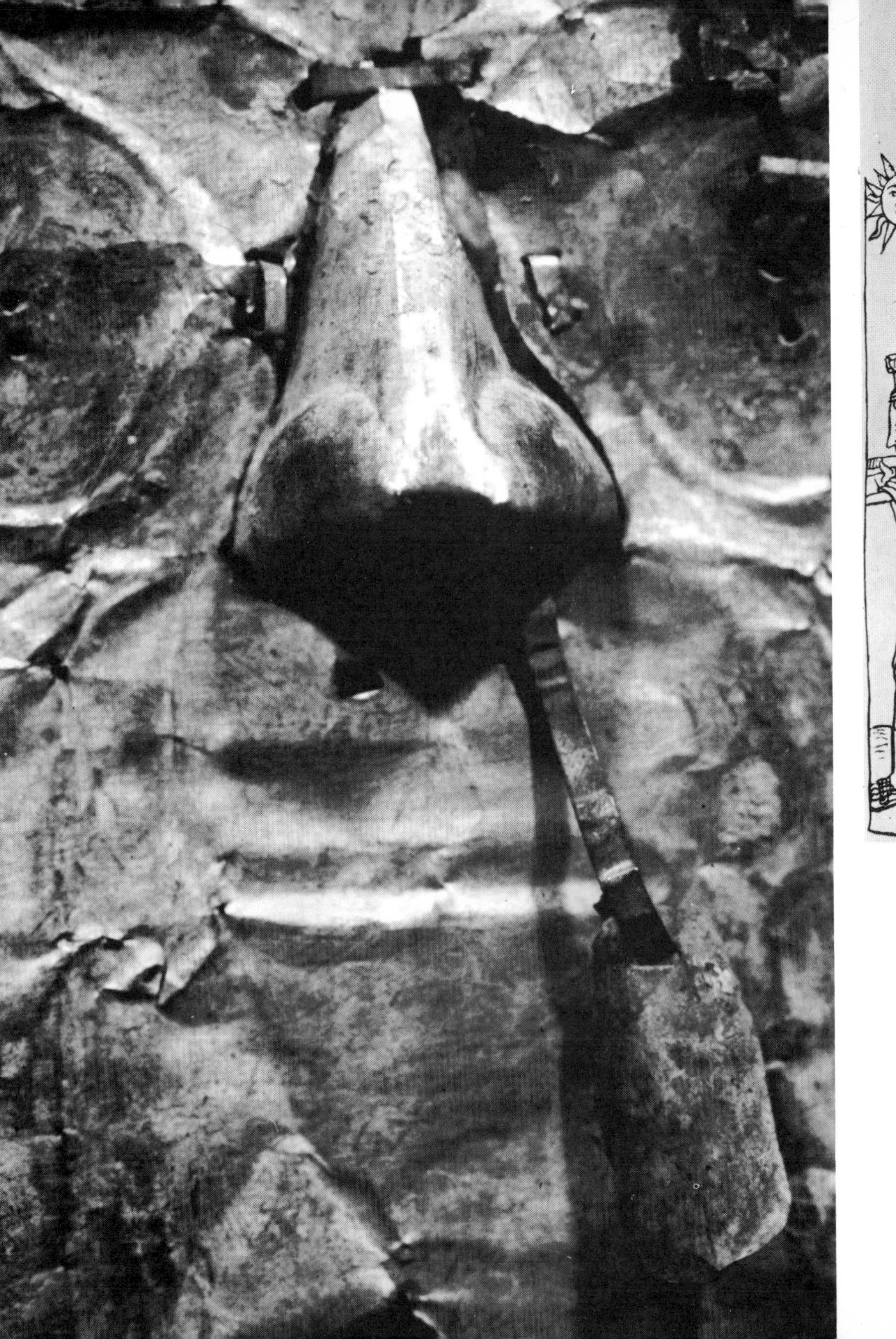

as the sun rose yet higher in the sky the Inca returned from time to time to lead an increase in the volume of the chanting. Later, as the sun declined, he correspondingly marked the stages of descent by softening the chant.

Looking on throughout the day were the mummified bodies of the past Incas. All of them were present to be part of the material descent from the sun to the present Inca. Some were grim bundles of skin-covered bones, but the more recent ones appeared almost alive, with even the eyelashes in perfect condition. All were attended by their servants in splendid clothes, and the bodies were also dressed in royal robes of golden splendour. They watched the great altar platform, on which was a growing tree. To this symbol of the upward path offerings were made in honour of the sun himself. All day for eight days joints of meat were burnt to ashes. Llamas were brought and slaughtered so that the bodies could be seized and eaten by the crowds of Cuzqueños at the feast.

Then came an army of beautiful girls. Each carried a large pot full of chicha on her back. The girls marched in rows of five, walking proudly despite the weight of five gallons of beer. This was a procession of offering, and the drink was first ceremonially offered to the sun, and then poured out for the drinkers in the crowds. One chronicler notes that the Peruvian Indians had the fortunate habit when drunk of going to sleep instead of fighting, and says that the stone walls of the city were lined with dozing Indians overcome with happiness.

At sunset the bodies of the past Incas were taken in procession back to their cells in the temple Ccoricancha. All the gathered people wailed a lament for the setting of the bright sun.

The festival was repeated with mass singing and dancing for each of the eight days. The dead Incas were each attended by fifteen ladies of rank, and all day the servants were busy fanning away the flies from the sleeping faces. All was noble and splendid.

At the end of this particular festival Inca Manco gathered his nobles, and on a specially prepared patch of ground he turned the first sod with his digging stick for the first maize to be sown. But this was in fact out of season—this should have waited for another ceremony in July. Perhaps this departure from the rules had a magic significance which the Spaniards could not understand. One would guess that it was a prayer for early food to assist some plan to destroy the invader; and indeed Manco was later to revolt against his oppressive masters.

But Manco left no record. And the Spaniards later destroyed Inca history when they burnt the painted story-boards which were preserved with the mummy of each Inca. The mummies they also burnt in their splendid attire. Nevertheless the story of the Children of the Sun lived on.

Above: A procession bears the mummy of a previous Inca to the Sun Festival in November, from the book of Huaman Poma de Ayala

Left: A golden death mask from the Peruvian Chimú kingdom

It began a long time ago, when the golden man who was the sun hid in a cave underneath Lake Titicaca. He was to survive the great flood which the creator god Viracocha had brought on the impious earth people. There were also two people saved so that humans should live when the sacrifice had been completed. The water rose until even the great mountains were covered. Then the waters fell, and the land and seas, the rivers and lakes were all as now.

As the first human pair of the new world knelt and prayed to the great creator, he caused the sun to awake and leap golden in the sky as the light of day. He also brought rainbow and thunder into being and created the stars. The universe was made beautiful and the people lived and loved. They bore many fine children in this beautiful world. The numbers of people increased. Tribes formed and lived in many places, and spoke differing languages. Then Inti the sun sent his children to earth, so that the four quarters of the earth (Tahuantinsuyu) should be brought under a common and wise rule.

How this was done is reflected in legends which contradict one another: some say they came as last of a line of four hundred wise men from Tiahuanaco; others believed they came from the sunrise over the Amazon jungles; others, that they rose from Lake Titicaca. Most, however, agree that eventually the four children of the sun came to the four caves at Tamputocco. Thence they descended from the mountain on the road to Cuzco. Many strange events befell them: Huanacauri, for instance, was changed into a great rock in the form of a huge puma.

However, Inca Roca and his sister continued their journey seeking the navel of the earth. To this purpose Inti had given them a wedge of gold which they were to place on the ground each time they stopped. When they had reached the navel, the Cuzco, they were to stay and proceed to conquer all nations. They came to the hills above a small town inhabited by primitive mountain people. Inca Roca's sister, the Ccoya (queen), decided to terrify them. She slew a llama, and cutting out its lungs she hung them from her mouth, blew them up like balloons, and descended drenched in blood and looking like some cannibal spirit. The people fled. When they returned she had enthroned her brother. Together they assumed the rule, the Children of the Sun ruling from the Cuzco, for this is the place where the golden wedge sank from sight.

Gradually the Inca family, marrying only in the pure line of the sun, brother marrying sister, came to control all Peru for four centuries, until the fratricidal attacks of Atahualpa broke the myth and eased the way of the Spanish invaders. But always the sun was the guardian of his Inca children, and among their festivals they never neglected to celebrate his greatness.

Above: The shining face of Surya, the Hindu sun god

Right: Vishnu and his consort Lakshmi ride on the bird god Garuda

Left: The mummified head of a Maori chief: his tattoos denote rank

Right: Drawn by his many-headed horse Surya drives in his chariot: a Bundi drawing of the 18th century

K

And now to another warm land, north of the Equator, with seasons but without a significant period of winter. To India, where the gods were worshipped with great devotion and where each social caste was content to hold its place because so the gods had ordained the order of the world. But among the gods the generous beneficent sun god, Surya, was especially loved. His images show him giving and defending, but whatever his actions he has two arms, each holding the open blossom of a beautiful flower, for he caused flowers to live and made the harvests ripen.

It began with Agni, lord of Fire, who cleanses all that he touches. He helps the dead with warmth on their passage, devours evil things, and gives fire to the sun in the daily circuit of the sky. He has a hearth in the southerly direction (when the sun is farthest away from India) which is in the middle air and warms the home of the dead. But he has another power on the earth, Movement, the Lord Savitri. Savitri is the wind, the movement of the waters, and the marvellous dancing of the fire. Whatever has movement he is there; he is even within other gods, for they have movement from him, especially Surya, the ever-moving sun.

Surya is a warm deity. He is painted as a handsome man coloured a deep warm red. He has three eyes because he sees also with the mind, and four arms, for he not only holds the open lotus flowers, but he also showers blessings on his worshippers, and gives them encouragement in their devotions. Often he is enthroned upon a red lotus flower, and from that, like the red sun of the east, rays of gold flow all around him. Surya has twelve names of great honour, for each describes some great quality which comes from within him. He is the shining Indra, king of the gods; he is Dhata, the bringer of all things into being; he is Parjanya who sends the rain down to earth from where the sun rays pierce the clouds; he is Tvashta, who reveals the corporeal forms of all things; he is Puchan, the giver of food; he is Aryama who gives reality to sacrifices; he is the giver of alms in the spirit of love; he is Vivasvan who causes food to nourish; he is Vishnu, destroying the enemies of the gods; he is Ansuman who gives health in orderly living; he is Varuna, the life spirit in the great oceans of the universe; he is Mitra who from the moon governs the wellbeing of the three worlds. Those twelve are the glories of Surya, who through them enters the universe of created beings and gives light to the souls of men.

Surya, however, had his troubles, for he was too devoted to his wife. She was the daughter of Visvakarma, architect of the gods. Her name was Sanjna, and she was mother to the three children of the sun. A rift arose in the marriage. Surya lavished attention and love on her, but he continuously radiated light, ever blinding her with brilliance. So eventually she called on her companion Shaya to live with Surya while she went away to seek for peace.

Above: Vishnu in his incarnation as Surya the sun god, as seen at Konarak

Right: The god Indra rides his elephant in his aspect as a thunder god

(This probably refers to the coming of autumn.) Surya was so involved in his shining glory and his precise routine that for a long time he was unaware that his wife had exchanged personalities. But then he left on an adventurous trail seeking to find the beautiful Sanjna. While he was away Visvakarma planned with the gods that the brilliance of Surya should be somewhat dimmed. He took away a part of the brilliance of shining sunlight, making weapons for the gods with it. Then, when the lovers were reunited, the marriage was mended and there was happiness and lasting peace between them.

Thus at the coming of autumn shades began the hard way for seeking peace and reunion. It was the way of mysterious fate from which all changes and all renewal must follow.

Below. The pattern of fate, shown in the basic trigrams of the *I-Ching*, surrounds the Yin-Yang symbol of continuous change on a Taoist priest's robe.
Left: Contemplating the mystery of the Universe, Chinese scholars study the Yin-Yang symbol

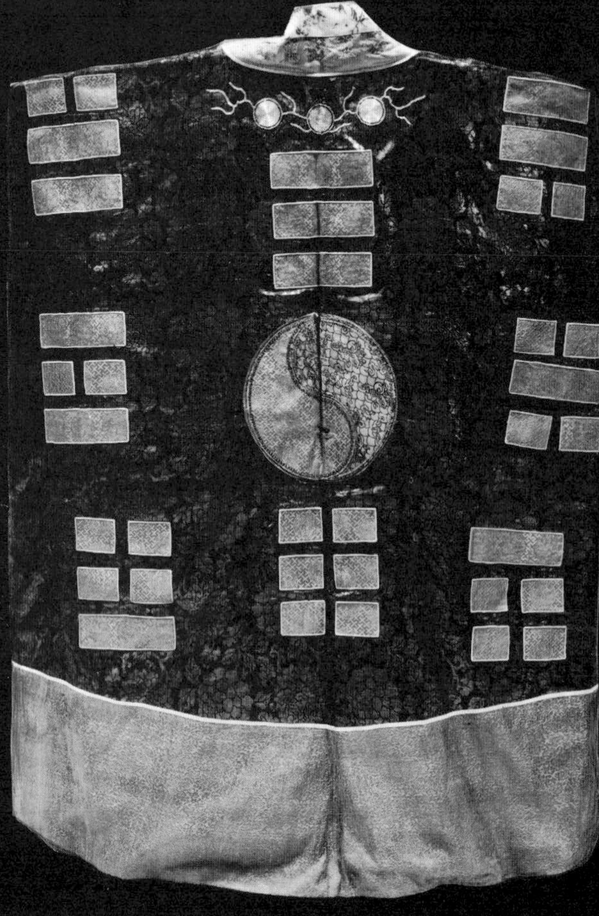

9. Autumn's Golden Equinox

The dimming of the sunlight after the brave shining summer; the coming of the quiet days when the leaves become coloured; the joys of the fall: these things are always a little sad. Will we see the rebirth of the year next time? We are aware that we are not part of the eternal round of the material world. Change is the key to it all, the orderly sequence of events, the reaping and the sowing, the growing and the declining. There has always been a hope of renewal and an understanding that the rhythm of the earthly life is but one aspect of all manner of rhythms in nature. The old astrological identification of the individual personality with the sun has always been mingled with the pictures of the inner mind. The sun of autumn is always glorious and always sad.

In Chinese thought there is a symbol which expresses it all to perfection, the Yin-Yang circle which has its three-dimensional sign in the little circles within each of the two elements. It reminds us of the constant change from light to dark and back again, and of the constant opposition of disparate elements which achieve success only if they can reconcile their differences in unity. But the only true unity is change. The experience of life is one of opposites which can unite, but only temporarily. Light and darkness, male and female, east and west, life and non-existence, power and weakness are but a few of the innumerable contrasts which comprise our universe of personal experience. The changes of emphasis and reversals of polarity are expressed in myths, but there remains the question of the two universes: the external one and the equally magnificent interior one which we enter sometimes in dreams. It is to be expressed in symbols because it too is ever-changing. Yet all our experiences are felt by a world-soul, say the philosophers of the east. The best example comes from the Chinese belief intrinsic to the book of changes, the *I-Ching*. It has a myth to tell us of its origin, but, as with the book itself, myth and reality are interchangeable. The idea of the trigrams, the three-line symbols, was ancient. They were attributed to the time of Fu Hsi, who was said to have been the inventor of the art of cooking food. Three lines, either broken in two or unbroken, can be arranged to give eight symbols. Thus they came to be assigned to the eight directions of the universe, the four cardinal points and the four intermediate points. But eventually seers were inspired to use the three-line combinations in pairs, giving the possibility of sixty-four combinations. With an accidental and unpredictable method of selection they were arranged to give oracles upon contemporary situations. What they came to mean at that time is not known, though there is a tradition that they were in a different order than in the time when King-Wen first used them.

King-Wen was a valiant warrior, renowned for seeking to bring stability and order in the time of corrupt government. The period was at the end of the Shang Yin dynasty. He fought against the tyrannical Chou Hsin. There was battle and eventually King-Wen was captured. All his honours were stripped from him and he was imprisoned. In a bare room with mud-brick walls he considered the changes of fate, the evil state which had befallen his country, and the hopes of change. The magical hexagrams were much in his mind. He could mark them in the dust and meditate. Using the stalks of the yarrow plant he worked out a way of dividing them irrationally, so that numbers could be produced as if by accident. These accidental patterns of numbers reflected the events in his inner world. They came to be predictions of the nature and course of change at any given time.

Eventually the armies with their weapons of bronze and jade clashed again. King-Wen's son the Duke of Chou conquered the tyrant and, as so often throughout her history, China had arisen from oppression and found a new life. The freed King-Wen, now an old man, wrote the first commentary on the meaning of the symbols of change. Later the work was added to by the Duke of Chou, and the *Book of Changes* was given a form which allowed it to speak. Eventually the thoughtful scholar, the great Kung Fu Tse (Confucius) added a series of commentaries explaining the inner meaning of each of the sixty-four hexagrams. Since that time the book has spoken for itself to those who have the right simplicity of heart.

The *Book of Changes*, the *I-Ching*, has chosen Tui the Joyous as the symbol of autumn, a sign associated with the idea of the youngest daughter in a family, of gaiety and contentment in awaiting the future. So men could accept philosophically the state of change in the world and see the declining of the autumn sun as an occasion for joy, the quiet joy which comes of understanding the hope which underlies all change. From the humiliation and sadness of prison the ancient forms were given soul by King-Wen, and with the changing of time they were enriched and given to the world. They can speak silently, exploring the world of the inner universe and bringing its mysterious hidden jewels of meaning to light.

There is a similarity of the theme of glory in defeat in the unexpected region of the stories of King Arthur, the Once and Future King. His was a story of glory, struggle against tyranny, and eventual defeat which ended in the voyage to Avalon, the Island of Apples, where he was laid to sleep until the dawn should come to bring victory once again to the Britons. His legend is not uncommon in the world, especially among people oppressed and awaiting a future freedom. But Arthur has a more complex character. The legends tell of his mysterious parentage, begotten by a great king who in another's guise lay with the Queen. His whole life is shown as a mystery, and one should not

The teacher Confucius dressed as a Mandarin, enthroned on a table as in a well-to-do Chinese home

be misled by chroniclers and poets into thinking that Arthur can be contained in history. Certainly he was an historical war leader of the Britons, who were trying to uphold some kind of Romano–Christian culture against the aggressive colonizing farmers from the north German and Danish coasts. He faced the West Saxons, led them into a trap at Mons Badonicus (probably near Bath), and destroyed their army so completely that they retreated to below Salisbury and did not even capture that ancient fortress (now Old Sarum) until two generations had passed.

But Arthur has many other faces. He is married to the White Wife, an aspect of the great goddess in her triple form; he is ruler over a vast imaginary empire which includes the older Celtic lands; he goes on his ship and conquers the terrible wild boar Trwch Trwth. These reflect a Celtic god figure. His final magical feat takes him to the entrance of the underworld where he has to slay a terrible witch, and does so by casting his dagger which cuts her in half, like two bowls. The historical king is slain in the battle against his treacherous nephew at Camlann (Cam Long Down in Gloucestershire?), but in legend he is later placed in a boat in which the nine black-draped maidens (the nine blackbirds sent by Rhiannon) take him away to Avalon.

There is yet another Arthur who dwelt on hills and mountains. In early times, and indeed in some places up to the eighteenth century, a village girl whom everybody liked was escorted before dawn to the Arthur's Seat. There, clad in white and sometimes crowned she held court. Her gown hung very wide so that as she parted her legs it swung into a white bowl into which the villagers put offerings of the wild fruits. This was a September festival. It had all the simple charm of the old folk festivals, and it helps to identify this other Arthur and place him as lord of the harvest of nature, and also as the sun god of autumn. Again, there is also a tradition that Morgan le Fay was half-sister to Arthur!

The oldest Arthurian story is the *Spoils of Annwn,* which tells the story of how Arthur three times sailed his magical ship *Pridwen* loaded with warriors to assault the island of the dead. As in the Marquesan story, he does not seem to have known that he was in another dimension of space. Annwn is treated as if it were but another island in the ocean. Its fortress was Caer Colur, and six thousand warriors guarded it. The invasion was a great success, but of the warriors who sailed with Arthur only seven returned. They brought the cauldron of Annwn which was ever full of nourishment, and from it only the valiant and true of heart could eat. One could equate this as a myth of the solar descent with the myriad stars into darkness, and the sun's re-emergence in the dawn with only the seven stars.

The horned god Cernunnos receives wisdom and gives gold in the midst of the sacred beasts

The earlier heroic stories, themselves garbled by five centuries of increasing ignorance following the fall of heathendom, still echoed the legends of the gods, and as the chivalric stories of Arthur developed the ancient god assumed another personality, an honourable and noble one of the great war leader of the Britons against the Saxon invaders. But by his very nature his decline was inevitable. The story of the king who was betrayed and is now in a far place, awaiting his return to save Britain, is also the story of the autumn sun, sorely wounded by time and declining until he is recalled to rise for another year.

There were some English folk customs surviving until a little more than a century ago which contained vestiges of the Arthurian story. In particular, the hunting of the dreadful boar, the Trwch Trwth, had degenerated into the dance of the Old Sow. In Derbyshire farm labourers at the harvest home chose one of their number to become the Old Sow. He wore a boar's head of wood on which were fitted spiny branches of furze. His function was to upset the harvest feasting and to tease the feasters. This he did by lowering his head and prodding the dancers with the furze spines which finally brought them to such anger that despite his spines they seized him and drove him outside, thus magically preserving the harvest for another year.

There was an element of joking in this which was far removed from the terrifying legend of the great boar who caused the death of warriors. Laughter was an important part of many harvest festivals. It was a way of releasing excitement harmlessly. Many of the American Indian tribes also found that it was important to have laughter at ceremonies: it helped to ward off evil and darkness. This probably conditioned the nature of the Okipa harvest festival which George Catlin observed among the Mandan of the Upper Missouri. He was rather shocked because the ceremony had so much of sex about it. But in a simple way the ceremony promised the return of the maize spirit after the harvest. It was a prayer for future harvests, turned into a symbolic dance.

When the maize was ripe the Mandan women held a meeting at which they selected an honoured matron to go out to the maize fields and prepare a special corn dolly. There was a festival on the day when corn was to be cut. The earth had given her fruit to save the lives of her children. The sun had ripened it, and now was the time to put the holy food into the granaries to give life through the coming winter.

The tribe would gather on the appropriate day, and there was much talking and waiting and hoping that all would be well. Then, coming over the sky line, they would see the harvest

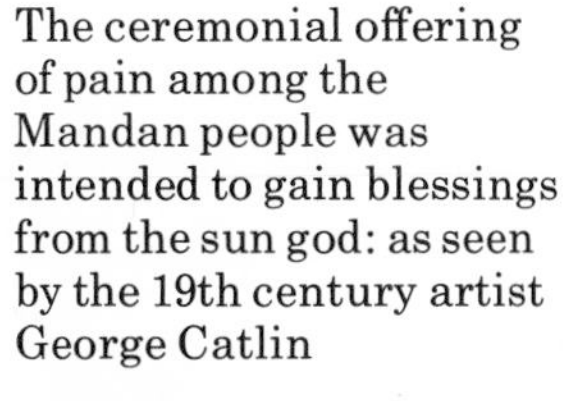

The ceremonial offering of pain among the Mandan people was intended to gain blessings from the sun god: as seen by the 19th century artist George Catlin

mother approaching with an armful of maize stalks with the ripe ears on them. As she came nearer they broke into rejoicing songs. Still nearer to the people she began to laugh, and so did the people, for every now and then she squeezed the bundle under her arm, and from the midst of the maize there slowly arose a huge penis, brown and with a bright red glans. It seemed wildly excited, and the people, particularly the women, laughed at it. Then it would sadly die down and disappear in the sheaf.

There were many jokes shouted out about the digging stick which planted life, and men were a little afraid of what their womenfolk would say about them. Every now and then the great penis would stick out and shake its crimson head, to renewed joking and laughter. There was a rush to possess it, but the women usually prevented this and the harvest mother was allowed to enter her house and hide it away. It was really a length of buffalo intestine carefully moulded and sewn so that it could be inflated from a bag of blood attached to it. But nevertheless it was sacred, a symbol of life and hope for the future. There was naturally laughter, because sex usually elicits laughter in public. It is an irrational happiness and a kind of dream magic. But most importantly for the Mandans, the ceremony was a mark that the time of plenty had arrived as the sun was moving lower in the southern sky.

Harvest is different in the tropics only because it has a different timescale. Where two or even three crops are harvested each year there is less contact with calendars or the stars. It is the planting, growth and final harvesting of the food staple that is the key to belief about life. But in some tropical areas the commencement of the year is tied to the safe gathering in of the staple food. An example is to be found in the ceremonies of the Kayan people of Borneo. This is an old account of a customary way of looking after the basic source of nourishment, the rice plant. The ending of the rice harvest was the beginning of a new year simply because people liked to begin their year with the granaries full and a feeling of freedom and richness within the family.

The whole of Kayan ceremonial life hangs on their belief in a spirit world in which ancestors, elemental nature sprites and some more exalted gods cooperate with mankind. The will of the spirits was expressed through the trance mediumship of dedicated priestesses. They were governed by a learned priest, an elder of great experience and knowledge. The spirits controlling rice lived in an underworld. They were naturally regarded as man and wife since no new life can start or grow without the care and protection of parents. They were believed to act according to the behaviour of their people. There was a sacred patch of ground set apart for growing rice for these two alone. The care given to

The sun spirit and the rain give life to the maize: a Pueblo Indian drawing

In a Kayan longhouse the sacred rice is stored in ancient jars

it and the offerings made by the people through the chief and the priestesses were thought to reflect the will to care for the sacred crop of food of all the people in the padi fields. If all was good and the people were polite, the parents beneath the earth would influence the balance of nature favourably. There was the village plot cared for by the chief, and each family in the long-house had a small family plot which was dedicated to the two deities. But there was also the padi area further out in which each family had its allotment for the good of the whole village as well as the family group. Just as they lived in their screened rooms in the longhouse as individuals within the great unit, with the chief's room in the centre, so their rice stores were expected to be shared if there were shortages.

Rice sowing began with a dance by the priestess who might be in a trance. After planting a few stems she delegated the work to the young villagers. The boys made holes with their dibbling-sticks and the girls planted the baby plants. Then on the sacred plot the priestesses danced and laid offerings in selected spots. The whole village swung to the booming of the splendid brass gongs, which were the main symbols of the wealth of the people. There were ten days of the festival and on two of them people

Right: Flooded rice fields in Indonesia

could not enjoy the daily bath in the river. For eight nights there was a harder restriction: people were not allowed to work or to go out to visit their neighbours. Each family stayed in its compartment in the one-house village. No visitors from outside were allowed. The intention was to give a period of quiet rest in which the souls of the rice, like those of the people, could be in repose. But during daylight entertainments were allowed. The whipping tops spun to the delight of the men, young and old, who showed their skill. Young men wrestled before the admiring eyes of girls who cheered them on from the verandah of the longhouse.

On the evening of the tenth day the forest demons emerged. A motley crew of masked figures covered with shaggy straw cloaks were followed by a team of other grotesques who performed a frightening dance with bare swords. The girls then joined the dance but with their heads covered by basket-weave masks with painted cloth faces. It looks like an old English mummers' dance, perhaps because the underlying intention was the same: the destructive forces are driven away and the feminine spirits bring life in their wake.

The night was then lit up by bonfires and the young men of the village performed a grand mime in which they hunted and pretended to slay a wild boar, a helmeted young man who was a specially skilled dancer. After he had been 'slain' the masked girls came on with a celebratory posture dance. The force of the darkness and savagery was destroyed and life had come back. (It reminds one of the famous hunt of Trwch Trwth in old Wales). While the rice was growing there were occasional processions when a priestess would bless the fields and lead the villagers in hoeing the ground. Eventually the harvest was ready, the rice was mature. After cutting the first ears ceremonially with little reaping knives set in carved wooden handles, the priestesses led the people in cutting the new crop. It was threshed and stored high up in great baskets in the houses, safe from mildew and mice. Now was the time for thanksgiving, and for eight days the village rejoiced. There was dancing, and the women of good family wore their brass corsages over their wrap-around skirts. Some of them lined up to dance holding the bamboo cages in which the heads of dead enemies were drying. They all wore their best ornaments. The men had turbans ornamented with hornbill feathers and ear pendants of carved horn. Their loincloths were beautifully woven with figures of spirits and heroes. The girls all wore skirts newly woven in *ikat* patterns. Their breasts, pointed with happiness, quivered firmly beneath the rows of necklets. They wore basket-weave caps of delicate woven designs in red and cream.

On the sixth day of the festival eight priestesses climbed on the sacrificial platform and danced with linked hands, invoking

A Kayan mother carries rice-seed to the storehouse in a rice basket decorated with cowrie shells, symbols of fertility

the spirits to come to join with the people in the great festival. They chanted a long prayer and told the spirits how good and brave the people of the village had been throughout the year. Then they opened a basket of dainties as offerings to these kindly spirit friends. After a while they knew that their invitations had been accepted. They closed the basket and danced over a gangway to the house of the chief and installed the basket, which now contained the spirits, on a throne of honour.

Another dance was held on the final day of the festival. Pigs were to be sacrificed. The priestesses, no longer wearing their long skirts and necklets, danced in a transvestite costume of men's loin cloths and war coats, rather like leather ponchos. They swung swords, but indicated that they were going to offer the pigs to the spirits and powers above. While they danced, two priests postured around them fully armed, fighting off the assault of evil powers from the wildwood. As evening drew near the pigs were taken up to the stage where the dancing was coming to an end. They were slain and their livers taken out and examined for good omens. It was hoped that the underside of each liver would be pale in colour, signifying good luck.

The end of the ceremonies was a general friendly mêlée, in which the men wrestled for the sport and for the acclamation of the crowds. The girls as well took on a sham fight in which they threw water over each other from bamboo containers.

When the festal time at last was over the people began to prepare for the beginning of another cycle of rice cultivation with the appropriate ceremonies for planting.

In this sequence of events in Borneo of some hundred and fifty years ago there is a unity between the people and the spirit world which makes the ceremony into its own myth. There was no need for anyone to have invented an explanatory poem for their actions. One notes that the Kayans had been separated from the world outside Borneo for many centuries. They were of Mongolian stock and in no way related to the people of the European world. Yet there are many points of coincidence in their ceremonies with the folk customs of western Europe. They were part of a worldwide series of fertility customs which ended with the falling of sacrificial victims, in this case the pigs. The final ceremonies often included a kind of saturnalia with transvestite dancing. This stems from the thought which links basic foodstuffs with the rhythm of human life. Even the transvestite dance has been a widespread custom all over the world. It is known from the Iroquois, the peoples of western Europe, some Arab countries, South Africa and most of Asia. Always it was a gay time and brought much happy laughter. The basis of this appears to be the necessity in times of good fortune to delude the spirits of bad luck and death so that they could not hold power

Right: The awesome visage of Mictlantecuhtli, the Aztec Lord of Death. Far right: A Chinese red lacquer panel with the Yin-Yang symbol surrounded by the eight triagrams, the key to knowledge

A wooden figure of a Luba girl, her beauty emphasized by cicatrization all over her body

over those upon whom they had set their desires.

The tutelary spirits of the granaries now had their role. They appear in art in New Zealand as little formalized figures of naked girls standing above the store houses. They were the essence of life and increased the life-giving, nutritional value of food stocks. Among the Bakota of the Congo Republic sacred baskets containing ancestral skulls and fronted by a metal-plated symbolic figure guarded the granaries of the chief. The ancestors still remembered the earthbound people and guarded their life force. In fact this care was quintessential in the belief of past and present as a continuous exposition of the life force. It was derived from the first creator who was ineffable, and could not be portrayed by mask or image. To a large extent the power over earthly life was delegated, but nevertheless the divine spirit was everywhere, in all things and people.

This spirit of the continuity of life is inherent in all African religions. The seasons of the year and the declining sun do not have great significance for the good reason that they make little impact on the orderly routine of village life. On the whole the gentle moon seems a more popular deity than the fierce tropical sun. The Luiya of Kenya, however, tell of a merciful sun god who took a human wife. It could be a story to explain in some way an eclipse, but time scales are not at all clear. But the important point is that the giving of light to the people on earth was decided by a woman.

The rule of marriage among the Luiya was that young women were expected to obey their parents' wishes and presents were arranged. One girl would not agree to this: no earthly suitor in her estimation was good enough, and she would not be persuaded to accept the young man chosen for her. She ran away, and journeyed to new lands. Suddenly she came across a rope hanging from the sky (a common dream form in European psychology). She was interested and began to climb the rope, but suddenly it moved of its own volition and whirled her up to the land beyond the sky. She was thrown down on the soft mess of the midden behind the house of the sun.

After a while a beautiful elderly woman came from the house and found the girl frightened and crying. She told her that she was the mother of the great chief of the skyland. It would be certain that he would wish to marry the girl and keep her among his other wives. The girl still did not want to marry and only wept. She was taken to the house, and the other young wives came to her, but she did not respond to their kind words. The elder lady told her not to be frightened when the world began to glow with light.

Then light began to come. It grew brighter and brighter until all that world shone with the brilliance of summer lightning.

Left: A Kayan longhouse, with a Balinese rice dolly (bottom right) made at the rice harvest

L

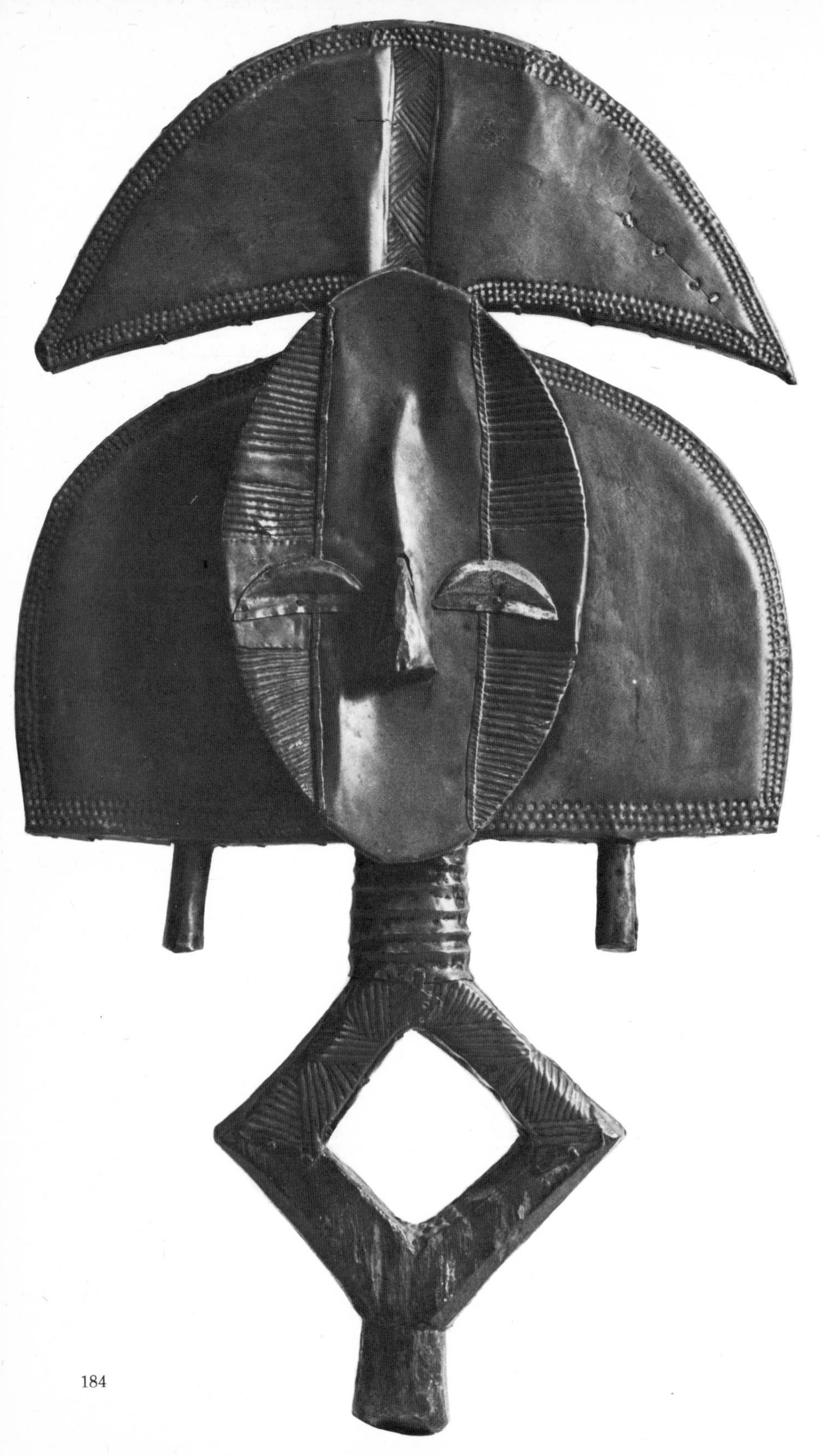

Left: This Bakota figure sits in front of a basket containing the skulls of ancestors

Above: Aztec boys joyfully prepare to climb the greasy pole to snatch the image of the war god, Huitzilopochtli, at the Festival of the High Sun at midsummer

The other wives came to the sun and told him that there was a girl with them whom his mother had brought to be a new wife for him. But the girl had thrown herself on the ground and covered her eyes. She refused to speak at all. The sun asked his chief servant the moon to speak to her but she did not speak, so one after another the sun sent the six planets to speak to her. Still she remained silent. Then they were sent again with a bride price of all the things which grew in the skyland. But to no avail. Then the sun decided on a great gift, and he took a wooden box and put the sun rays in it. After putting on the lid he gave it to the girl. She was delighted, not least because she could see in the less violent light. (At that time the rays did not shine on earth and therewas darkness.) At last the girl whispered that she would be bride to the sun. They married, and she became mother of three beautiful sons. She ranked high among the sun's wives.

However, in time the sun's wife felt lonely and asked if she could descend again to earth to see her family. So she was let down gently on a beautiful vine, and carried many presents to the darkened world. She was kind to her parents and they were delighted to hear of her wonderful marriage. But even the gifts she brought could not console her mother because the world was dark, and she could not see clearly and neither could all her friends. After a while the sun's wife had to return to her home in the sky. She found the vine had descended for her, and soon was back in her home with her happy companion wives. When the sun came home she asked him to allow her to release the sun rays again from the strong wooden box. He agreed, and light came back to the world so that people could once more see their work and recognize one another. One is tempted to add 'and so everyone lived happily ever after,' only we know better.

In ancient Mexico, the pattern of festivals placed the sun as patron of all warriors, and separated the agricultural side of life in a series of festivals mainly to do with the growth of the maize and involving the rain gods. The sun was a hot and thirsty being needed to ripen the plants, but experienced as an agency who dried up the ground and withered the maize stems after the harvest. The weeping for rain early in the year was followed by the horrific flaying sacrifice to Xipe Totec, the patron of the maize seed as it sprouted from the husk. And the victims, just like maize corns, were skinned and killed to bring forth new life.

Then, at midsummer, there was a dance in which a woman dressed as the salt goddess was suddenly, in the midst of dancing, slung on to the back of a priest dressed as Ehecatl the wind god. As she was lifted in the dance another priest sliced off her head; and as the dance continued the beautiful, pulsating fountain of blood sprayed all the bystanders and gave them new life just as the reaped cobs of the maize became their sustenance. The

The image of the old fire-god, Huehueteotl, to whom burning sacrifices were offered in August

deeper motive was to invoke the water gods to keep Mexico fertile and alive.

The August period, when the harvest was reaped in the old world, brought a Mexican festival to the fire god. The rite is so grotesque that it reminds one of the Roman story of the Britons stuffing wicker idols with war captives and setting fire to the lot. Prisoners, usually slaves, were painted in the yellow and red of the fire god. They were taken to the temple pyramid and dragged up the staircase by their hair. The warrior who had captured them was responsible for getting them safely to the top platform, where a great stone bowl filled with blazing pine logs was waiting just behind the sacrificial stone. On the way, the victims were liberally dosed with a powder which made them insensible to pain and saved a certain amount of agony, for they were to be just alive enough to have beating hearts for the ritual's climax. They were tied to poles and after being carried round the fire were one by one cast into the flames. The bodies were burnt free of the poles and writhed and twisted as the muscles contracted in the heat. Then, when thought to be still just alive, the grotesque scorched creatures were stretched over

The heart is snatched from the human victims at a temple decorated on its roof with the fire butterflies of Huehueteotl

the stone for the heart to be lifted out. It was offered to the fire god, for warmth and life for the people. He was of tremendous importance, though favoured with few festivals, because he was the earthly representative of the creator who put sparks of divine fire on earth to be the souls of newly born humans. The bodies of the victims of this sacrifice were cremated, not eaten. Their souls were taken into the heavens, towards the Pole Star, symbol of the giver of life.

This dramatic ritual was enacted at every temple. When the slaying had ended there was a great festival of dancing and singing. In the courtyards of the temples poles were erected which bore gifts on top, and the young men scrambled to climb the poles and snatch the gifts down. After this display of strength, arrayed in their new finery they danced wildly, singing and rejoicing in the blessings which the lord of fire had given to Mexico.

For all the terror of his ritual this god was a high and good god. But there were truly evil beings around, the 'adversary who goeth like a roaring lion' was abroad in Mexico as elsewhere in the world.

10. The Everlasting Shadow

The year suddenly changes, the autumn leaves fall, the skies become grey, and a sadness covers all, for the delights of summer are come to an end. So the mind is conditioned to dread the coming of winter. There is an area of our inner mind which houses a dark fear expressed as a shadow personality. It is usually the truly shadowed part of our mind which we do not wish to acknowledge: a kind of Freudian dustbin in which we hide something contrary to our notions of cultural excellence. From this shadowy area inside us come many devils. In West Africa it used to manifest itself as violence when a king was expected to have his subjects slain as a sign of his omnipotence. In the classical world it was a destructive underworld being. The American Indians found a dark fatality driving on the warriors in the search for death or glory. In western Europe the shadow seems a mixture of sex and brutality. Everywhere there is a feeling that some unknown shadow personality takes over and destroys the works of light. Because the drive comes from regions beyond consciousness it produces abnormal effects like the burning of witches, punishment for quite innocent eroticism, and the wholesale destruction of cities described as victories of right and goodness.

To look at the world is to see this irrational force of negation everywhere at work. In the magical scheme of directions this is the region below. In our myths we have expressed it as a personality of great power, of infinite and endless evil. The things we are afraid of in our soul are personified as the Devil sitting on one's shoulder whispering evil thoughts into the mind. This image, of a very real and very destructive influence, is shared among ancient Mexicans and modern Puritans.

In a most extraordinary way the devil-figure is often credited with the creation of the visible world. One finds the thought, among Gnostics as well as early Christians, that the world is basically evil, though it is a concept far removed from the teachings of Christ. The Gnostics thought of the creation by Ialdabaoth as an event in opposition to the high God. As far away as Mexico the black Tezcatlipoca brought the earth up from the waters, and lost his foot in the process. But this terrible deity was not the giver of life, nor was he good.

The great pyramid temple in Tenochtitlan (Mexico City) is now left only as the sad ruins of foundations, though it still has an uncanny atmosphere. Once the great brilliantly painted pyramid towered over the city in a lake. There was beauty and music all around. At the top of the 114 steps were two glorious houses. One in blue and white was dedicated to the lord of rains, the fertility god, Tlaloc. The other in red and white was the home of Huitzilopochtli, the southern form of Tezcatlipoca and the patron of the Aztecs. The god had four forms, for he was lord

The immortal head of the moon goddess Coyolxanhqui, from the great temple of Tenochtitlan

The foot of Tezcatlipoca is torn off by the earth monster, from the Codex Fejervary-Mayer. Below: The greatest of Mexican pyramid temples: the high house of the sun at Teotihuacan

of the four directions over the surface of the earth. There was an eastern form in yellow and black; the southern form was blue and yellow; the western was red and white; and the northern form was blue and black. But essentially the god was thought of as a great shining black figure with the yellow bars across his face.

Bernal Diaz was with Cortes when the Aztec ruler Moctecuzomatzin led them to see the great god. They climbed the steps and noted the blood from sacrifices running over the top ones. In front of the house of the gods was the sacrificial stone. Then they stepped under the gilded beams of the glorious house, into the gloom. As their eyes became accustomed to the light reflected from the sun-scorched pavement outside they grew aware of the huge figure of an enthroned giant. He was black, covered with jewel-encrusted ornaments which glittered like coloured stars. Beside him stood his messenger Ixtlilton who carried a jewelled shield and was dressed in black feathers. The whole place was caked with dried blood. The priests climbed short ladders in order to pour fresh blood from gilded-cane tubes over the god and his treasures. Hearts were tipped out before the god from golden bowls. To the Aztecs this was a wonderful place, the shrine of the great 'Smoking Mirror', the god who protected them and gave them glory. One of his feet was missing, replaced by a marvellous ornament of humming bird feathers. He had given them the lovely earth to live in, so they repaid his sacrifice with the hearts of captured warriors. This was splendour and glory; but the Spaniards were sick and distressed, for this was truly a black devil in his hellish house. The walls were caked with red-black layers which rotted and stank of corruption as the maggots writhed among them. The glorious temple was inwardly terrible, a horror set with jewels.

Now this god had been born of the Earth Mother and came into the world fully armed. He was the sun and destroyed the stars. He also cut off the head of the moon goddess, but when he realized she was his sister he managed to keep the head eternally alive. Then he saved the universe by making earth rise from the waters in the form of a great alligator which he forced to remain on the surface by tearing off her jaws. He was the god of material things, and of bravery and war. His children were the warriors who were trained by his priests and who sacrificed their captives to him. They were ever willing that their hearts in turn might be offered to him if they were captured by other tribes who worshipped him.

But this great god Huitzilopochtli was a false creature. He promised all *anahuac* to the Aztecs and that promise was kept, but when the Spaniards came he prevaricated and allowed the nation to be defeated and brought to ruin. He could not withstand the Christians and fled from the blazing ruin of his house when Mexico fell in 1521.

The god Tezcatlipoca was called He-Who-is-at-the-Shoulder, and Lord of the Innermost Nearness; he was the inspiration of valour, sitting always so close that he whispered thoughts of bravery and cruelty into the ears of young men. He inspired wars, and stood in direct opposition to the cult of the gods of light and peace.

The Mexicans believed that their terrible patron god would be finally defeated by the return of Quetzalcoatl, the Morning Star and the Breath of Life. On one of the possible days of this reversal —which would mean disaster for the Aztec domination and freedom for mankind—Hernando Cortes landed in Mexico. The great Moctecuzomatzin recognized the inevitability of change and his dilemma and final despair were reflected in the slow disintegration of Aztec rule.

Above: The head of the moon goddess, torn from her body by the demonic Tezcatlipoca, in the form of a pendant

The story of the Aztecs is one of the few occurrences in history when a whole people believed themselves to be protected by a divinity of such malevolence as Tezcatlipoca, Lord of Sorcery. It seems to have originated in a deep-seated reverence for fate, and an assumption that time changed in a regular manner by which the powers of light were replaced by grim black powers. The later philosophers among the Aztecs believed that the last change of the rhythm had occurred just after the election of the great chief Quetzalcoatl II of the Toltecs. The king saw the end of the time coming and made some as yet unidentified change in the calendar. Through his unfortunate love affair, which raised the nations in revolt against him, the Toltec Empire was broken up, and the last official leader of the nation was the execrated Huemac, who switched the religion of Quetzalcoatl to a minor role and gave dominance to the worship of Tezcatlipoca. This occurred around 980 AD, so the reign of the black Tezcatlipoca among the gods of Mexico lasted only five and a half centuries.

Below: The Aztec king Tizoc, dressed as Tezcatlipoca, conquers enemy chieftains on a large stone used for combat sacrifices

However, the beliefs of the Aztecs were simple compared to the philosophies of ancient Persia. There the classic duality of Ahuramazda and Angra Mainyu ran from the creation up to the end of the material universe. In later times Angra Mainyu is known by the name of Ahriman. This in old Persian could be taken as feminine, and suggests that once the mysterious dark power was an ancient mother goddess. But in all historical periods Ahriman has been thought of as male, a twin soul of Ahuramazda, but for ever in conflict with the Light. The legend tells us that in the beginning was the Light, Ahuramazda. He thought of creation, visualized those who would come into being. Thus he saw Ahriman emerge from darkness when he thought of him. He was, and had existence. At first the Light sought to come to an agreement with Darkness, but this was not possible and as the one

The dual birth of light and darkness: Zurvan bears Ohrmazd and Ahriman

created good things, the other made the evil beings. In the late seventh century BC the prophet Zarathustra was enlightened. The spirit led him before the formless Light of Ahuramazda, and the deity revealed to him the story of creation.

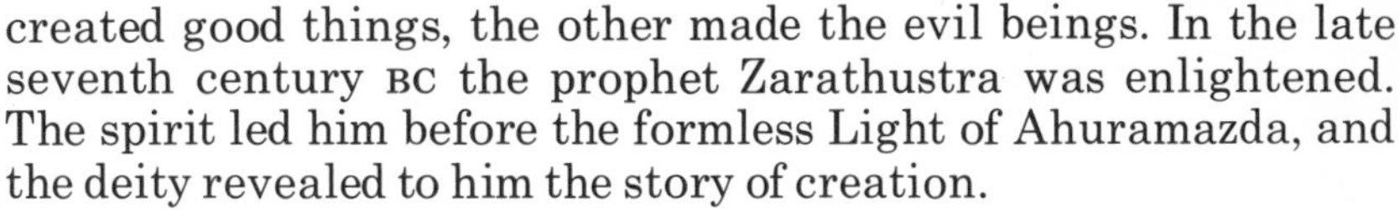

Ahuramazda created the world from nothing. This world is the world of life, but Angra Mainyu also created a world: a world of death (this seems to have been the far northern world, for there the summer was but two moons long and evil flourished in the cold darkness). Then Ahuramazda created paradise, Ghaon, where roses ever flourish and the humming birds shine like rubies. But Angra Mainyu then created harmful insects to destroy and harass all living creatures. Ahuramazda in turn created a great city for men to live in prosperity, but the Dark One introduced lies and deception. Pastures were created for the great herds of cattle, but wild beasts were sent to destroy and maim them. A place for loving prayer was made, but the Evil One introduced doubt into men's hearts which worked to destroy their gentle faith. In the city where work and merchandizing flourished Angra Mainyu introduced sloth, so that there should be poverty and misery. Thus the creation of the good and beautiful Light was marred by Darkness bringing death and misfortunes to mankind. He even introduced the dreadful custom of burying or burning the bodies of the dead, which should have been exposed to sun and air in the Towers of Silence.

The teaching of Zarathustra revealed that after the three thousand years of contemplation there were three thousand years of creation, then three thousand years of learning between the creation of the first man and the time of Zarathustra. The fourth period of three thousand years began with the teachings of Zarathustra and was a period of preparation for the final victory. Then, with the destruction or ultimate separation of Ahriman, Ahuramazda would rule in truth and justice and the old creation would pass away.

The world was populated by spirit beings of great power as well as humans and animals. They are the equivalent to angels and devils in Christian thought, except that for the followers of Zarathustra each group was created from a part of the soul of the creator. They were simply diametric aspects of the spiritual unity. But it was known that the shadow would eventually be destroyed. Psychologically this is true, since as the human being approaches true integration there must remain less and less room for the shadow.

In the Zoroastrian hierarchy of spirits there are six Amshaspends, angelic spirits of immortal goodness, a greater number of personifications of the forces of nature, the Yazatas and Fravashis, and six Daevas, the spirits of evil and contrariness who were aided by a great number of lesser devils divided into cohorts of Drujs, Pairikas and Yatus.

The spirits of the dark side of being were the opposites of their counterparts of the light. There was a balance of good and evil up to the ending of the universe (believed to be in about 2400 AD). The Daevas (devils) are under the command of Ahriman. They are liars and cheats and look after all those unhappy souls who have a like character; Ako Mano was the prince of these

Ahuramazda gives the symbols of power to a Parthian king, Ardashir

A bronze statuette from Iceland of Thor grasping his hammer

dark powers. Indra (not the Hindu deity, but a ghastly shadow) had the duty of watching human souls coming to cross the bridge Sinvat, leading to the other world. As they passed full of hope, he would leap out and try to cast them into the depths of the river of perdition which flowed beneath. Sauru strove against good government, overthrowing kings and encouraging anarchy and usurpation. Naonhaithya entered ordinary folk and filled them with pride and rebellious irreverence. Taurvi and Zairisha combined to tempt men into sinful self-indulgence and corruption, while Aeshma was the spirit of rage and anger who caused war and devastation. Such were the motley crew who led the forces of Ahriman, seeking to darken the light and spoil the beauty of creation.

Such a hierarchy of demons is part of the mythology of many civilized lands. In the system of Zarathustra the main demons were aided by hordes of lesser beings who dragged humans down into sinful excitement and despairing loss of hope. But the same process of demon-fear is visible in western European medieval art, and also in Chinese pictures of the underworld. The chains of diffusion were the overland trade routes and the movements of semi-nomadic peoples. One of the fruits of the teaching of Zarathustra was the emergence of another prophet, Manes, who under the Sassanid King Sapor I evolved a system which linked Christian ideas with the older beliefs and eventually spread from the South of France to China as the Manichaean tradition. In southern Europe it was simple and high-minded, but undoubtedly heretical. Its suppression was accomplished with such brutality that the extirpation of the Albigenses was a blot on the name of both the French King and the Christian Church that has never been forgotten.

But areas fearing the Devil were not the only parts of the world in which an evil being was thought to have been in the company of the gods. In the old Germanic religions there was the disgraceful dissembler Loki who was responsible for the slaying of Baldur. No one ever wrote a good word about him, no *skald* sang of any noble deed performed by Loki. Yet he remains a minor deity in the glorious company of Valhalla. Loki is a typical shadow figure; he is the antithesis of all that the leaders of the heroic society valued. He is master of cowardice, lying and cheating; traits that no warrior hero would dare admit lurked in his own soul, though he might well know that a half-seen strain of such evil lurked somewhere—somewhere out of mind, whence it might creep into the ultimate stress of combat as a moment of weakness or cowardice. For a blood-glorious slayer of men this was anathema.

Yet we of a more civilized time might pause to think that Loki had an excuse for his malevolence. He was the son of the giant

Left: A Northumbrian version of the escape of the wolf Fenrir at the Götterdammerung, the end of the world, on the Gosforth Cross

Below: Valhalla, home of the Valkyries and the souls of Norse heroes, as seen on a grave-cover

Above: The old gods remembered on a tapestry depicting Odin, Thor and Frey from Skog Church, Hälsingland, Sweden

Farbauti and his wife Laufey. He had three brothers, but he was the handsome one in the family. He married a faithful and kind wife, Sigyn, and they had a son. However, Loki also took to wife a giantess whose name meant Coming of Sorrows. They had three children, the wolf Fenrir, the great serpent Jormundgant, and third the lady Hel who was half flesh-coloured and half black. The other gods in their city Asgard heard prophecies that they could be harmed by the children of Loki. They held a council and decided that they must defend themselves by acting first. They found that the children were in Giantland and planned a raid. They swept down from their mighty fortress and seized all three.

Hel was treated well by the Aesir. They cast her down to the lowest realm of darkness, but there she was a queen, sharing out food to the poor unhappy souls who were sent to her realm, those who had died of disease or old age and not in battle, the unfit souls who could never enter the brilliant glory of Valhalla.

The great serpent was taken by the gods, and Odin All-Father lifted it and cast it afar into the depths of the western Ocean. There it grew but could never escape to land. It grew until its mouth and tail met. The great circle it made encircled the whole habitable earth. Once Thor was deluded into trying to lift it and

thereby sank the boat from which he was trying to haul up the monster. Only at the end of the world would the serpent son of Loki be set free to take his revenge.

The remaining son, the wolf Fenrir, was taken to the palaces of heaven, but he could not be tamed. The gods planned to imprison him, but having brought him into the courtyard they dared not go near. He snarled and fought every move they made—two great iron fetters were shattered in moments. The Aesir were perplexed, and sought out an unbreakable chain. It had to be made of six impossibilities: the noise of a cat walking, the beard of a maiden, the roots of a mountain, the breath of a fish, the saliva of a bird, and the sinews of a bear. The cord was woven, thin and smooth and quite unbreakable. First they had to trap the wolf, and this was impossible until Tyr grasped its jaws. His action allowed them to get the rope around the mighty animal. It snapped the hand off Tyr's arm, but it was bound and the ropes were tethered to great stones which were buried deep in the earth. Thus the three children of Loki were imprisoned and for the time being made powerless.

The Aesir did this to protect themselves, even though Loki had once helped them gain their fortress without paying for it. He had cheated the giant who did the work and brought death to him. Nothing that Loki performed was good or altruistic. But although his lies were the result of his own nature, he became even more destructive because he in turn had been cheated by the Aesir.

Finally the gods decided that Loki himself must be imprisoned and disgraced. But Loki had expected this and built himself a house with four doors so that he could watch for trouble from any direction. If he saw the vengeful Aesir advancing one way he escaped in the other direction as fast as he might. He was also endowed with the protean gift of changing shape, and often sought quiet refuge under a waterfall in the form of a beautiful salmon. When he returned to his house he tried to work out what kind of thing the Aesir would make to trap him, and in doing so happened to make the first net from flax stems. Then he heard the clatter of horses and knew his cheating foes were upon him. Quickly he threw the net on the fire and assumed his salmon guise.

The gods broke into the house, and Kvasir the Wise saw the pattern of white ash left by the net. They copied it and fished in the river, but Loki evaded them several times. Once, afraid to swim into the sea, Loki leapt over a fish weir, but Thor grabbed hold of him; Loki became thinner and slipped through the iron grip. Ever after that salmon were slender towards their tails.

There were several further escapes, but at last Loki was cornered and captured. The gods decided to imprison him in a

Loki stands chained to the rock, on a Viking memorial stone from Kirby Stephen, Westmorland

Right: Blake's vision of Satan, the prince of the Christian hierarchy of demons, rousing his rebel angels

Overleaf: left: A modern Mexican Tarahumara dancer's headdress closely resembles those of the Aztecs in Cortes's time. Above and below right: The Zoroastrian Towers of Silence near Yazd in Iran, in which were exposed the corpses of the dead

house of great stones. They seized Loki's human sons, slew them and with their entrails they bound the tricky god to a trilithon by neck, loins and knees. From above they suspended a poison-dripping snake so that its venom should drop on Loki's face, but they were thwarted by the devotion of Loki's wife who held a bowl over him to catch the fatal drops. And there he lay bound unjustly by the cruelty of the Aesir, although of course they felt justified in what they had done. His predicament, however, did not stop Loki from spreading thoughts of evil around, and he never lost his hold on the minds of men.

But the evil done by the gods against the spirit of evil was to be amply revenged. Even Odin All-Father knew that the final doom would come. Even while Loki was tied to the rocks he sometimes shuddered, and the whole earth would shake. It was a premonition that the day of retribution would befall: Ragnarok could be avoided neither by the Aesir nor by mankind. Doom would be signalled by the terrible winter, which would last for three winters one after another without summer's interruption. Mankind would abandon itself to evildoing. War upon war would shake the earth, incest and adultery would be rife, creating yet more strife. It would be an age of battles and storms. Then two wolves would come to devour the sun and moon and cast down the stars. Earthquakes would break up the solid earth, and at last the wolf Fenrir would break his fetters and grow and grow until his jaws spread from sky to earth. The serpent, freed from his bondage, would spew poison throughout the atmosphere. Then would the skies burst asunder, and into them the giants from Muspell would throw their fires, and ride with the released souls of the dead, led by Hel herself, to the rescue of Loki, as they stormed to their assault on the gods. Nothing but struggle would be left, gods and all would fight to the death, and at the end the dark forces of Surt would cast the final fire, consuming the whole world in the downfall of the gods.

Yet heaven would remain, the place of the just and the good. After a time earth would rise again out of the dark seas and a few of the gods would return. Then from the darksome wood where they were hidden, Lif and Lifthrasir would come forth. These two new humans were to repopulate the earth and usher in an era of new growth and life. Even the old sun would be in labour and bring forth a beautiful golden daughter to be the new sun and give life and happiness after the evils of the old world of Odin. And Loki and all the monsters would have been overcome.

The story of the Götterdammerung belongs to a world which we hope has passed, one of power and violence which poets knew must revert to a balance. It is the final theme which emphasizes that fears of the evil powers can only lead to catastrophe followed by an eventual return to the light.

Winged Peris, or Pairikas, on a Gujarati embroidery from Western India

But there have been people who could not believe that the evils of this world were caused by a single great and frightful being. There were many peoples living in an environment of technical merit equal to that of the Norsemen, and even approaching Persian standards, who did not take such a determined dualistic standpoint. In Africa the break in tradition traverses the southern fringe of the Sahara. In the north there were people of Mediterranean character, who later codified their dualism into the complexities of the Gnostic gods and demons, while the Egyptians preserved a simpler approach and had a contrary deity in opposition to life. He is represented as Set, the opponent of Osiris and father of evil. He may well have been some ancient god of misfortune from further south, but in historic times Set was the evil tempter, father of lies and the murderer of Osiris. He smacks of black magic. Set was drought and darkness and destruction of life. Just how he acquired his strange features similar to the head of a giraffe is uncertain. In some sculptures he has a head rather like that of a smaller creature, the *ichneumon*.

Set was once a less markedly evil being, but as Egypt became more hierarchical he was fitted into the theological scheme as the evil twin of Osiris. (One finds the dualistic twins in many mythologies, usually as Morning Star and Evening Star.) With seventy-two helpers Set went to a great meeting at Memphis for the installation of Osiris into the kingdom. He brought with him a beautifully painted casket and promised to give it to anyone who most nearly fitted its measurements when they lay in it. Osiris obligingly did so, whereupon the followers of Set shut the casket and hammered in its wooden dowels. Then Set threw it into the Nile. The coffin floated, and drifted to Byblos in the land of the Syrians. There it was sheltered and eventually incorporated into a marvellous tamarisk.

Isis divined the coffin was in the tree and the body within. But Set found the body as well and cut it into fourteen parts, casting them away all over the land of Egypt. Isis found them all, all that is except the sacred penis, which had been stolen by a crab. But she mummified the reunited body and nurtured her son Horus until the time came for him to confront and destroy the earthly rule of Set. For ever afterwards Set was regarded as the implacable adversary of life and of vegetation. Set was the desert, the dry season, the night.

Such philosophical translation of ancient mythology was not attempted in the lands beyond the Nile. African mythology contains no supreme evil. Although there are many stories of misfortune, of the coming of death and the betrayal of good, they are all associated with a temporary event: no African spirit has been made the eternal force of evil and destruction. Sometimes,

Isis suckles her son Horus

indeed, God the overshadowing creative power is made into a villainous, self-willed king, but at the same time he is still a loving, if distant friend to his creation.

The sad aspect of the kingly God is seen in a story from the Ba Ila of Rhodesia. It is about the creator and sustainer Leza who is said to sit on the backs of all humans, keeping them as his unquestioning servants with no hope of their ever being able to make their own way through life. There was an old woman, who had been left an orphan when she was a child. Many of her relatives had died one after another and she was alone in the world. Then she found a husband who was kind to her and she had some children, but suddenly her husband died. The children married and she became a grandmother, happy amid the laughter of the youngsters. But her troubles were not over; first the children died and soon after them the grandchildren were taken away. There was no happiness for the old woman alone without a hope for the future.

Her sorrows were great and the old woman thought to die, but even this was denied her. Instead she became stronger and younger looking. Eventually she was able to travel far and was very determined as well as healthy, so she set out to seek God and tell him of his monstrous injustice in causing all her people to die. She went to a far country and cut down great trees hoping to make a ladder to climb into the sky, but before the work was finished the lower trees rotted and her work was wasted. So she went still further seeking to find the place where earth and sky met. There she hoped to find her way upward to confront Leza with her questions. She passed through the lands of many tribes, and all asked her where she was going. But when they heard they let her pass on with a dour comment on her madness. They said she had no reason to quarrel with Leza, for he ordered everything, always planning for life and death to follow one another according to his own wisdom. Still she wandered on ever seeking, until her time came and God called her to her own death.

It is a hopeless story, but another tale from the same part of Africa tells of a man who was allowed to see Leza and meet his dead relatives, all shining bright and happy, but quite unwilling to return to sad earth. So perhaps we may think the old woman also found her relatives awaiting her arrival in that happier world.

Again from Rhodesia comes a Barotsi story in which one almost takes pity on the creator. It seems that God created all living creatures and was content, so, with his wife, he lived among them. But there was a man Kamonu who believed God to be just another human. When God took iron and hammered it to make a hoe, Kamonu did the same, and his hoe was equally good.

Figures of protective spirit beings. The large one (near right) riding on an elephant protects the crops from damage by animals

The trouble came when Kamonu became a great hunter. An antelope was slain by an iron spear forged by Kamonu. God protested that all living beings were like brothers and one should not slay the other, but Kamonu pleaded that he would become a farmer instead of a hunter; so he was allowed to live in that country once again. For a while all went well, but suddenly buffalo attacked the farm and Kamonu was forced to kill some. Then Kamonu was afraid the deer would devastate his farm, so he hunted and killed some. Then bad luck came, he broke a precious storage pot, his dog died, and finally his son died. Kamonu thought this was unfair and marched off to tell God about it. He was surprised to find pot, dog and boy all in the house of God. He begged for medicine to make them come back, but God refused. Kamonu became so troublesome that God's wife demanded that they should move to an island away from him. Undeterred, Kamonu made a raft and continued complaining. Then God made a great mountain and lived in Olympian isolation—until Kamonu found a way to scale the mountain. But other men were around. They kept on making love and having children so that their numbers were making the country uncomfortably overcrowded.

Then God and his wife called a little bird to advise them, and he in turn brought in the spider. The spider helped by floating a silken thread which reached all the way to the sky. Then God and his family climbed up and ever since have lived in the sky in peace.

Luckless Kamonu still tried to ascend but everything he tried to pile up collapsed like the Tower of Babel. Nowadays men no longer try to climb into the sky, but they salute the sun as the sign of God, and the moon as the wife of God.

Such gentle tales with their note of sadness are characteristic of the pastoral tribes of Africa. The autocratic behaviour of God in the tales is a simple reflection of the status of the chief in African iron age pastoral society and in the city states of West Africa. A certain flamboyance was demanded from the chief, and a century ago this still included the right, almost the duty, to show godlike powers by the destruction of life from time to time. But this could only develop in an economically stable society where the hierarchy was regarded as possessing magical powers as great as those of an Egyptian pharaoh.

In simpler societies where life was hard, the tribe small, and leadership strictly democratic in agreeing where the hunters should move next in the continuous search for food, there was still less belief in a centralized power of evil. The Australian aborigines had ancestors, misfortunes, sorrow and joy, but no determined spirits of evil. The aborigine was possessed of a totemic spirit. His ancestors in the dream-time had a duality of form, being animals and yet able to act and think like humans. Eventually the great changes came about which divided the beings into humans and animals, but the ancient mystical links remained. No one would willingly hurt his totem animal, though he might eat its body if it had been slain by a man of another totemic group.

One of the tales of the dream-time concerned the koala bear, who was blamed for causing drought—perhaps because nobody had seen a koala bear drinking from any stream or pond. It was very important to treat the body of a dead koala with great respect for fear that it might cause the waters to dry up and the tribe to starve. Long ago in Victoria there was a tribe of selfish people. Among them lived an orphan boy, Koobor. He was ill treated, given only scraps of food and never much water. He learned to live by eating leaves and grass, but was often ill and people thought that he would soon die. He was just a nuisance to them. Nevertheless he had some magic songs; in those times most people had special powers which have now been lost.

One day Koobor came to the camp after the people had gone out on a hunt. He saw that they had put several bark buckets full of water in a hollow under a tree. At last he had enough to drink! So he emptied one delicious bucketful. Now he was stronger and decided to hide all the water so that he could drink whenever he was thirsty. He sang his magic song and a eucalyptus tree began to grow beside him. On its branches he hung the water buckets like fruit, and then jumped up on a bough. The tree grew high, as high as several men, and Koobor and the water were safely away.

When the little tribe returned they found their water was stolen. Then they saw the new tree and Koobor with the water buckets far above them. They tried to climb it but with no success. So they called two of the elders who were great magicians. The two men half-climbed, half-floated up the tree, took Koobor and beat him, breaking his limbs and cursing him, and threw him down to earth. The body broke up and Koobor was dead. Yet his magic was still powerful. The broken bones came together, smaller and covered with fur. The body of Koobor changed into his totem animal, and he became the first koala bear.

There was a drought after that. In the end rain came, but the people proposed a new custom, that a hunted koala must never be skinned nor his bones broken until after he had been cooked in the fire. If they did otherwise they feared that the koala magic would cause a drought and their water would go away again.

This little story makes a small creature into a threat to those who treated it wrongly. That is about as far as the Australian aboriginal mind could think of evil: it was not part of their natural world. Such was the simplest approach to evil.

11. Sad November

In the northern hemisphere November is necessarily sad. But how the Peruvians got their annual penitential ceremony in November is less obvious. It may be that they had brought the tradition from some previous northern homeland, or else they perhaps were following an almost universal custom of commencing the year when the Pleiades were overhead at midnight, or when they set as the sun was rising. This unique cluster of stars is associated in many lands with the beginning of the year, and so also with the ending of the old year. The end of the old year universally implied mortality, and especially in the northern hemisphere. The leaves had fallen, the chill grey skies were warnings of the snow time to come. November was the month of the dead; it opened with the Day of the Dead, and ended as the sleep of nature set in.

Nobody expected the gloom to last for long. It was a symbol of change: the sun would sink before rising again and the ones who went down to the underworld would be replaced with new life. In many places the dead were expected to rest until the time for resurrection was come. But, Peru apart, the November period as such did not influence many peoples south of the equator. They could not experience the onset of winter darkness; in fact most of them saw little change in the light even in the corresponding period in May when the sun was approaching the northern tropic. In addition they were not far advanced culturally, being mostly simple hunters and farmers. Yet they all knew well that they expected the end of human life to be followed by some form of new living experience.

The most southerly people whose thoughts we may now share are the Polynesians. We have already seen that the transition from this world to the land of the dead was for them a voyage to new islands, and the idea of above and below was ill-defined. But common to most of the Polynesian islands was the belief that the souls of the dead waited a few days and then joined the continuous stream of travellers who walked to the most westerly point of land in the island and plunged into the sea. In many islands, they were instead taken by canoe to a beautiful western summer land. But the Maori in New Zealand feared that their souls must go into the dark night, into the abyss called Te Po. The souls of chiefs were more honoured than those of their followers, and slaves might not exist at all after death. But it may be that after centuries of missionary teaching the idea of a hell for the heathen had superimposed itself. They were in no doubt that everyone did meet death because when in the beginning the hero Maui had sought immortality, and he crawled into Mother Earth's vulva, her vagina contracted and crushed his head. Thus mankind had no hope of return to this ever-beautiful earth. Of course, souls might return for a time. The islands were full of ghost stories,

The head of Maui is crushed by the contracting vagina of Hine

and on Puka Puka the priests made sinnet rings into soul traps so that ghosts could be captured while flying through the rings. It became a source of revenue: the price was high for trapping a harmful spirit or, conversely, for freeing the soul of a beloved relative.

In Africa, too, there was a social division of the dead, and generally speaking, chiefs held court in the sky and commoners went to a land beneath the earth. In Egypt the Fields of Heaven were open to all who possessed the appropriate ritual knowledge; hence the care spent in preparing the *Book of Going Forth by Day* which accompanied the mummies of the dead to the tomb. The dead person was identified with Osiris. Just as the Lady Isis sought out the mortal remains of Osiris and reassembled them in unity before burial, so would the mummified body be unified and subjected to the rituals which made it like the god. It was believed that while the body lived in the tomb something new grew and arose from it, to become a spiritual double living in the Heavens. In earliest times the abode of the gods was thought to be above the iron dome of the sky; but later the priests thought that the land of the dead must be where the sun shone at night, underneath the earth. But that did not deter the Egyptians from holding the parallel view that the dead went to the blessed lands of the west where the sun went down. Whatever the place of that wonderful land where the souls lived with the gods the salient point was that the soul was identified with Osiris himself.

The whole Egyptian nation mourned for Osiris at about midsummer. This was the point in the agricultural year at which the corn was reaped and the land lay fallow and empty of life—much as in the northern November. On the horizon just before dawn the people saw Isis seeking for her slain brother. She was symbolized by the brightest star in the sky, the one which we call Sirius. It was thought that a tear fell from heaven to match the tears of the people, invoking a proper burial and the eventual resurrection of the beloved Osiris. All was sorrow and yet all was hope. Even the great Pharaoh himself had a duty to weep, and in addition would come to the sinking Nile and throw a written instruction to it that life must be brought back, and therefore the holy river must rise and spread its life-giving silt over the land.

Osiris not only had the primary role of the lord of the dead, but was also the lord of the corn. In common with other farming peoples, the Egyptians saw that the seed was apparently dead and dry and that later something grew out of its heart and became the new plant bearing a great increase in seed.

So it was with the life of the other world: the soul passed through its ordeals, answered the examining gods in turn and was weighed in the balance. For this the heart—the intentions

A dead man enters the Egyptian underworld and must reply truthfully to the spirit guardians

and will—was balanced against absolute truth. If it proved to be as light as truth the whole spiritual personality was glorified, and passed through the gateway to the heavenly fields. But, if the heart was heavy with sins and false desires, the soul was seized upon by Am-mit who devoured it and the personality lost existence.

To those who had recited the charms and made the statements written in their guide, the *Book of Going Forth by Day*, was given eternal bliss. They came to another Egypt where the gods were enthroned and where men and women were spirits as real as when they inhabited their earthly bodies. Sometimes, indeed, part of their personality visited earth as a beautiful bird with a human face and feathers of rainbows. They watched over the mummy hoping that it would remain secure until the time of reunion.

In the heavenly land, the Field of Reeds, the spiritual body

Isis, as protectress of the dead, gives support from the foot of the coffin

lived in a beautiful cool house in the midst of an estate. Rivers flowed through the peaceful fields, and the crops were more bountiful than those of earth. Flowers abounded and the strong vines clustered their grapes on the terraces. Happiness filled this land. Even labour was provided by magic, for the little figures buried with the owner were brought to life and did all the hard work of caring for the fields and cattle, and even the domestic chores. The dead were men and women who loved and feasted happily and naturally. This land of the Field of Reeds was but part of the *Sekhet Hetepet,* or Fields of Peace. In the heart of it all the gods lived and the souls were able to see them and be alive among them in the House of Eternity. The dead were one with Osiris, though retaining their individual personalities.

Each day in the Fields of Peace the boat of the sun passed on its serene way. Those who wished accompanied the sun disc and his attendant gods and spirits as he passed through the land.

The scribe Ani and his wife worship Horus, the rising sun

There was singing and beauty amid the happy feasting. The soul chanted hymns of praise, and added words of self-glorification:

> 'I have gained the mastery of all the things which were commanded to be done for me on the earth, according to the prayer which thou hast spoken for me, "Behold, let him live on the bread of Seb the Earth God." That which is evil for me I shall not eat. I shall live upon bread of white corn, my beer shall be made from the red grain of the Nile. In a clean spot I shall sit on the ground beneath the date palm of Hathor who dwells in the great Disc.'

The glory of the chant in the sixty-eighth chapter of the *Book of Going Forth by Day* is hard to beat:

> 'The doors of heaven are opened for me. The doors of earth are opened for me. The barriers of the underworld have been opened for me, and the first temple has been prepared for me by the god Petra. Behold, I who was kept under guard and watched continually am now released. Behold, his hand had tied me with cords and he had cast me down in the earth, now the canals of heaven are opened for me. The passage has been given to me and I shall come forth by day into whatever place I wish.'

In other words the dead are alive and have qualities which can place them with the gods. They may farm their heavenly fields and live in love and feasting, or they may travel in the boat of the sun, happy for ever. Pharaoh himself was a god happy among his fellows, but the peasant farmer was also raised among the gods, provided that the purity of his heart and his innocence of evil deeds had opened the way for him.

It is hard to find much sadness in Egyptian religion. There was hope always that the soul would prosper and find a perfection of all earthly joys in this spiritual world. True, there was weeping at the tomb. People sobbed and beat their breasts. The professional mourners came weeping and pouring dust over their heads. There was a rapid funeral feast and after the priest had finished his ceremonies people dispersed quickly home. But they departed with much hope.

The Egyptians did not have the hosts of angels and demons of their Semitic neighbours to the east. They were satisfied with a pantheon of gods who were in many respects autonomous. But among the peoples of Palestine, Syria and Mesopotamia attitudes were different. Most of them had no share in the sublime belief of the souls conducted by the angels, the thoughts of God, to the bosom of Abraham to wait in peace until the day of the

The soul worships Horus, son of Osiris, before the herd of heaven

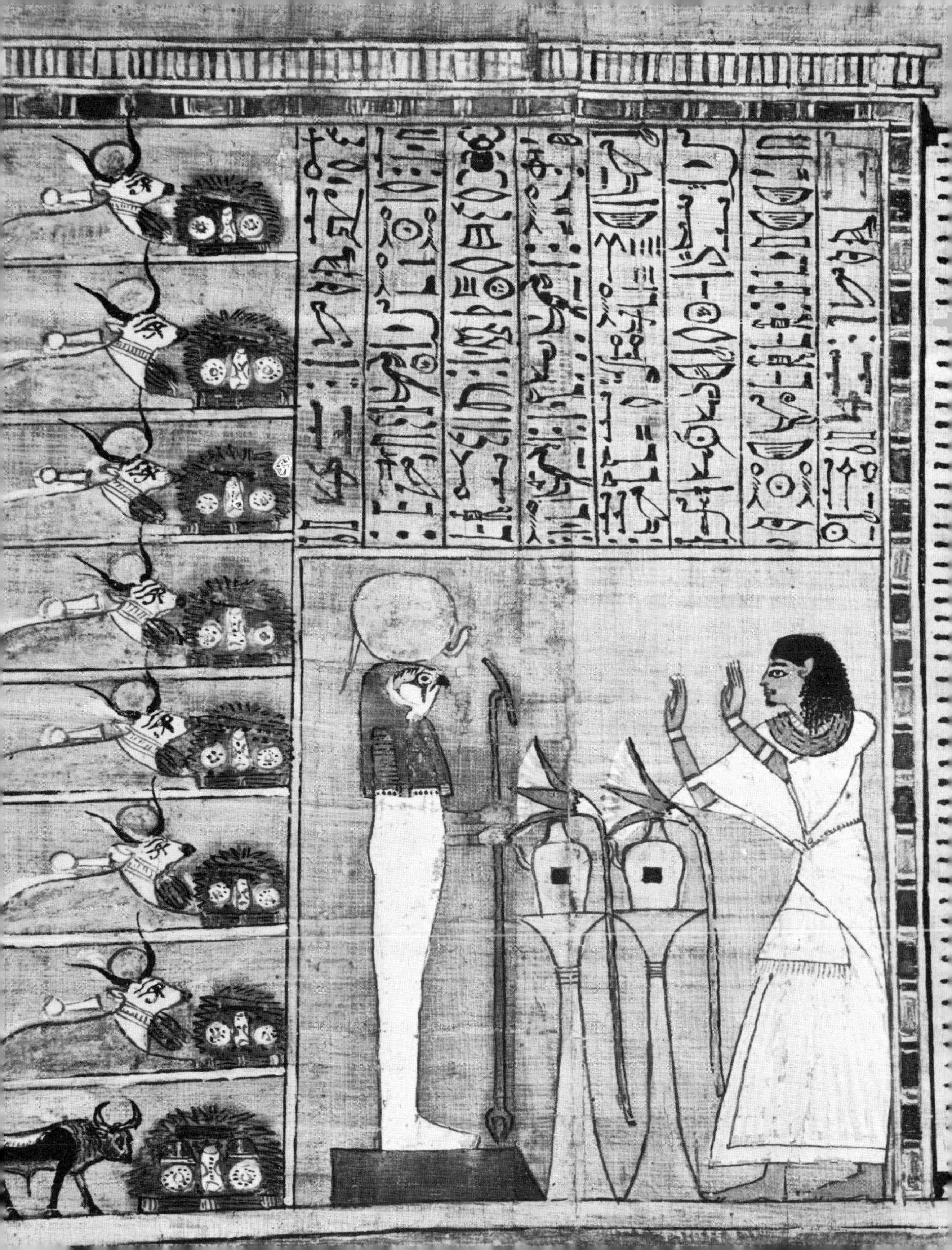

final judgement. Rather, they thought of the place of the dead as a sad, gloomy abode. Instead of the glorious presence of the sun in his celestial boat the people of Babylon dreaded a dark passage to a murky, dusty underworld where all the spirits could hope for was to avoid chaos and destruction. This attitude to the world of death is closely related to the classical beliefs portrayed in the journey of Aeneas in the underworld, yet they seem to have lacked a paradise. Perhaps kings escaped, since they were the viceroys of the gods on earth. But in the story of the departure of Enkidu, an important section of the *Epic of Gilgamesh*, we find little hope for a happy future. The hero must accept his doom, as his friends accept it, albeit with sorrow at his passing.

The doom was decreed by the goddess Ishtar. After Gilgamesh's alliance with Enkidu the two mighty heroes entered the cedar forests, felled great trees, slaughtered the giant who guarded the forests and returned through the beautiful cedarwood gate to boast of their prowess in the ancient city of Urukh, which was the domain of Gilgamesh.

Gilgamesh cleansed himself after his toils. He washed his hair and perfumed it, he put on the robes of royalty and the embroidered crown. He was then the noblest and most handsome of all mankind. The Lady Ishtar gazed on him and longed to enjoy his strength and to feel the warm seed of his body enter her. She promised him all power and dominion. Even the winds should

Above right: Anubis weighs the heart of the deceased.
Below right: Agricultural activity in the Elysian Fields, from the Theban *Book of the Dead*

Overleaf: left: A Babylonian terracotta figure of Gilgamesh. Right: The Plutonium at Eleusis, from where Persephone (bottom right, holding a pomegranate) was carried off into the Underworld

Priests perform the ceremony of opening the mouth of the dead man when he enters the other world, in order to give him speech and knowledge

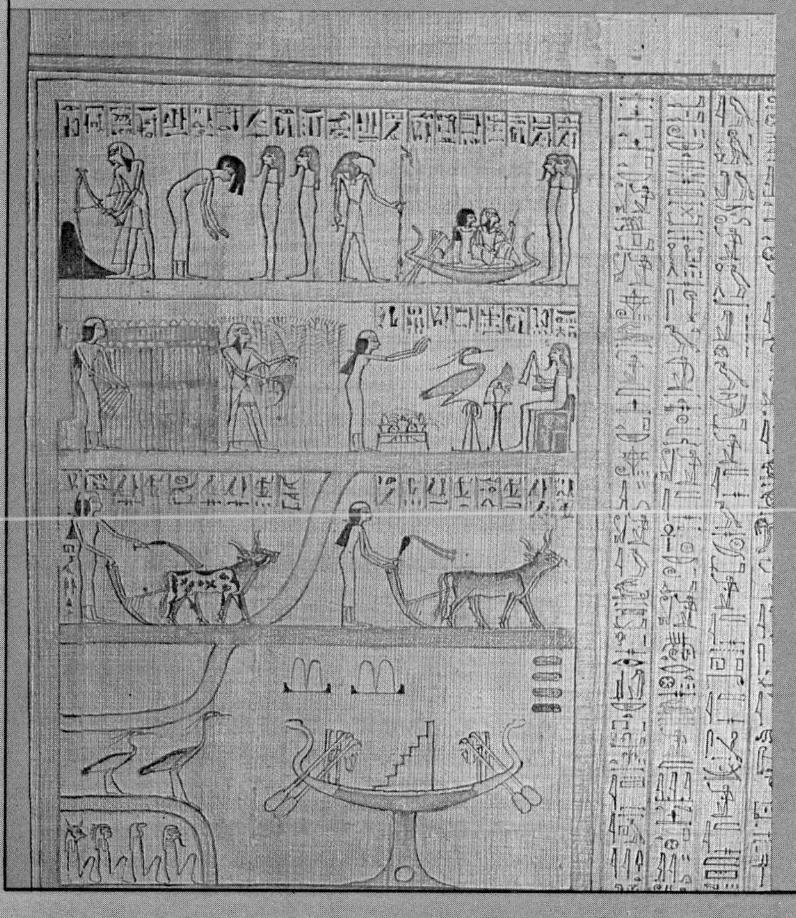

Above left: The goddess Demeter and Persephone send Triptolemos with the gift of corn to mankind. Below left: Hades carries Persephone away to the Underworld

obey him, and his flocks and herds should increase beyond anything hitherto known. All glory on earth could be his.

But Gilgamesh interrupted. What could a mortal king give to a goddess for a dowry? How should he clothe such a bride, or how should she be feasted? If he should mate with the queen of heaven how could he give her happiness? He reminded her that he could not expect a future of joy from her. He lamented that she had chosen him to be tempted. Then he told her of her previous loves, the beautiful shepherd boy Tammuz, for whom she had commanded the world to weep each year on the anniversary of his death, the beautiful bird, the mighty lion, the glorious white stallion. All had been destroyed because of the inordinate desire with which she had inspired them. Even her gardener had been lured to love and then changed into a blind mole, ever seeking something in the darkness. Then the great goddess was hurt, she raged like a mortal woman. And she flew up into the heavens to complain to the gods.

The lord Anu chided Ishtar, reminding her that it was her own lust which had brought these insults upon her. But she pleaded and then suddenly reminded the great god that he had made her a promise to give her the bull of heaven to chastise the earth. He hesitated, but she commanded his attention with a great threat. She who had descended into the very depths of the land of the dead threatened to force open the gates of hell, to release the spirits kept there under her sister Ereshkigal, so that the earth should be full of the dead among the living. Anu sensibly decided that her wish must now be granted. Gilgamesh must be

Below: Gilgamesh and Enkidu destroys the Bull of Heaven and other monsters, on a plaster cast from an early Mesopotamian cylinder seal

N

filled with pride so that he should attack the great bull and be destroyed by it. But Anu warned Ishtar that there would be a drought on earth and that she must make sure that her stores of food were sufficient to sustain the people. But she assured him that she had reserves of grain sufficient for those seven years.

Then Anu created the great bull, a creature of might and beauty. It was cast upon the earth and came to its feet in anger. Its breath slew men by hundreds as it snorted and pawed the earth in anger. It came beside Urukh, and there was Enkidu before it. Enkidu did not wait, he rushed forward and seized its horns. Such was his marvellous strength that he bent down that terrible head, and called to Gilgamesh to slay the bull. Gilgamesh seized the bull by the root of its tail and swung his dagger to pierce the neck between the vertebrae. The bull fell dead. Then they opened the bull and took its heart as an offering to the Sun.

Once more Ishtar was hurt and enraged. She descended to earth and ascended the walls of Urukh. High on her ziggurat she stood and laid a curse on Gilgamesh and his companion Enkidu. But the feud was to go on: Enkidu seized the corpse and cut off the left thigh. He cast the bloody flesh of the bull full in the face of the goddess. Then he threatened that if he could come up to her he would also tear off her thigh and tie her entrails beside her. But he could not reach her. She called all the women together, the temple prostitutes and the dancers and singers, and they lamented at the death of the bull of heaven.

Again Ishtar pleaded with the gods to take away the life of Gilgamesh for destroying the holy cedar trees and for slaying the bull of heaven. But as Enkidu had assisted it was determined that Gilgamesh was to remain on earth and that Enkidu the mighty hunter should tread the paths of death.

A dream was sent to Enkidu, and he understood the meaning. He told it to Gilgamesh, and together they lamented the decision of the gods; and then waited. He fell sick, and bemoaned his fate, that he must die of illness and not in the bravery of battle. Gilgamesh lamented also, for he was unhappy that he must always remember his friend as he sat by the doorway of the ghosts, unable to manifest his presence. It would be a long parting, almost for eternity.

Enkidu cursed his victories and the days when he was led by the temple prostitute to become a great and sophisticated man after his happy early life in the wild forests. He cursed the great gateway to the cedar forests, and then all that fine raiment and jewellery, and even the kind prostitute who had taught him the graces of civilized life. But the gods heard, Shamash the sun heard and shone on Enkidu telling him how the woman had helped and given Enkidu his great position in the world of men and brought glory to his memory. He also prophesied that

Left: Ishtar, marked by her star headdress, rides on her lion

Gilgamesh would mourn and abandon his riches to wander in the deserts.

The words of the sun were kindly and so Enkidu revoked his curses. He blessed the prostitute instead; calling down on her much love and youthful pleasure, the gifts of jewels and jealousies of other women; and an entry through the prayers of the priests to the house of the gods. Then more at peace he fell asleep again. The gods sent him another prophetic dream. He found himself standing before a terrible being, black and with beak and claws like an eagle. He seized Enkidu and stopped his breath; Enkidu was led to the house of Irkalla, the Lady of Death, and from there he went down the path from which there is no return. He came to the house of the dead where they sat in eternal darkness. They were clothed in dark feathers, sitting in the dust. Dust they ate for bread and clay for meat. Among them Enkidu saw the great kings of former days. They stood in the dust waiting to carry food and drink to the gods of that terrible place as if they were slaves. There too were the priests and prophets, the enchanters and the temple servants. Enkidu also saw the demigods and eventually came to the place of the queen of the underworld, the terrible Ereshkigal. Before her sat her scribe Belit-Sheri. Enkidu was asked who had sent him, but before he could reply he awoke from the vision.

Below: Enkidu living among the wild beasts, on a Mesopotamian stone vase

He told Gilgamesh of the dream, and together they lamented. But they also thought the dream was a wonder, for at last mankind had been told about the nature of existence after death. It was clear that in the end misery came to all men, however great and powerful.

For a day, then another day, for twelve days Enkidu lay on his couch suffering pain. Then Gilgamesh went out and made a public prayer, answered only by the silence of death. The heart of the mighty Enkidu stopped beating, and Gilgamesh covered the body with a veil as if it had been a bride going to the other world.

Then he burst into a terrible rage of despair. He destroyed his royal regalia and tore his hair. He lost all care for his appearance and simply mourned his friend. For seven days and nights the body lay there because he would not have it moved; but finally the maggots swarmed over it, and he was forced to bury what remained of Enkidu.

A great statue of Enkidu was made of precious materials, and offerings to the gods were placed before it. But Gilgamesh would not be pacified. He let his hair grow long and loose, forgot cleanliness and eventually ran into the woods clothed only in the skin of a lion.

This was not the end of the saga, for Gilgamesh was so affected that he later went in search of the gift of everlasting life. Alas, he failed, and so we must all follow the path that Enkidu trod. All

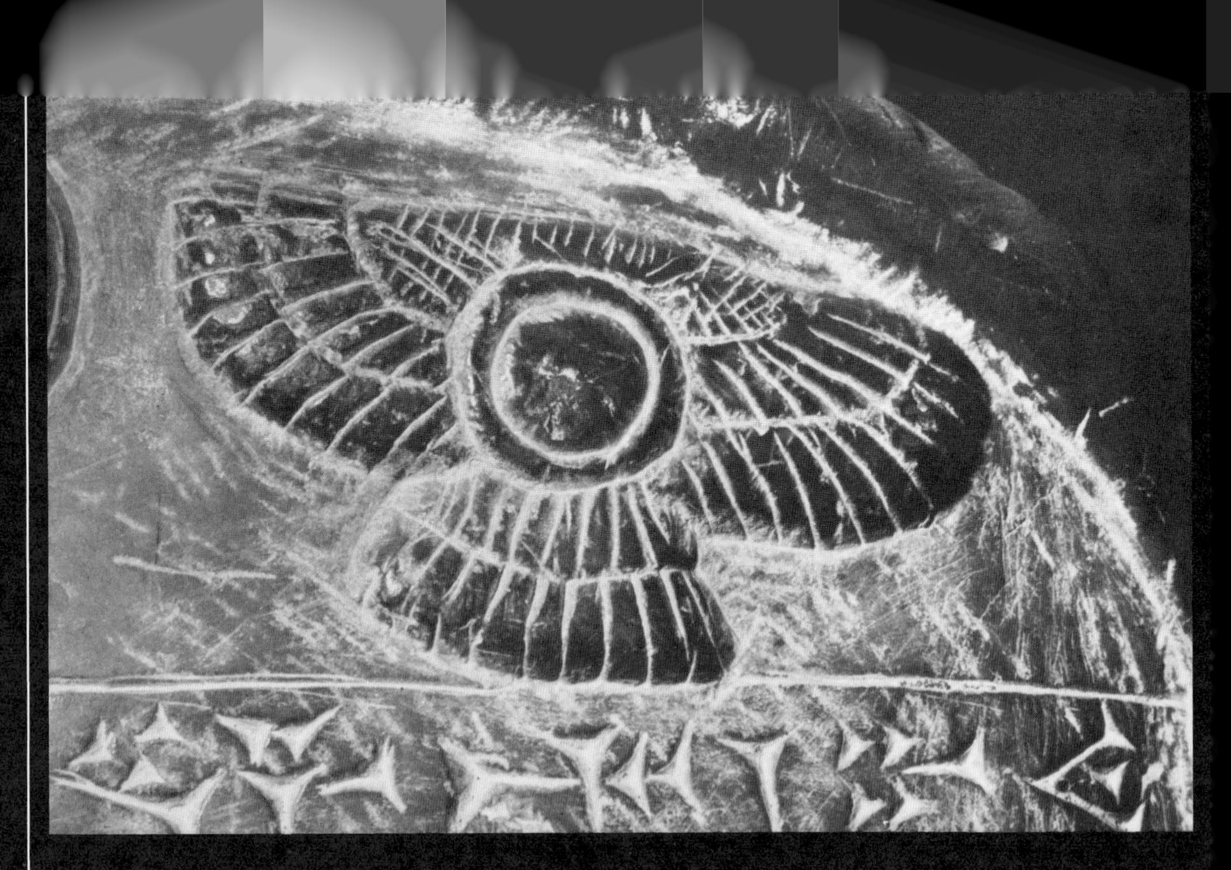

The winged sun of Shamash (above) and the star of Ishtar protect a boundary stone

that Gilgamesh was able to discover on his own terrible pilgrimage into the mountain and through eight days in the darkness among the dusty feathered dead was that there was a land not unlike that visited by the Roman Virgil, where a few of the dead, singled out by the gods, resided in palaces among fine gardens. No others could hope to get to this place unless the gods should intervene. It was in this paradise island that he met his ancestor Uta-Napishtim who, like Noah, was saved from the great flood. The island of the blessed was in the east, in a land where the star of Ishtar rose just before the sun. It was called Dilmun but nothing was known about it since the lands were only accessible at the express will of the gods.

While there Gilgamesh dived into the sea to win the marvellous herb of eternal life, the true elixir. But alas, on his return journey he was cozened by the serpent who eventually stole the herb and so left mankind without any remedy for the inevitability of death.

The desperate unhappiness of the Sumerian and Babylonian stories of death and the underworld may have spread in ancient times, notably to the Mediterranean. The story of the bull of heaven may perhaps have some echo in the bull of Minos and so have entered the Greek world from the marvellous Keftiu civilization of Crete. But the stories are also similar to those told in old Scandinavia where the souls of the ordinary, unheroic citizens descended below the world into the care of the frightening goddess Hel. They were far away from the earthly paradise of the Celts, the lovely Island of Apples; yet the Celts believed there was a second world under the earth from which the red hounds came to summon souls, and which was visited by

The Sumerian gods with Ishtar (on the mountain) above the rising sun, Shamash

Right: The Epic of Gilgamesh is written in cuneiform on tablets such as this

the noble-hearted Pwyll. But when one looks further back to the beginnings of the Bronze Age in Britain some forty centuries ago, one finds that the long-barrows have an entrance, or at least a hole, facing the sunrise, as if the souls would one day face the sun again after their time in the tomb. So also in Mycenaean legend there was a priestess of Artemis living in the courtyard before the tomb. She represented life as contrasted with death, a symbol of resurgence.

The cycle of life and death was the central theme of the ancient and secret Eleusinian mysteries. The story of Demeter and Persephone, which was celebrated in Eleusis, concerns the death and return of vegetation, the way to the underworld where Hades was the king, and its relation to the seasons and the way of life of humanity.

Left: A king (left) pours offerings on the tree of life before the sun god, Shamash

Zeus the great ruler of heaven loved the goddess Demeter, the Corn Mother. By him she had a beautiful daughter, the Spring Maiden, the *Kore* Persephone. In those days when the world was

still young, Persephone went to the fields with the Nereids, the daughters of Ocean. They danced in a round, singing and happy. But a plot had been laid. The mighty Hades had fallen in love with his brother's new daughter. She was now a beautiful maiden, light of foot and gay of heart, and he determined to take her for a wife. To that end he created a beautiful multi-headed flower, the sweet-scented narcissus. He caused it to grow in the Nysean fields so that when Persephone danced there she would be sure to see it. As soon as she plucked it she would be in magical contact with him. So dancing with the waves Persephone came singing to the flowery field of springtime, where crocus, violet, hyacinth and iris grew. There was another flower, pale and yet rich, scented with such a heavenly odour that she must come to take one. As she touched it there came a roaring, and from the earth burst a chariot with black horses driven by Hades. He seized Persephone, and then in the chasm of an earthquake they disappeared beneath the earth. In the underworld she found a place was prepared for her, a golden throne beside that of Hades himself. She was not ill-treated; rather she was given the treasures of the earth. Gold, silver and precious stones were her new raiment. It turned out to be a love match and Hades was wonderful, yet Persephone ached for the blue skies and soft grass of her home in Sicily.

Demeter was dumbfounded when the Nereids came back with their story of the stealing of her daughter. She wept, and prayed, but no sign came. Then she travelled around Sicily looking for clues. In one river she saw a girdle that had belonged to her daughter, but she had to wait until she came to the river of the curly-headed nymph Arethusa. The nymph came from her stream and told of the strange news brought by a stream from deep under ground. It had seen the underworld of Hades, and there beside the dark god sat Persephone, beautiful but sad. Knowing the greatness of that god Demeter felt almost hopeless. The cry of Persephone when she was first abducted was still echoing in the heavens. Demeter was disconsolate. She flew away to search the earth. While she was gone no plants grew, no flowers blossomed, no food plants thrived. She went carrying two torches to seek through the darkness. She ascended to the sun and enquired of Helios, only to be told that she had a worthy husband for her missing daughter. She then flew down from the heavens again and once more roamed the earth lamenting.

Thus Demeter on earth looked like a sad old woman, grey-haired, clad in black and woebegone. A young man dared to laugh at her, and he was turned into a lizard. Eventually she came to Eleusis, a town not far west of Athens. As she sat by the wayside, she was met by the four daughters of the king Peleus. They took her to the palace and she was met by the Queen,

A sacred bull with a beard of lapis lazuli, from a Sumerian harp found in Ur of the Chaldees

Deianira. She seemed to become larger and full of power. The Queen welcomed her as an equal and offered her wine, but Demeter would drink none. She asked for a drink of barley-water flavoured with mint. She sat sorrowing on the stool covered with white lambskin which was brought to her.

Later she tried to reward her hostess secretly by making her baby son immortal. She had to dip him in a fire; but Deianira noticed what was happening and screamed. The goddess put the child down, scolded the mother for causing her child to remain merely mortal, though she predicted a famous life for him. Then she revealed herself in her true majesty and beauty and stalked out of the palace, leaving Deianira fainting from terror and the princesses comforting their baby brother. They told the king, and he commanded all the people of the kingdom to build a new temple to the beautiful sorrowing goddess.

There in the temple at Eleusis the goddess sat alone, apart even from the gods. For a whole year she sat there meditating on her sorrow that Persephone was gone away. Nothing grew on the earth. The people were without food and in their distress they came to pray to the goddess for aid. Alas, she refused to give anything until she was once more beside her beloved daughter. The prayers of the people ascended to Olympus. There Zeus on his ivory throne heard their lamentation and was sorry for them. He called Hermes to him and gave command that the Messenger should fly down beneath the earth and enter the palace of Hades in order to persuade Hades with his silver tongue to return the Spring Maiden to earth.

Above: Persephone leaves the underworld to return to her mother Demeter

No persuasion was needed, for Hades was sitting disconsolate beside the bed of Persephone who was ill from home-sickness, wishing only to visit her mother. As Hermes gave his message, Hades found a new hope. He told Persephone to return to her mother, promising her that if she should return to him in due season she should be forever honoured among the gods. Here he cheated, for he slipped a single pomegranate seed into her mouth, and she swallowed it. Now she had eaten the food of the dead and was bound to return. In blissful ignorance she stepped into the golden chariot and Hermes took the reins.

Suddenly they were there, under the blue skies of sweet earth. Demeter and the *Kore* Persephone embraced, and became for a moment like one person. But on enquiring if Persephone had eaten she was told of the pomegranate. That was fixed then, no total return would be possible but for a third of each year Persephone would return to her husband to rule with him in the underworld. They told each other of their sadness and hopes. Then the powers of heaven descended and made the fair earth fruitful again. Before Persephone flew up to Olympus she took a second son of Deianira, young Triptolemus, and in the presence

Left: Persephone holds the pomegranate given to her by Hades

of the great goddesses she gave him three ears of wheat, told him how it must be planted, and then sat him in a holy chariot drawn by two flying serpents so that he could teach mankind how to grow grain for food. Thus with the return of Persephone the earth was blessed and people given food. All was well, and when darkness came with the approach of winter Persephone once more descended to her noble husband to stay until she came forth again, bringing the spring flowers, the crocus, hyacinth, iris, and narcissus to show the happiness of her annual return.

Far away from Greece there was an annual ceremony of sadness in November, apparently for astrological reasons. The Ayamarca in Peru was a period of penitence and sorrow held just before the sun reached his highest point in the sky. The apparent key was the passage of the Pleiades through the zenith at midnight, when they were opposite the sun. In many lands this little cluster of stars marked a turning point in the year. In the north, of course, it reminded people of the old age of men and the death of the seed in winter. But these considerations were not so

Right: Holding their gifts to mankind, Persephone and Hades sit in the underworld

Triptolemos is given his message and is sent to earth by Demeter, as seen on a sculpture from Eleusis

Above: The Inca consecrates the black llama as a scapegoat to remove sin

obvious in Peru. A period of penitence and fasting is not unusual in advanced societies: the Jewish fast at Yom Kippur, Moslems fast for the moon of Ramadan, and the Christians during Lent. The Peruvian ceremony, however, was a great national effort to dispose of the consequences of sinfulness—disobedience to the social code or to the sun.

When the sacred festival approached all strangers were sent outside the boundaries of the sacred city of Cuzco, and all became silent. In the morning people assembled in the great square, all of them veiled and most weeping. They sat down and the Sapa Inca brought before them a llama and some black alpacas. There was a general recital of sorrow before the rising sun. The high priest sacrificed the llama, and read the prognostications for the coming year from its entrails. Then with more lamentations the sins of the people were tied up in bundles, probably knotted up in *quipus*. These were then tied on the black alpacas. To great shouting the alpacas were chased out of the city and beyond the river, and left to wander in the mountains until they met their death. If any were seen they were driven away. The city was purified, and in a thoroughly chastened spirit the people returned home and hoped that the gods would accept their offerings and take pity on the plight of human beings. There would be a better future and the ceremonial errors of the past would be forgotten.

In outlying towns the Peruvians celebrated the sad festival by tying their sins into bundles which were placed in little rafts and boats of reeds and thrown into the rivers. Their sinfulness was swept away, either to the great sea, or down the gorges into the mysterious forest of the Amazon.

The cleansing of the country from sin was most important in Peru. The powers of nature were personified and appeased. But how death and the underworld were pictured in ancient Peru is not clear, mostly because there were few records. At this festival of mourning, the Ayamarca, the mummies of the ancestors were brought out and mourned. They were thought of as part of life, though no longer active on earth. In general, the noble and powerful souls, who might be of any social class, would go to the heaven of the sun, but the mass of souls went down to a cold and dark underworld. It might not have always been unhappy because on some coastal Peruvian pottery we find representations of skeletons merrily dancing and playing music.

The Ayamarca ceremonies stated that the past would be destroyed and the future made open for new blessings. In its way it echoed the hope that the Greeks found in the return of Persephone to the world of flowers. And at the depth of the year in the north lands and in other places where the sun was still high there was hope, and ceremonies marked the return to new life.

Below: Demeter as Ceres (centre) carries an ear of corn, in an Etruscan tomb painting

12. Festivals of Light

As the great circuit reaches its end there is hope for a new beginning, a re-emergence of light and hope. Even when the legends tell of a great deity who has become oppressive there is very often a story of escape to light. The story of Persephone was an example of this promise. The Egyptians were aware of the facts of death and the break-up of the body but they also had the fields of heaven awaiting the just. The Aranda of central Australia were sure that the soul imprisoned in the stone *churinga* was free to find itself a new mother. It is true that many peoples think that the nonentities, the nameless slaves and other untouchables will simply fade away and be no longer known in the other world when they are forgotten in this. Yet for some, even in those class-conscious primitive societies, there is to be resurrection and glory. As we reach the end of the spiral of time and the dance of the four directions, the wise men of the past see a new hope. One may in fact ascend into a state of such perfection that earthly things have no reason, so that one cannot be apprehended in material terms. Such was the reasoning of the Lord Buddha. Islam and Christianity tell of a period of waiting and hope for eventual revival and life, at best in paradise, at worst in a dreadful spiritual torment for the unjust. But for many there is to be salvation. We symbolize our hopes with festivals of hope. We listen to the first singing of the birds.

The birds sing a Celtic song, for they are the birds of Rhiannon singing us to sleep, or waking the dead in the western island, the Apple Orchard. The goddess Rhiannon presides there, her hair the colour of honey, her robe the blue of the sky edged with white swans' down, and her eyes of such a mystery that those who look in them will ever hope, and find solace in the song of her birds. They were the birds desired by Ysbadadden the giant to sing him to sleep on the night before the heroes slew him, before the lady on her white horse took him away to the land of souls.

The most primitive of peoples had stories of happiness and escape from the shadow of dark death. Somewhere there was always a song and a symbol of continuing life. Charles Mountford, a great friend of the aboriginal peoples in Australia, came across the story of Purupriki.

Before the Milky Way there were no trails in the heavens. But after it had been fixed up there a bright star called Purupriki appeared. It was high in the northern sky at the depth of the year in early June, when the sun was furthest away from the hunting grounds of the blackfellow. Purupriki had been taken to the sky because of his rashness in hunting the fruit bats. Throughout the land he was admired as a great singer and dancer, and people came from the camps to the great corroboree whenever they knew Purupriki was to dance. They learned his songs and dances, for he was the maker of happiness. Then one day he

At the festival of St Lucia on 12 December in Sweden, the winter darkness is dispelled by maidens bearing candles

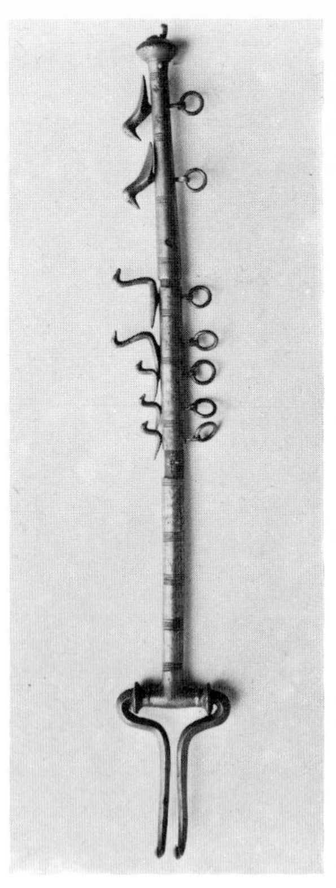

Left: The churingas harbour the souls of Aboriginal tribesmen awaiting rebirth.
Below left: The four directions protect the weaver of this Plains Indian beadwork.
Above: The sacred ravens and swans of Rhiannon, Celtic messengers from the other world, decorate an ancient Irish fork

Right: The prow of a mock Viking ship blazes at the modern Shetland festival of Up-helly-aa

Left: The perfect expression of Indian erotic love and the seeking for life

danced and sung and the people ate much food, feasted and some made love for sheer happiness. After the great festival they slept. Purupriki woke early while the darkness was but lightly tinged with sunrise. He moved into the woods to find some food, and on a tree he saw great numbers of flying foxes preparing to settle down to a day's sleep. Rashly he threw his club at them. In anger the whole great flock swooped down chattering and seized on Purupriki. They carried him off and flew higher and higher through the skies. They formed a great trail through the stars, and one can now see them shining in the night as the Milky Way, and just beside them one can see Purupriki the great singer always dancing as the bright star Antares.

One hopes that such beauty and poetry may always shine on the people. But humans also feel the need of a magical protector to help them escape whatever fate may bring. Perhaps the protector is not always successful, for when fate is Death he is likely to win the last trick. A story about it comes from the Krachi of Togo in West Africa.

There was a famine, and a young man was searching in the forest for something to eat. Suddenly he came upon a strange great rock like the head of a sleeping giant. It had green hair, long and strong like forest lianas. The boy walked a little further, and then tripped over a creeper. The giant awoke and stood up, towering high above the trees. The boy was not very frightened

Below: The Aboriginal soul starts on the pathway to the land of the dead

P

and asked for some food. The giant gave him some dried meat and took him home. The boy became his servant and often enjoyed succulent fresh meat. But after a few years he became homesick. The giant told him he could go home, provided he brought his brother back to take his place. He did so, and then went home and stayed a while. When he came back his brother was not there. The giant told him that he had sent the lad off to a far country on an errand. So all was well. They ate good meat, and many people settled near them into a village. The boy was content enough, but after a while wished to return home again. Once more the giant made him promise to bring another helper; this time it was to be his sister. So the girl stayed and the boy spent a while with his parents.

When the boy returned he was given more fresh sweet meat. It was delicious, and he was happy and busied himself with work; but one day the giant was resting, and when the boy asked him for another meal the giant told him to go to the storehouse and bring the meat. So he entered the dark cool room. There he lit a torch and saw the meat neatly laid out, and beside it, a little pile of fresh bones. Among them was an arm bone with a slight deformity. He recognized it as his sister's arm. So death had been feeding him on his own relatives. Death was an ogre living on human flesh! The boy rushed out and went to the village to tell his lurid story.

The remains of sculptures on a wall in the sacred city of Tiahuanaco

The villagers waited till night when the giant was sleeping and then, led by the boy, they set fire to the great house. The giant slept, merely tossing and turning as the flames surrounded him. Then the house fell in and the giant was dead, completely burnt up except for his head. In the green hair the boy saw a leaf-packet of powder. The people had heard of a story that there was a powder which could bring back the dead. The boy put some on his sister's arm bone, and suddenly there she stood, just as delightful as when she was alive. Then he found some more bones, and instantly there was his brother. More bones, more powder, and other children appeared. It seemed miraculous and all were happy. But the boy wondered and threw a little powder at the giant's head. It fell on the eye. Suddenly the baleful eye blinked open and someone died. They all ran away, but it was of no avail. Even now when the eye of death glances at a human he dies. Everyday someone dies, and people do not know why. It is merely that death has looked upon them.

So for a brief moment it had been possible to thwart death, but in the end fate had intervened in a foolish experiment. Accordingly we must all die and go to the land of spirits, which need not always be such a bad place. The peoples of Babylon and Greece may have thought it was, but not the Navajo Indians of Colorado. They knew that the ancestors had come up, ever changing,

through four underworlds, each of which was good in its time. In the last of these they became real people, and camped beside pleasant waters, but they were asked to climb for the last time the tree-trunk ladder through a hole in the sky, to emerge into this world under the sun. The skies were blue with little fleecy clouds, and the four sacred mountains protected their holy land. But rising waters threatened them because of the evil doing of Coyote: he had stolen the children of the water monster. People made a mound in the centre of their land and prayed. As a result Coyote was forced to return the children and the floods receded. But now the sun stood still and the land was too hot. The sun could not be placated unless someone died and left this world. It happened that the wife of the great chief was ill, and she lay down and her breath went away. Then the sun moved, and everyone now knew that death caused the sun to move. But they also discovered that death was not so bad: the people looked down through the hole of emergence, and there below in the previous world they saw the chieftainess sitting happily working on a fine buffalo hide. She told them that when they died all the people of the fifth world must return as she had to the fourth world. Soon after, her husband died, and then the moon moved in the sky.

Coyote the trickster had great wisdom. He understood the pattern and told the people that day and night must ever follow each other. Every day one of the Navajo would die, and every night a member of some other tribe would pass to the fourth world; and so it has been ever since.

Farther away in South America, the higher civilizations of Peru had developed a richer mythology than the Navajo farmers. But alas, most of the stories are lost or tied in the knotted *quipus* which no one can read. Many refer to the ancient ruined site of Tiahuanaco, which was named by an Inca ruler. While seated among the ruins the chief received a messenger who had traversed the mountain roads from Cuzco at an incredible speed. So he rewarded him and said, '*Tiay huanacu*', which means 'Sit down, fast runner.' No one knows the original name of the ancient city. The local Indians tell of it as the heart of the world, the place where the creator Tiki Viracocha had his home. Some tribes had a story that their ancestors had found the ancient city populated by white people with white hair and beards, and that they had destroyed them all in battle.

This may have arisen as an explanation of the strange appearance of the Viracocha, who was both white and bearded as depicted on a few Mochica pots from the Peruvian coast of about the fourth century A.D. But there he is, an old man in the ordinary clothes of the country. It may be possible that there really was a group of people who grew white beards in ancient Peru and that

the legend was not a simple reference to the rays of the sun. But, as usual, the few relevant stories surviving are hardly clear. Meanwhile we do have a little information about the land of the dead. The defeat of darkness and the rising of hope comes from the story of creation.

Long ago the earth was dark and grey. There was a diffuse light, but no sun. In those days the ancient people were able to live and work, but the world was savage and the people prone to war among themselves. Then, without warning, a great lord came up out of Lake Titicaca. He had many followers with him. They marched a little way from the shore to Tiahuanaco, and while they were there Viracocha made the sun and set it on its course. Later he made the moon and stars and set them in their courses. This was his second coming to earth, for he was the creator who had made the grey world and the first race of uncivilized people. It is said that the people insulted him because he looked poor, and that in angry retribution he turned them to stone. They may still be seen, strange figures of grey rock in the mountains. Then he returned to Tiahuanaco and made stone models of the people he intended to create, for he was the breath of life, the foam of the sea, Kon Tiki Viracocha, the very creator. Then in another place he made more figures. Some five times he did this. He made stone men, stone women and stone children. He painted them in their garments in bright natural colours. Then he called the people who had come with him out of the lake to help him in a great ceremony. He pointed to the regions of Tahuantinsuyu, the four quarters and the centre, and commanded that the stone figures should become people. Then each of the five groups were sent to caves and springs, one in each region. There they were to come forth, live as human families, have children and gradually fill the land. Then he commanded his followers to go among the different peoples, giving each their names and their customs and confirming them in the lands they had been given. In each region he placed a Viracocha in charge of the people.

Then at Tiahuanaco, Kon Tiki Viracocha called to all the land: 'Come forth, come forth, and people this land which is deserted; come forth to the command of Kon Tiki Viracocha who has made this world.' The first creation was of the people towards the east, then came those of the south and west. Then he turned to the north and followed the royal road which the Incas were to complete in later times. He seemed strange to the Indians for he was like a man, but with white hair and beard. He wore a long white robe held by a broad girdle. He came to within fifty miles of Cuzco. There he called forth the district of Cacha where he had established the Cañas. Alas! They saw only a man with a white beard and a worn, torn white robe. They thought it was a

Above: The gateway of the sun at the entrance to a sacred enclosure which was said to be founded by Viracocha.
Below: The stone columns of an ancient building at Tiahuanaco

madman and threw stones to drive him away. As they ran nearer, intending to kill him, he turned and lifted his staff. Suddenly fire streaked down from the sky and set a mountain peak in their path ablaze. It roared and melted in the terrible heat. The Cañas were terrified. They cast away their weapons and came to throw themselves at the feet of Viracocha. Then he accepted their sorrow for their actions against him. He strode to the mountain and struck it twice with his staff: the fires died down and the molten rock cooled. In awe the Cañas made a platform of stone blocks upon which they set a huge statue of the god, and promised that they would ever more pray to him and bring regular offerings. This they did for many centuries until the coming of the Spaniards. They remembered his name as Kon Tiki Viracocha Pachayachachic, the creator of the world.

After this display of might, Viracocha came to within fifteen miles of Cuzco, at the Tambo of Urcos. There he climbed to the highest mountain peak, and sat still while he created the Indian tribes of that region. There again the Indians made a sacred place and within it they made a throne of pure gold. Upon it they placed an image of Viracocha, also of the finest gold. The god then descended to Cuzco, the navel of the earth, left instructions for the future of the land, and then passed over the mountains and down to the coast where his followers were already waiting in their boats. Then they departed, travelling smoothly and rapidly over the waters, far beyond the horizon.

Thus Viracocha brought light to dispel darkness, and put life and creation into action. The cycle would always recur, and Viracocha need not again descend to his earth.

The theme of light after darkness is the key to all midwinter celebrations in the northern hemisphere, and all over Europe fire was used in the days of darkness to invoke the return of the sun. Fire wheels were popular, rolled down hills to mark the descent and the hope of ascent of the sun. There was new hope in the candle-lit Christmas tree and the crown of candles on the head of a Swedish maiden. In the Shetlands there is a modern festival, the Up-helly-aa, which recalls a very ancient tradition of lighting fire barrels and marching with them in procession. But about a century ago a local journalist added the ceremony of burning a Viking ship in a reconstruction of a ship burial from the Norse sagas. It has become a famous and beautiful custom with its songs and fireworks and the sight of the longship blazing on the waters. Wassail is drunk to wish health and prosperity, and it is a night of gaiety and excitement.

The list of fire processions to mark the New Year is almost limitless. One may find them in many a fairy tale, and they express the same hope of a happy future as the tales which tell of unexpected gifts. There is a pleasant little story collected by the

A doorway leads from a paved road into a palace in Cuzco

brothers Grimm. A little boy who was very poor left his house to look for some firewood. The wood pile was very low and covered by drifted snow. So he grubbed down to reach the wood, and as he did so he came across a little golden key. Then as he dug a little further he found a box. He looked it over and took it in with him. He put the wood on the fire and by the light he saw a tiny key hole, very tiny indeed but certainly there. He put in the key and turned it. The box opened and it was full of silver coins.

It is a charming little vignette, and it belongs to winter and to hope. Was the golden key the little winter sunshine? Was the silver the moons of the coming year? We are not told: the mystery is perhaps the important point.

Most people, however, have not the direct simplicity of the peasant farmers of old Europe. We must have the great gods, and the powers of nature acting in a great epic. Where better to go than to the earliest literature? We go to the mud-brick cities of the great plain of Mesopotamia. There are the clay tablets which tell of the Sumerians and their structured religious mythology. Six thousand years ago, they knew well the need for mankind to be in touch with nature. They also knew of the terrible power of love which destroyed and recreated. Their great goddess Inanna (who was later Ishtar) was the mother of a legend which in itself was the forerunner of many other myths.

The story is of dark death and magical revival. It tells of the return of the goddess from the depths. It seems that she had loved and lost the beautiful Dumuzi and descended through many terrible adventures into the realm of death. On the way she had been stripped of jewels and clothing until in the great depths before her sister Ereshkigal she was stripped of life itself. Her rotting corpse hung on the stake which was thrust through her from anus to mouth. (One can see such corpses of defeated victims in the Assyrian sculptures from Nineveh.) After three days and nights the angel of true speech, Ninshubar, proclaimed the horrible news. He rent his garments and poured dust over his head and full of lamentations went to the house of the god Enlil. He called on him for help: 'Let not your daughter be destroyed in the depths. You would not permit jewels to be ground into powder, nor the precious wood for caskets to be made into laths by the wood workers; do not then let the young daughter be dead in the underworld.' But the god replied that his daughter was insatiable in her lusts, and as she had gone through the rituals of the underworld she must accept death.

Then Ninshubar went away lamenting and came to Ur, where in the house of divine Nanna, the temple Ekishnugal, he repeated his plea. But likewise Nanna the moon god replied that the beautiful maiden had sought the ways of death and must abide by the laws. Alas for Ninshubar, who spoke only truth. He

Before a table of offerings an Assyrian warrior casts a freshly decapitated head upon a heap of trophies, in a sculpture from Nineveh

went away and came to the house of the Lord Enki in Eridu. There again he raised his plaint, humbling himself in the dust before the god.

In Eridu he received help. Enki heard the sad news and wept for his daughter the young queen of the earth and beloved of heaven. For a moment he thought how he could help. He worked great magic. He took dust from his finger nail, he took lacquer from his finger nail. The black and the red became Kugarru and Kalaturru. To one he gave the food of life, to the other the water of life.

Enki commanded them to descend to the gates of Hell. They were to be like flies, buzzing and flying around until they could enter the gates. There they would find Ereshkigal writhing in the pains of childbirth.

They descended and found her naked and yet beautiful in her agony. They called to her entrails and to her divine presence, and she learnt their intention. She promised them blessings if they were gods, and good fortune if they were human, but they were to swear by heaven and earth. They gave the oath that she desired. Then they were offered drink from the river of the dead. They refused. They were offered the food of the dead. They refused. They only asked for one favour: 'Give us this rotting body.'

'It is your queen,' said Ereshkigal, 'and, as this carrion was your queen, you may have it.'

Then they stepped up to the stake and scattered the black powder and the red powder upon it and Inanna stood up, alive and beautiful.

The spirits of the underworld assembled and declared that she might not leave the underworld unless a substitute was found to replace her. But she was powerful, and she arose with a horde of demons around her. They took her to the cities of the land. In each they found a sad penitent, whom she would not give up to death. Further they searched until she saw her lost love Dumuzi. Then she told them to take him away, to take him down and torture him. They took him, and Inanna flew up to her rightful place among the gods. Her naked beauty she covered with fine raiment and was herself again.

As for Dumuzi, he was wept for by all people. Breasts were beaten and cheeks slashed weeping for the loss of his beauty. Eventually he went to the depths, but it was arranged that each year, like Persephone, he should spend half the year in the underworld and that the other half of the year his sister should descend in his place; and so on for ever. The women wept each year for Dumuzi and rejoiced again at his return.

This story refers in reality to the change of the seasons, but it exalts the goddess of love and beauty, the bright life with all its

Eros shoots his arrow into the future for his mother Aphrodite

charm and terror rising again in the world, and the eternal resurrection of Inanna, Ishtar, Venus, Diana.

And now we come to the end of this book with some remarks on the nature of the light, the light of the seeking for life. They come from India, from one of the Upanishads.

The King Janaka asked a question of Yajñavalkya: 'What is the light of mankind?'

'The sun is his light, by it a man lives his life, rests, works, and returns.'

'And after sunset what then is the light of man?'

'Fire then becomes the light and he performs his tasks in its glow.'

'When sun and moon and fire are all asleep then what is the light of man?'

'Voice is the light then, even when he can no longer see he can follow the sound and advice of the voice.'

'When the voice is silent, then what is the light of man?'

'The soul becomes his light, and by its light he rests, works, and returns.'

More wisdom is in the poem, but here we leave the world of myths at the point of hope.

Epilogue

Our mystery tour is over. Yet it will never end. We hope the stories will lead to thought, and dreams. There is poetry tucked away in every corner of our world. If one sought out the myths of mankind there would be a library of millions of volumes and a great gathering of songs. The material is seemingly endless, and it is also eternal, at least as far as the human soul can dream.

Some of our teachers have told of life as a continuous cycle of birth, death and reincarnation, some have told of final judgements, but everywhere there is hope that spring will come again and life be renewed.

From all the material of our experience we must each take an individual path and seek for true awareness. This book can only show other peoples' ideas. We find myths from poor savage wanderers and from noble philosophers living in splendid palaces. All have their say. There is a development of the story as civilization has progressed, and the greater communities reflect their social complexities in the life of their gods. Perhaps we can only think of our gods as exemplifications of forces in our own experience. But we can always seek to find our own myths, our own beliefs about the path. Like the initiates at Eleusis we have seen the blue skies, and rejoicing have entered the temple. We have faced the darkness and sat on the woolly sheep skins to hear secrets and experience visions of life and resurrection. At the end may we go out into the world as they did, rejoicing in a new unity with the universe.

Further Reading List

Brandon S. G. F. (ed.) *A Dictionary of Comparative Religion* (Weidenfeld and Nicolson, 1970)
Budge E. A. Wallis *The Book of the Dead* (Routledge and Kegan Paul, 1960)
Bureau of American Ethnology *Bulletins* (Smithsonian Institute)
Burland C. A. *North American Indian Mythology* (Hamlyn, 1968)
Burland C. A. and Forman W. *Gods and Demons in Primitive Art* (Hamlyn, 1974)
Dutt, R. C. (ed.) *The Ramayana and the Mahabharata* (Dent Everyman)
Frazer J. G. *The Golden Bough* (Macmillan, 1936) 12 vols.
Griffiths J. Gwynn *The Conflict of Horus and Sett* (Liverpool University Press, 1960)
Grimm J. L. K. and W. K. *Grimm's Fairy Tales* (Penguin, 1971 and others)
Guerra Francisco *The Pre-Colombian Mind* (Seminar Press, 1971)
Homer *Iliad* trans. E. V. Rieu (Penguin, 1970)
I-Ching or *Book of Changes* trans. R. Wilhelm and F. Baynes (Routledge and Kegan Paul, 1968) 2 vols.
Ions Veronica *Egyptian Mythology* (Hamlyn, 1968)
Ions Veronica *Indian Mythology* (Hamlyn, 1967)
Jackson K. H. (ed.) *A Celtic Miscellany* (Routledge and Kegan Paul, 1951; Penguin, 1971)
James E. O. *The Ancient Gods* (Weidenfeld and Nicolson, 1960)
Karkala John B. Alphonso- (ed.) *An Anthology of Indian Literature* (Penguin, 1971)
Kerenyi Carl *Asklepios* (Routledge and Kegan Paul, 1967)
Kerenyi Carl *The Gods of the Greeks* (Thames and Hudson, 1951)
Layamon and Wace Robert *Arthurian Chronicles* (Dent Everyman)
Mbiti John S. *African Religions and Philosophy* (Heinemann, 1967)
Mylonas George E. *Eleusis and the Eleusinian Mysteries* (Routledge and Kegan Paul, 1962)
Osborne Harold *South American Mythology* (Hamlyn, 1969)
Parrinder E. Geoffrey *West African Religion* (Epworth Press, 1961)
Parrinder E. Geoffrey *Witchcraft, European and African* (Faber and Faber, 1968)
Pinsent John *Myths and Legends of Ancient Greece* (Hamlyn, 1969)
Poignant Roslyn *Oceanic Mythology* (Hamlyn, 1968)
Pritchard E. E. Evans- *The Nuer* (O.U.P., 1940)
Radin Paul *The Trickster: Study in American Indian Mythology* (Schocken, N.Y., 1972)
Rattray R. S. *Ashanti* (O.U.P., 1969)
Roberts Ainslie and Mountford Charles P. *The Dream Time* (Angus and R., 1970)
Ross Anne *Pagan Celtic Britain: Studies in Iconography and Tradition* (Routledge and Kegan Paul, 1967)
Sandars N. K. trans. *The Epic of Gilgamesh* (Penguin, 1960)
Sandars N. K. trans. *Poems of Heaven and Hell from Ancient Mesopotamia* (Penguin, 1971)
Spence Lewis *The Mysteries of Britain* (Aquarian Pub. Co., 1970)
Sturluson Snorri *The Prose Edda: Tales from Norse Mythology* (Univ. California Press, 1966)
Sykes Egerton (ed.) *Everyman's Dictionary of Non-Classical Mythology* (Dent, 1962)
Virgil *Aeneid* trans. W. F. Jackson Knight (Penguin, 1969)
Wentz W. Y. E. (ed.) *Tibetan Yoga and Secret Doctrines* (O.U.P., 1958)
Werner Alice *Myths and Legends of the Bantu* (F. Cass, 1968)
Wind Edgar *Pagan Mysteries in the Renaissance* (Faber and Faber, 1968)
Winstedt R. O. *The Malay Magician* (Routledge and Kegan Paul, 1961)

Index

All numbers in italics refer to illustration captions

The publishers would like to thank the following for permission to reproduce their photographs:

Aerofilms Limited, 90 b: Art Gallery of Ateneum, Helsinki, 38, 39: American Museum of Natural History, 13 b: Antikuarisk Topografiska Arkinet, Stockholm, 113 l: Ferdinand Anton, 119: Ashmolean Museum, Oxford, 90 t: Belzeaux-Zodiaque, 30 t, 31 b: Brissonas, Geneva, 234: Trustees of the British Museum, 15 b, 21 tr, 21 tl, 30 b, 40 t, 58, 74, 77, 98, 99 b, 117, 136, 168 l, 190 t, 192 t, 215, 225, 227, 229, 238 tr: C. A. Burland, 14 t, 14 b, 23 b, 46 b, 80, 99 t, 126 l, 130 t, 154 t, 154 b (Pat Vinnicombe), 155 t, 155 b, 157, 161, 173, 183, 185, 187, 235 t: City of Liverpool Museum, 100 t: Collection Gudrun Schwegler, 33: Collection Viollet, 120: C. M. Dixon, title page, 13 tr, 17 l, 26 t, 31 tr, 35 b, 55, 60, 61, 64 t, 68, 82 tl, 88 tl, 88 bl, 91 t, 94 r, 95, 97, 103, 111 t, 114, 118, 121, 136 r, 138, 152 t, 152 b, 153, 163, 164, 172, 195, 197 t, 202, 213, 218, 219 t, 219 b, 222 b, 232 t, 232 b, 235 b: Dominion Museum, New Zealand, 76 t: Dunbarton Oaks, Washington, 101 t: Robert Estall, 54 t: Les Films du Chateau, 106: Giraudon, 105, 228, 250: Susan Griggs, 72 l, 82 b, 83, 84, 94 tl, 239: The Hamlyn Group, 12, 40 b, 42 c, 56 b, 72 t, 101 b, 107, 108, 126 r, 135, 137, 166, 174, 193, 206, 214, 238 b: Sonia Halliday, 72 r, 89, 94 bl, 221: Robert Harding Associates, 35 t, 54 b, 176, 179, 190 b, 200, 201: Michael Holford, 13 tl, 17 r, 23 t, 53, 56 l, 56 t, 71, 79, 86 t, 88 r, 93, 111 b, 112 l, 112 r, 140, 146 t, 146 b, 167, 181 r, 184, 199, 204, 217, 220 l, 222 t, 223, 226 t, 226 b, 230, 240, 248: J. F. Huckel Collection, Taylor Museum, 46 t: Horniman Museum, 162: Instituto Nacional de Antropologia e Historia, Mexico, 192 b: Larousse, 49, 50: Clare Leimbach, half-title page, 142, 143: Linden Museum, Stuttgart, 66, 67: The Mansell Collection, 10, 15 t, 34, 37 t, 37 r, 73 t, 73 r, 75, 86 b, 92, 96, 110: Metropolitan Museum of Art, 168 r: John Moss, 145, 156, 158, 160: Musée Guimet, 120: Musée de l'Homme, Paris, 130 b, 159: Musées Nationaux, 224: Museo Aracimal, Mexico, 188: Museum of the American Indian, Haye Foundation, 42 t: Museum of Fine Arts, Boston, 25: Museum of Primitive Art, 203: William Rockhill Nelson Gallery of Art, Kansas City, 21 b: New York State Museum and Science Service, 64 l: Nordisk Presse Foto, 113 r: Axel Poignant, 11 t, 26 b, 32 t, 32 b, 42 n, 76 b, 81, 100 b, 128, 133, 147 t, 147 b, 149, 181 l, 182, 186, 196, 197 b, 198, 210, 236, 238 tl, 241: Popperfoto, 124: Rijksmuseum voor Volkenkunde, Leiden, 20: Secretary of State for Commonwealth Relations, 78 t: Brian Shuel, 62, 91 b: Spectrum, 11 r, 28, 44, 65, 74 t, 150: Suprintendenza alle Antichita della Calabria, 233: Universitets Oldsaksamlung, Oslo, 115, 116: University of Pennsylvania, 51: Victoria and Albert Museum, 78 b, 165: Roger Wood, 123, 194: Pictor-ZEFA, 8, 18, 31 tl, 36, 144, 177, 242, 244 t, 244 b, 246